Improving the First Year of College

Research and Practice

Improving the First Year of College

Research and Practice

Edited by

ROBERT S. FELDMAN
University of Massachusetts, Amherst

LEA LAWRENCE ERLBAUM ASSOCIATES, PUBLISHERS

2005 Mahwah, New Jersey   London

Lawrence Erlbaum Associates, Inc., Publishers
10 Industrial Avenue
Mahwah, New Jersey 07430
www.erlbaum.com

Cover Photo by Kevin Mattingly,
  Northern Virginia Community College
Cover Design by Sean Sciarrone

Library of Congress Cataloging-in-Publication Data

Improving the First year of college : research and practice / edited by
  Robert S. Feldman.
     p. cm.
Includes bibliographical references and index.
ISBN 0–8058–5575–0 (cloth : alk. paper)
ISBN 0–8058–4815–0 (pbk. : alk. paper)
1. College student orientation—United States—Case studies. 2. College freshmen—United States.   I. Feldman, Robert S. (Robert Stephen), 1947–
LB2343.32.I57 2004
378.I'98—dc22   2004050063

Printed in the United States of America
10   9   8   7   6   5   4   3   2   1

May 27, 2005

Contents

Preface

The first year of college represents an enormous milestone in students' lives. Whether attending a four-year or two-year institution of higher education, living on campus or at home, enrolled in a highly selective Ivy League school or a college with an open-admissions policy, students are challenged in unique and demanding ways during their first year.

Although many students rise to the challenges they face, for some the demands are too great. Retention rates beyond the first year are disappointing: One third of first-year students seriously consider leaving college during their first term, and ultimately only half of all students who start college complete it.

What are the factors that impact students during their first year? How can the academic and social experiences of first-year students be optimized? What can we do to improve retention rates to maximize the number of students who complete college? This book addresses these, and many other questions, as it examines the first year of college from a variety of perspectives. Drawing on a broad array of experts, it systematically considers the factors that produce success during the critical first year of college.

The main goal of this volume is to present, in an integrated framework, the newest, most contemporary perspectives on the first year of college. The book includes empirically grounded work and educational theories that are central to our understanding of the cognitive and social processes that underlie the first-year experience and its consequences.

The volume has several secondary aims, as well. One is to highlight the newest subareas in the domain of the first-year college experience that hold much promise, such as the development of learning communities. The volume also examines how technology impacts on students' first-year experience. Finally, the book provides examples of "best practices," determined through research by leaders in the field, to permit educators to draw on their experiences.

In order to accomplish these goals, each of the chapter authors has been asked to show explicitly the link between their research, its theoretical underpinnings, and potential applications. Each author also was charged with presenting new data, theory, and perspectives, assuring that the book makes a unique contribution to the literature.

LESSONS LEARNED

What are some of the general themes that emerge from the volume? There are several:

- *The first year of college is critical in ultimately producing college success.* As all of the chapters in the book make clear, the experiences that students encounter in their first year plays a crucial role in determining their ultimate success. A supportive environment (academically and socially) can spell the difference between a successful college career and one in which students do not reach their potential, fail, or even drop out. As one example, Cuseo (chapter 2) describes how the quality of advising in the first year influences student success in important ways.
- *The likelihood of student success can be increased through carefully constructed first-year experience programs.* As Petschauer and Wallace (chapter 8) and Laufgraben (chapter 9) discuss, good programs targeted toward first-year students make an enormous difference in terms of ultimate student success. These programs are not simple to implement, nor are they inexpensive in terms of dedicated personnel or dollar costs. But careful evaluation indicates that they are successful in enhancing student achievement and reducing attrition.
- *Not all good programs are alike.* Considered collectively, the chapters in this volume illustrate the point that a variety of different types of first-year programs produce positive outcomes. There is no single "gold standard" for successful programs for first-year students. Instead, good programs are tailored to campus strengths, constraints, and norms. At the same time, one factor appears important: buy-in from campus administrators and faculty. The more that first-year experience programs are seen as an essential

component of first-year students' educational experience—and not as a supplemental window dressing—the more effective they are.

- *Accountability and assessment are critical.* All educational institutions are facing increasing pressures for accountability arising from state legislatures, grant and funding agencies, and even from organizations representing specific disciplines. In order to demonstrate the efficacy of first-year programs within the context of pressure for accountability, extensive formal assessments are crucial. As Schuh extensively documents in chapter 6, institutions of higher education must—and can—demonstrate through data that their educational offerings are producing the intended outcomes.

- *The experience of first-year students is enhanced by multiculturalism.* Pope, Miklitsch, and Weigand (chapter 3) and Nagda, Gurin, and Johnson (chapter 4) demonstrate that exposure to other students who represent a broad range of cultures, ethnicities, and races is crucial to a full college experience. Not only do students benefit socially, but their cognitive development is also enhanced.

- *Money matters.* As King (chapter 1) documents, financial considerations are one of the central factors that affect the success of first-year students. The ability to attend college, as well as persistence in college, is associated with the financial decisions that students make.

- *Technology provides alternatives to traditional pedagogies.* An increasing body of research shows that technology may, compared with traditional educational approaches, provide alternate means of addressing the needs of first-year students. Specifically, Poirier and Feldman (chapter 7) show the promise of first-year experience courses taught completely online. Similarly, Pascarella (chapter 5) discusses the efficacy of computer-based instruction.

THE CONTENT OF THE BOOK

The book is divided into four parts. In the first part, the consequences of decisions made by first-year college students are considered. King (chapter 1) reports the findings from a comprehensive study carried out by the American Council on Education examining the impact of financial factors on first-year college students. In chapter 2, Cuseo discusses choices made by first-year students in terms of identifying a major and the effects of those choices on retention and academic achievement.

In Part II, we consider issues involving diversity. Pope, Miklitsch, and Weigand (chapter 3) discuss the development of multicultural competence and its importance in the context of the first-year college experience. In chapter 4, Nagda, Gurin, and Johnson provide findings on the influence of pre-college diversity on the outcomes of first-year college students' participation in multicultural learning communities.

Part III of the book examines the assessment of the factors influencing the first year of college. Pascarella (chapter 5) provides a comprehensive overview of the educational outcomes of college, summarizing a great deal of data. In chapter 6, Schuh provides a roadmap on assessment. He summarizes the necessary steps and provides several case studies.

The fourth and final part of the book looks at some specific programs and the lessons that can be drawn from them. In chapter 7, Poirier and Feldman discuss a program at the University of Massachusetts, Amherst, in which students participate in an online, distance-learning first-year experience course. Chapter 8, by Petschauer and Wallace, describes the nationally recognized first-year programs at Appalachian State University in North Carolina. Finally, in chapter 9, Laufgraben discusses the creation of first-year learning communities at Temple University in Philadelphia.

A FINAL WORD

As this book illustrates, the first year is a crucial period in the life of college students. Socially, economically, and academically, college students face enormous pressures when they begin their higher educational experience. If there is a single lesson to be drawn from the variety of approaches espoused by the authors in this volume, it is that these issues must be addressed intentionally and vigorously. Without a concerted effort, the promise of the first year of college cannot be attained.

I

First-Year Student Decisions

1

Academic Success and Financial Decisions: Helping Students Make Crucial Choices

JACQUELINE E. KING
American Council on Education

INTRODUCTION

Every day, students make decisions that affect their ability to complete a degree. They weigh some of these choices carefully, such as which college to attend. Yet they underestimate the impact of many other choices, such as whether to drop a course or accept more hours at work, not understanding the cumulative effect these decisions might have on their likelihood of completing a degree. Information on the consequences of student choices can help institutions refine their counseling interventions and other programs to better influence students to make decisions that improve their chances of persistence. The data presented in this chapter will demonstrate that, by working long hours and studying part-time, students not only lengthen their time-to-degree, but also increase their likelihood of dropping out. Given that more than half of all undergraduates attend college part-time and 80% work while enrolled (U.S. Department of Education, 2002), it is crucial that institutions understand and confront the effects of student choices on academic success.

This chapter examines the most recent evidence on the effects of students' choices on their prospects of succeeding in college. It attempts to describe students who are entering college, the resources they use to pay for their education, and the potential effects of their choices on the likelihood that they will graduate. The chapter pays particular attention to the characteristics and financing choices of low-income students, since these individuals are at greatest risk of dropping out.

The chapter addresses the following questions:

- What are the demographic characteristics and academic background of entering students, and how do low-income students differ from those with greater financial resources?
- How do students pay for college, and how do the financing patterns of low-income students differ from those of other students?
- What is the impact of students' financing choices on their academic success?

Why should the answers to these questions matter to campus leaders? They matter because colleges increasingly will be challenged to maintain and enhance graduation rates and, in many cases, to shorten time-to-degree. As the student population becomes more diverse in terms of age, race/ethnicity, and socioeconomic status, improving graduation rates will become more difficult. Understanding as much as possible about the critical links between students' financial decisions and academic success — especially for low-income students — will help campuses continue to refine their efforts to help all students succeed.

Data and Limitations

The data presented in this chapter come from two national studies conducted by the U.S. Department of Education's National Center for Education Statistics. The National Postsecondary Student Aid Study: 1995–96 (NPSAS) provides a comprehensive national picture of how students pay for college in a single year. It includes data from college records, student interviews, and federal student financial aid files for more than 35,000 undergraduate and graduate students. Approximately 12,000 students included in the 1995–96 iteration of NPSAS were first-time freshmen. These students were questioned again in fall 1998 and spring 2001. The resulting longitudinal data set is called Beginning Postsecondary Students 1996/2001 (BPS). This chapter relies on the BPS data to examine the effects of student choices during their freshman year on persistence and degree completion after six years.

Definition of Low-Income Students

Several student characteristics should be considered to make a fair determination of which college students truly are low-income students. The characteristics considered in this chapter are dependency status, attendance status, and family size.

The first step in assessing family income is to divide undergraduates into three groups: dependent students, independent students without dependents, and independent students with dependents. Dependent students are under the age of 25, unmarried, not veterans, and they do not have children. When dependent students apply for financial aid, their parents' income and assets are considered in the determination of their financial need. Students are considered independent—and count only their own income and that of a spouse when applying for aid—if they are 25 or older, married, a veteran, or they have children. Independent students are further divided into those who do and those who do not have dependent children. These distinctions are critical when assessing student income.

The second consideration is attendance status. This characteristic is particularly important when assessing independent students' income. Some independent students may seem quite poor, but if they are attending college full-time, this "poverty" may be a temporary condition. To control for this problem, this chapter uses students' income from the year prior to entering college.

Family size is the third characteristic used to determine which students can be considered low-income. A family of four with an income of $30,000 usually is worse off than a family of two with the same income. The analysis in this chapter takes family size into account by converting income to a percentage of the federal poverty standard, which varies by family size. Because the federal poverty thresholds are very low, this chapter considers students to be low-income if their income is at or below 150% of the poverty threshold. Eight out of 10 entering students falling into this income category who attended college at least half-time and applied for aid received a Pell Grant, the primary federal grant for low-income students. Throughout the chapter, low-income students are compared with middle- and upper-income students, who had incomes of at least 300% of the poverty level.

DEMOGRAPHIC CHARACTERISTICS

Thirty-two percent of undergraduates who began college in 1995–96 came from families with incomes at or below 150% of the poverty threshold, and 41% came from families with incomes of at least 300% of the poverty threshold. These two groups of students will be compared throughout this chapter because they provide a contrast between those at the lowest and those at the highest ends of the income spectrum. When dependency status is considered along with income, most of these students fall into one of three groups: low-income dependent students (17% of all beginning students); low-income independent students with dependents (11%); and middle- and upper-income dependent students (37%). The average income of students in these three groups ranged from $8,900 for low-income independent students with dependents to approximately $82,000 for middle- and upper-income dependent students. It is important to consider dependency status as well as income because dependent students and independent students with dependents have different family obligations that affect their range of financing options.

Low-income undergraduates differ from other students in several ways (see Table 1.1). They are more likely than their middle- and upper-income peers to be female, African American, Hispanic, Asian American, or American Indian; 48% of low-income students are racial or ethnic minorities, compared with only 20% of middle- and upper-income students.

Low-income and middle- and upper-income undergraduates also significantly differ in age. Low-income undergraduates tend to begin college later in life than their middle- and upper-income peers. Only 56% of low-income students began college at age 19 or younger, compared with 85% of middle- and upper-income students. Almost one quarter of low-income students enrolled in college for the first time at age 25 or older, compared with just 9% of middle- and upper-income students. Low-income students also are far more likely to have started a family. More than one third of low-income students are married and/or have children, and almost one quarter are single parents. The vast majority of middle- and upper-income students are single and have no children.

TABLE 1.1

Demographic Characteristics of Beginning Postsecondary Students,
by Income, 1995–1996

	Low-income (%)	Middle- and Upper-income (%)	All Undergraduates (%)
Gender			
Male	40.3	50.0	45.5
Female	59.7	50.0	54.5
Race/Ethnicity			
White	52.0	80.0	68.0
African American	18.0	6.0	11.0
Hispanic	21.0	9.0	14.0
Asian American	8.0	4.0	5.0
American Indian	1.4	0.6	1.0
Other	0.8	0.4	0.0
Age			
19 or younger	56.0	85.0	71.0
20 to 24	21.0	5.0	12.0
25 or older	23.0	9.0	17.0
Family Status			
Not married, no children	65.0	93.0	81.0
Married, no children	3.0	4.0	4.0
Not married, children	23.0	1.0	9.0
Married, children	9.0	3.0	6.0

Note: Data are from U.S. Department of Education, National Center for Education
Statistics, National Postsecondary Student Aid Study: 1995–96; analysis by author. Figures
may not add to 100% due to rounding.

ACADEMIC BACKGROUND

Many academic background factors negatively affect persistence. Students
who do not take rigorous high school courses, who earn a nontraditional
high school credential, who do not enter college immediately after high
school, or whose parents did not attend college are more likely than other
students to drop out before earning a degree (Adelman, 1999, U.S. Department of Education, 1995). Unfortunately, low-income students are more
likely than other undergraduates to possess each of these "high-risk" characteristics.

Two thirds of low-income beginning students come from families in
which neither parent attended college (12% did not complete high school

and 52% earned only a high school diploma or GED), compared with 33% of middle- and upper-income students. Conversely, half of middle- and upper-income students have at least one parent who earned a bachelor's degree or higher, compared with less than 20% of low-income students. First-generation college students face many disadvantages: They have far less experience and information on the social and academic culture of higher education, and they may not be able to rely on their parents for assistance in these matters.

Previous research has shown that students who do not earn a traditional high school diploma and those who delay entry into higher education after high school are more likely to drop out of college than other students (U.S. Department of Education, 1995). Although the vast majority of entering students have earned a regular high school diploma, low-income students are more than four times as likely as middle- and upper-income students to have earned a nontraditional certificate (13% of low-income students versus 3% of middle- and upper-income students). More important, low-income students are much more likely than more affluent students to delay entry into higher education after completing high school. More than half of low-income students delayed entry into higher education, compared with 23% of middle- and upper-income students.

The BPS data include extensive information on the high school curriculum and achievement of students who began college in 1995–96. Adelman's research (1999) shows that one of the most important factors influencing college success is the rigor of a student's high school curriculum. This variable is even more important than high school grades and test scores. BPS only includes this information for students who took a college entrance examination; since only four-year institutions require these examinations, no information is available for students who had determined in high school that they would attend a two-year or less-than-two-year institution.

With regard to admissions test takers, the difference in high school curriculum between low-income students and their peers is not as large as one might expect. Twenty-two percent of low-income students completed at least a moderately rigorous high school curriculum (four years of English; three years each of math [including Algebra II], social science, and science [including biology, chemistry, and physics]; and two years of a foreign language). In comparison, 36% of middle- and upper-income students completed at least a moderately rigorous high school curriculum.

In summary, low-income students are more likely than more affluent students to have earned a nontraditional diploma and to have delayed their entry into postsecondary education. In addition, most low-income students are first-generation college attendees. Among those who take admissions tests, low-income students are less likely than middle- and upper-income students to have completed a rigorous high school curriculum.

Previous research suggests that students who devote most of their time to their studies and to developing a close connection with their campus community are most likely to persist (Pascarella & Terenzini, 1991). Given the deficits in academic preparation and experience they must overcome, devoting adequate time to studying and forging ties with the campus community is of particular importance to low-income students. The financing resources available to these students — and the financing choices they make — can either facilitate this process or erect roadblocks that make achieving academic success even more difficult.

COLLEGE FINANCING

Students rely on many different resources to pay for college. Most begin with a certain amount of family resources — primarily in the form of income — and choose institutions that vary in how much they charge and how much grant aid they have available. Students also make choices that determine their living expenses, such as whether to live on campus or at home. Then, they make up whatever difference exists between their family's resources and their total student budget (adjusted for their attendance pattern and living situation, and reduced by any grant aid they may have received) through a combination of work, student loans, and commercial credit. The BPS data describe the different means and financing choices of low-income students and their more affluent peers.

Institutional Type and Price

Whether for academic or financial reasons (or a combination of the two), low-income students are more likely than their academic peers to choose institutions that offer programs of two years or less. Low-income students are somewhat more likely than their middle- and upper-income peers to attend public community and vocational colleges (50% versus 42%) and are far more likely to attend two-year and less-than-two-year for-profit institutions (21% versus 4%).[1] Conversely, low-income students were less

---

[1] The 1.5% of first-time freshmen attending private not-for-profit two-year and less-than-two-year institutions and for-profit four-year institutions are excluded from this analysis.

Price Definitions	
Total Student Budget	Also called the *total price*, this figure includes institutional charges for tuition, fees, and on-campus room and board for a full-time/full-year student, as well as institutions' estimates of expenses for such items as books and supplies, transportation, and entertainment.
Adjusted Student Budget	This figure is the *total student budget*, adjusted to reflect attendance status and housing choice.
Net Price	The *adjusted student budget*, less any grant aid received.
Unmet Need	The *adjusted student budget*, less all aid (including loans) and the student's expected family contribution.

likely than middle- and upper-income students to attend public and private not-for-profit four-year institutions. More than half of middle- and upper-income freshmen began at four-year institutions, compared with 29% of low-income freshmen.

Analysts define the price of attending college in many ways. The definitions of total price and net price used in this chapter are based on the total student budget. This budget includes institutional charges for tuition, fees, and on-campus room and board for a full-time/full-year student, as well as institutions' estimates of expenses for such items as books and supplies, transportation, and entertainment.[2]

Low-income students save money by choosing institutions with shorter academic programs — not substantially lower annual total prices. Overall, low-income students in 1995–96 chose institutions with an average annual total student budget that was only about $1,500 less than the average

---

[2] These estimates reflect the institution's best approximation of the amount students reasonably should spend on these items. They cannot reflect the wide variance in student choices.

total price of institutions chosen by middle- and upper-income students. Low-income students are somewhat more likely to attend lower-priced community colleges and are less likely to attend more expensive four-year institutions. However, 21% of low-income students chose for-profit institutions, which carried an average annual total student budget of $10,000. Low-income students face annual total prices that are similar to those paid by their middle- and upper-income peers but, because they are more likely to attend two-year and less-than-two-year institutions, their total multi-year educational costs are less.

The finding that low-income students do not tend to choose less expensive institutions than their middle- and upper-income peers is not as surprising as it may appear initially. Price is only one factor among many that students consider when choosing an institution. Location, selectivity, and curricular offerings all play a major role in student choice. In fact, when asked to name the most important factor influencing their choice of institution, low-income students were no more likely to name a price-related factor than middle- and upper-income students.

Attendance Status, Living Arrangement, and Adjusted Student Budget

Other factors influencing the prices that students pay are attendance status (whether they attend on a full- or part-time basis and for either a full or partial academic year) and whether they live on campus, off campus, or with their parents. The beginning student population is split almost evenly between those who study full-time/full-year (53%) and those who attend part-time and/or part-year (47%). Low-income beginning students are less likely to study full-time/full-year than middle- and upper-income freshmen (42% versus 64%). Of course, the prevalence of less-than-full-time/full-year attendance varies by type of institution. For example, one quarter of entering students at for-profit institutions attend full-time/full-year, versus nearly 80% of entering students at private four-year institutions.[3] At all institution types, low-income students are less likely than middle- and upper-income students to attend full-time/full-year.

In terms of living arrangements, 30% of all beginning students live on campus, 27% live off campus, and 43% live with their parents or other

---

[3] In this analysis, a full academic year is considered eight months. Many programs at for-profit institutions operate on a shorter schedule. Students attending such programs full time are not considered full-time/full-year.

relatives. Most two-year and less-than-two-year institutions do not offer on-campus student housing. At four-year institutions, almost two thirds of beginning students live on campus. Low-income students are far less likely than middle- and upper-income students to live on campus at four-year institutions (45% versus 75%). Some low-income students are older and have their own families; these students may prefer to remain in their existing homes or apartments, or the institution they attend may not offer suitable accommodations. Another explanation is that low-income students are twice as likely as middle- and upper-income students to choose to live with their parents. At four-year institutions, 35% of low-income freshmen live with their parents, compared with 16% of middle- and upper-income beginning students. There are many reasons why students might choose this option, but the cost saving is likely a primary reason for living at home.

When the total student budget is adjusted for students' attendance status and housing choices, the average price for all entering undergraduates drops by 20%. At community colleges and for-profit institutions, where the majority of students study part-time and many live at home, the average adjusted student budget is lower than the average total student budget by $2,700 and $3,000, respectively. At both public and private four-year institutions, where students are somewhat more likely to live on campus and study full-time, there is less of a difference between the average total and adjusted student budget. At public institutions, these choices reduce the average student budget only by approximately $1,300. Low-income students at private four-year institutions fare slightly better; their average adjusted student budget is approximately $2,200 less than the average total student budget. Of course, averages can mask great variation; some students reap significant savings by attending part-time and/or by living at home. Nonetheless, in general, students' living and attendance choices save relatively little money.

By contrast, students' attendance and housing choices can significantly affect their ability to succeed in college. Attending full-time may result in higher annual costs, but it also can shorten time-to-degree, resulting in lower total expenses over a college career. In addition, research has consistently shown that, after other contributing factors such as family income and prior academic preparation are taken into account, students who attend college full-time are more likely to complete a degree than those who attend part-time. Studies also have shown that students who live on campus are more likely to persist than students who live off campus or with their parents (Pascarella & Terenzini, 1991).

Grants and Net Price

Eighty-three percent of low-income freshmen applied for financial aid for the 1995–96 academic year. In contrast, 62% of all middle- and upper-income freshmen applied for assistance. Most students—and especially those with incomes less than 150% of the poverty threshold—will likely receive assistance if they apply for financial aid. In general, 69% of incoming students who applied for aid received grants averaging $3,006. Among low-income freshmen, 86% of those who applied for financial aid received grant assistance averaging $2,857. In contrast, 52% of entering middle- and upper-income students who applied for aid received grants, but the average amount that these students received was slightly greater, at $3,322. This difference in the average grant aid received reflects the fact that a higher proportion of middle- and upper-income students attend more expensive private not-for-profit institutions that offer significant amounts of institutional grant assistance, some of which is awarded using criteria other than financial need.

When grant assistance is taken into account in addition to living situation and attendance pattern, the average net price for all entering students (whether or not they received grants) is reduced by 33%, compared with the total price. Grants reduce the average price for low-income students by 45%, or by $3,700 to $7,750, depending on type of institution. When grants are deducted, low-income students face substantially lower prices than middle- and upper-income students—especially at public and private four-year institutions. This pattern reflects the fact that most grant assistance is awarded based on financial need—low-income students, of course, demonstrate more need than students with greater financial resources. Despite this grant assistance, low-income students still must pay an average of $5,400. This is equivalent to 42% and 61% of family income, respectively, for low-income dependent students and independent students with dependents. In contrast, the $8,745 average net price faced by middle- and upper-income dependent students is equivalent to 11% of their average family income. Clearly, despite lower net prices, low-income students will experience far more difficulty paying for college than their middle- and upper-income peers.

Student Loans

Despite the financial burden faced by low-income students, they are not much more likely to borrow than their middle- and upper-income peers.

One third of low-income freshmen borrowed student loans in 1995–96, versus 27% of middle- and upper-income entering students. Because annual borrowing limits in the federal student loan programs are relatively low ($2,625 for dependent freshmen and $6,625 for independent freshmen), the amount borrowed by low-income students and that borrowed by middle- or upper-income students varies little. For both groups, the average loan is about $3,000. Relying on student loans is a less popular choice for both income groups than either attending part-time or living at home.

Although many low-income students avoid student loans, those who do borrow often accrue substantial debt over the course of their academic careers. Low-income students who persist to graduation are more likely to borrow and accrue more debt than their middle- and upper-income peers.

Unmet Need and Employment

When the expected family contribution (EFC), grants, loans, and other assistance (such as employer aid) are deducted from the adjusted student budget, the remaining amount is a student's unmet need.[4] When students have no unmet need, it means that they have received enough aid to pay the entire net price of college, less the EFC. Low-income students face a lower average net price than middle- and upper-income students. However, because low-income students' average family contribution is very small, their average unmet need is more than three times that of middle- and upper-income undergraduates ($3,556 versus $994). The $3,556 in unmet need faced by low-income undergraduates is equivalent to 28% and 40% of average annual income for low-income dependent students and independent students with dependents, respectively. In contrast, the $994 unmet need of middle- and upper-income dependent students is equivalent to only 1% of annual family income. Except for students at for-profit institutions, low-income freshmen have approximately $2,400 more average unmet need than middle- and upper-income freshmen. At for-profit institutions, low-income students face $4,000 more in average unmet need than their middle- and upper-income peers.

Most students work during the academic year, at least in part to compensate for their unmet need. Despite their higher unmet need, low-income students are somewhat less likely to work than their middle- and upper-income peers: 63% of low-income freshmen worked during the 1995–96

---

[4] EFC is defined by a federal formula that takes into account student income and parent income, assets, family size, and number of family members in college.

academic year, compared with 71% of middle- and upper-income students. However, low-income dependent students are as likely to work, and to work about the same number of hours per week, as middle- and upper-income dependent students. Low-income independent students with dependents, who account for more than one third of low-income freshmen, are less likely to work than their dependent peers—most likely because of their child-rearing responsibilities.

In addition, differences in income seem to have little impact on the role that work plays in students' lives. Students were asked whether they consider themselves primarily a student who works to meet college expenses or primarily an employee who also is attending classes. Only one third of working low-income students and one quarter of middle- and upper-income working students consider themselves employees who study. Despite the fact that they consider themselves students first, these students work an average of 24 hours per week.

In summary, low-income students generally do not choose institutions that are significantly less expensive than those chosen by middle- and upper-income students. Low-income students' most popular strategies for lowering their college expenses are, in order of frequency: applying for aid, working, and attending college part-time (see Fig. 1.1). The least popular strategy for students at all income levels is borrowing student loans.

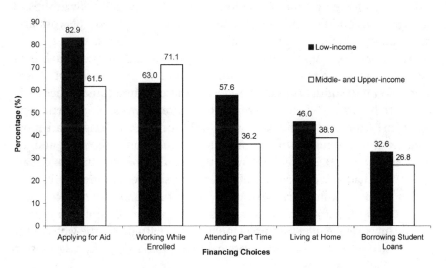

FIG. 1.1.   Financing choices of beginning postsecondary students, 1995–1996. (Data are from U.S. Department of Education, National Center for Education Statistics, National Postsecondary Student Aid Study: 1995–1996, analysis by author.)

FINANCING CHOICES
AND PERSISTENCE

The financing choices students make can have a substantial impact on their academic success. Table 1.2 shows the percentage of 1995–96 first-time freshmen who had either attained a certificate or degree, were still enrolled, or had dropped out by spring 2001, for each of the financing choices detailed earlier. It shows that, in general, 35% of 1995–96 entering freshmen had dropped out with no degree by the spring of 2001, 14% still were enrolled, and 51% had earned a degree or certificate. In general, students who were least likely to drop out pursued a very traditional pattern: They began at four-year institutions, studied full-time, lived on campus, and worked part-time (1 to 14 hours per week).[5]

This basic pattern varied somewhat by income. Middle- and upper-income students were less likely to have dropped out than low-income students. Twenty-nine percent of middle- and upper-income freshmen had left college without a degree by 2001, compared with 38% of low-income freshmen. For both groups of students, starting at a four-year institution, attending full-time, living on campus, and working part-time were associated with better-than-average persistence. Borrowing student loans and working part-time produced the lowest dropout rate for both groups of students, but middle- and upper-income students who did not work also persisted at high rates, regardless of whether they borrowed.

Among both groups, students who worked part-time persisted at higher rates than students who did not work at all. This finding, which at first seems counterintuitive, has been replicated across numerous studies (Pascarella & Terenzini, 1991). The research literature suggests that students who work part-time (and particularly those who work on the campus) are more connected to the institution, manage their time more effectively, and are more focused on their academic work than students who don't work at all. Borrowing had a stronger correlation with persistence among low-income students: Those who borrowed and worked part-time were much more likely to persist than those who worked part-time but did not borrow.

The importance of combining student loans with part-time work to the persistence of low-income students may be explained by the relationship

---

[5] Twelve percent of postsecondary students began with no intention of completing a degree or certificate program. In addition, some students who had dropped out as of 2001 will return to complete their degree.

between work and borrowing, on the one hand, and attendance status and institution type, on the other. Low-income students who borrowed and worked part-time were far more likely to attend on a full-time/full-year basis; 82% of these students attended full-time and for a full year. In contrast, only 27% of students who did not borrow and worked 15 hours per week or more attended full-time/full-year. Interestingly, low-income students who did not work at all were less likely to attend full-time than those who worked part-time. Of course, some low-income students—especially single parents—simply did not have the time to work or may have jeopardized government benefits, such as food stamps, by working. Even among dependent students, those who worked part-time were more likely to attend full-time/full-year than those who did not work. Low-income students who combine borrowing with part-time work can best afford—both financially and in terms of time—to attend on a full-time/full-year basis. Those who forgo borrowing and work more than part time may have every intention of attending full time but drop to less than a full-time course load because they cannot manage full-time attendance *and* a heavy work schedule.

For low-income students, borrowing student loans and working 1 to 14 hours per week also are highly correlated with attendance at a four-year institution—another important predictor of persistence. Three out of four students who borrowed and worked part-time attended a four-year institution, compared with just 18% of those who did not borrow and worked 15 hours per week or more. Most likely, both work and borrowing were necessary for low-income students to afford a four-year institution. Nonetheless, low-income students at two-year and less-than-two-year institutions who borrowed and worked part-time were far less likely to drop out than other students at these institutions. Thirty-six percent of students who worked part-time and 38% of those who borrowed had dropped out by 2001, compared with 45% of all low-income students who began at two-year or less-than-two-year institutions.[6] The pattern is even more dramatic at four-year institutions. Thirteen percent of low-income students at four-year institutions who borrowed and worked part-time as freshmen had dropped out by 2001, compared with 27% of all low-income students at these institutions.

Borrowing and working part-time are clearly associated with success for students at all income levels, especially for low-income students, yet

---

[6] The share of low-income students at these institutions who combined part-time work and borrowing was too small to return a reliable estimate.

TABLE 1.2

2001 Degree Attainment and Enrollment Status of Beginning Postsecondary Students, by First-year Choices

	All Beginning Students			Low-income			Middle- and Upper-income		
	No Degree, Not Enrolled (%)	Still Enrolled (%)	Attained Degree or Certificate (%)	No Degree, Not Enrolled (%)	Still Enrolled (%)	Attained Degree or Certificate (%)	No Degree, Not Enrolled (%)	Still Enrolled (%)	Attained Degree or Certificate (%)
All students	34.8	14.4	50.8	38.2	14.0	47.8	29.4	14.6	56.0
Institution type									
Public two-year or less	46.5	17.1	36.4	44.6	15.6	39.8	45.8	19.0	35.2
Public four-year	22.5	17.3	60.2	26.5	22.5	51.0	19.1	14.7	66.3
Private four-year	17.2	9.4	73.5	27.1	14.3	58.6	12.6	7.6	79.8
For-profit two-year or less	36.7	3.0	60.3	39.2	3.1	57.7	28.4	4.7	66.9
Attended full-time/full-year	20.1	12.6	67.3	24.6	13.9	61.5	16.8	11.6	71.6
Attended less than full-time/full-year	50.2	16.6	33.2	47.7	14.2	38.1	50.6	19.9	29.5
Residence									
On campus	17.3	11.2	71.6	23.6	14.7	61.7	14.2	10.4	75.4
Off campus	44.7	14.7	40.6	42.7	13.0	44.3	47.1	15.3	37.6
With parents or relatives	38.4	17.7	44.0	39.3	15.7	45.0	36.1	20.2	43.7

Filed financial aid application	32.0	13.4	54.6	36.5	12.9	50.6	23.2	13.5	63.4
Did not apply	41.3	16.9	41.8	46.7	19.5	33.7	38.2	16.2	45.7
Borrowed federal student loan	26.4	11.7	61.9	32.1	12.5	55.4	20.0	10.4	69.6
Did not borrow	38.2	15.5	46.3	41.5	14.8	43.7	32.5	16.0	51.5
Hours worked per wk. while enrolled									
None	29.1	10.0	60.9	36.1	10.8	53.1	19.7	8.9	71.4
1 to 14	18.8	12.1	69.1	25.5	16.9	57.7	16.2	8.7	75.1
15 to 34	33.6	17.8	48.6	38.6	16.2	45.2	29.0	18.9	52.2
35 or more	52.2	16.2	31.7	47.5	14.6	37.9	55.4	19.2	25.5
Working and borrowing status									
Borrowed, did not work	25.8	10.0	64.2	33.1	10.4	56.5	19.3	8.4	72.4
Borrowed, worked 1 to 14 hours	12.9	10.6	76.5	15.0	14.7	70.3	10.6	9.3	80.1
Borrowed, worked 15+ hours	32.6	13.1	54.4	35.2	12.8	52.0	28.1	13.2	58.7
Did not borrow, did not work	30.8	10.0	59.1	38.0	11.0	51.0	19.9	9.1	71.0
Did not borrow, worked 1 to 15 hours	24.6	13.4	62.0	35.2	19.0	45.9	21.3	8.1	70.6
Did not borrow, worked 16+ hours	44.1	18.5	37.5	46.0	16.9	37.1	40.3	20.3	39.4

Note. Data from U.S. Department of Education, National Center for Education Statistics, National Postsecondary Student Aid Study: 1995–96, analysis by author. Figures may not add to 100% due to rounding.

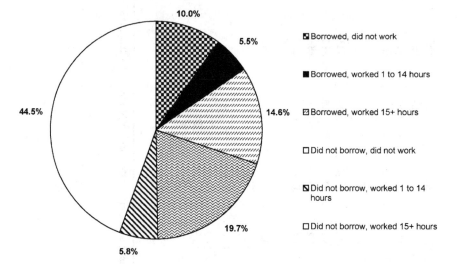

FIG. 1.2.   Distribution of beginning postsecondary students, by work and borrowing choices. (Data are from U.S. Department of Education, National Center for Education Statistics, National Postsecondary Student Aid Study: 1995–1996, analysis by author.)

less than 6% of freshmen adopted this strategy (see Fig. 1.2).[7] In fact, the largest group of freshmen (45%) chose the financing strategy that is least associated with success: borrowing nothing and working 15 or more hours per week. As discussed previously, this pattern varies little with student income. Even those middle- and upper-income students who could afford to follow this strategy chose instead to avoid student loans and work 15 or more hours per week.

Why are students making counterproductive choices? One explanation may be that students assume it will be less expensive in the long run to attend college part-time and avoid student loan debt. For many students, this is not the case. Of course, for those who drop out because they cannot adequately juggle college with work, the cost of working too many hours while enrolled is enormous. These individuals will pay for the rest of their lives in lost earning power. However, even those students who simply extend their undergraduate career will pay in opportunity costs because they are delaying their entry into the job market as full-time, college-educated workers.

---

[7] It is important to note that 15% of freshmen borrowed and worked 15 or more hours per week. These students would require additional grant assistance in order to reduce the amount they work.

To better understand the cost of this approach for students attending a public four-year institution, consider two hypothetical students who choose different financing options. Wendy does not borrow, works 25 hours per week, and, as a result, must take an extra year to graduate. Once her extra educational expenses are deducted from her earnings, she nets $5,800 during her fifth year of college.[8] Paul borrows $2,500 each year to allow him to work only 14 hours per week and, as a result, to graduate in four years. During the fifth year, Paul, who has graduated, earns $30,000. Even if the total cost of his $10,000 loan is assigned to that first year after graduation, Paul nets $15,756. In this scenario, working 25 hours per week cost Wendy about $10,000. Each student's situation will differ, and this simulation ignores many other costs that students may incur when they either stay in college or move into the workforce. For some students, working longer hours and taking a longer time to graduate may be unavoidable and, in some cases, might even be in the student's best financial interest. The concern is that students appear to be making these choices without considering the direct and opportunity costs associated with extended enrollment.

Many students may make crucial choices based on misinformation or faulty assumptions about the relative cost of the various options. These choices have serious consequences for all students, but they deal the hardest blow to low-income students, many of whom are first-generation college attendees who are not adequately prepared academically for college.

Student choices also have important consequences for institutions. Every institution wants — and is expected — to maximize its graduation rate. If a large proportion of the student body is working and attending part-time, achieving this goal may prove very difficult. In many states, colleges and universities also are experiencing significant growth in enrollment. Colleges are implementing numerous strategies to accommodate the influx of new students, such as offering courses year-round and via the Internet. One of the most efficient, cost-effective means to accommodate growth is to lessen time-to-degree. If students move through their academic programs efficiently, they graduate and make room for new students. When students carry less than a full-time load, they extend their time-to-degree, placing additional strain on campus resources. Helping students make wise financial decisions will pay dividends not only for individual students, but also for institutions.

---

[8] This analysis assumes that the living expenses of both students are the same and so excludes those costs.

In summary, the five choices identified in this chapter that are related to student success are: type of institution, attendance status, housing arrangement, student loans, and employment. The message from these data is that the traditional choices—living on campus and studying full-time—remain the factors most associated with academic success. This traditional approach is more expensive, but it pays off in the long run in several ways: increased likelihood of graduation, shorter time-to-degree, and lower opportunity costs. Unfortunately, for many low-income students, family obligations place these choices out of reach: One third of low-income freshmen are independent students with dependents. Nonetheless, two thirds of low-income freshmen do not have dependents; more students in this income category conceivably could make at least some of the choices that are associated with degree attainment if they had better information about how their choices can affect their academic progress.

Many middle- and upper-income students also could choose to work less and borrow student loans to pay their expenses. Given the higher unmet need of low-income students, it seems illogical that middle- and upper-income freshmen work as many hours per week as their low-income peers. Some middle- and upper-income students may be working to pay part of the EFC because their parents cannot or will not contribute as much as the formula suggests they can afford. Others may be working to support a lifestyle that costs more than the amount estimated in the college budget. In many cases, both explanations may apply.

Another possible explanation of students' work and borrowing choices, but one for which we have little systematic data, is that students at all income levels are compounding the cost of their lifestyle choices by using credit cards to pay for these purchases. The BPS survey does not contain any information on credit card use, but the 1999–2000 version of NPSAS contains several questions on credit cards. The responses reveal that more than half of dependent freshmen in 1999–2000 possessed at least one credit card.[9] Among those with a credit card, nearly half carry a balance each month, and that balance averages $1,400. These debt levels could push many students into working longer hours, thereby sacrificing their ability to reach their academic potential.

While credit cards offer convenience, if students carry a balance, they usually would be better off using a student loan instead. There is no data on the interest rates that these students pay on their credit cards, but it is

---

[9] Independent students are excluded from this analysis because, like other American adults, most of them possess credit cards.

safe to assume that, in most cases, the rates on their credit cards exceed the maximum interest rate on student loans of 8.25%. Because the federal reserve has kept the prime rate low to stave off inflation, the interest rate on federal student loans in 2003 is at its lowest point in history, making these loans more affordable than ever. Moreover, student loans need not be repaid until six months after a student leaves school, while credit card payments begin immediately. As noted, in 1999–2000 more than 50% of dependent freshmen possessed a credit card. Only 27% of these students took out a student loan. Many students appear to be choosing a more expensive form of credit that may be exacerbating their need to work.

CONCLUSION

This chapter has described the demographic and academic background of students entering college and discussed how these students pay for college. It also has delineated the choices students can make to improve the likelihood that they will complete a college degree. The data show that low-income students arrive at college with many strikes against them. Among other characteristics, they are more likely to have children, to be the first in their family to attend college, and to have completed a high school curriculum that is not rigorous. Even after receiving grants, they must find an average of $5,400 in additional resources to meet their college expenses.

The data presented in this chapter suggest that students often make choices that may negatively affect their academic performance for several reasons: to contain the price of attending college; to support lifestyle choices, such as living off campus or carrying a credit card balance; and, in some instances, to devote time to their children. Students also may be making certain choices because they do not have adequate information about the possible consequences and available alternatives. The question that these data pose for institutions is how to steer students toward making choices that suit their individual needs *and* maximize their likelihood of academic success.

Low-income students especially may find it difficult to make better choices because their level of unmet need is so high. Continued efforts to moderate college price increases and provide additional grant funding will help these students face lower levels of unmet need. That said, improvement in college affordability alone is not sufficient to solve this problem. More time and attention must be devoted to counseling students on college campuses, in high schools and community-based organizations, and through federal TRIO programs about the costs, benefits, and consequences of making various financing choices. Counseling students to attend college full-time and work part-time is not helpful if students do not have enough grant funding to make such a choice. However, additional grant funding will be most effective if students are counseled on the best ways to invest that money in their future academic success. Likewise, additional borrowing can only be helpful when students understand how to use the credit wisely.

An important option that campuses can pursue to assist low-income students (and their middle- and upper-income peers as well) is to forge stronger links between academic and financial advising. How often do students approach professors or other academic advisers asking to be released from a course because their work schedule does not allow them to handle a full course load? How do faculty members respond? Can the academic adviser refer that student directly to a financial counselor? Could the academic adviser help a student determine if dropping a course is in his or her financial—as well as academic—best interest? Is the importance of making the right choices about work, attendance, housing, and borrowing emphasized in student and parent orientation programs, academic advising sessions, and other such opportunities? Could work-study jobs be more closely linked to students' academic coursework? Do faculty understand how many hours students spend working and the effects of that work on their academic performance? Do students know how to use credit cards responsibly? What special programs are available to low-income students who so often enter college under-prepared academically and with so few financial options?

There is no "right answer" that will suit all students or all institutions, but every student can be helped by having a clearer understanding of the costs, benefits, and potential pitfalls associated with the various options. Such a shift in thinking will help individual students reach their academic goals and may free vital space and resources at institutions that must accommodate a large influx of new students.

ACKNOWLEDGMENT

This chapter is adapted from King, J. (2002). *Crucial choices: How students' financial decisions affect their academic success.* Washington, DC: American Council on Education. Adapted with permission of the American Council on Education.

REFERENCES

Adelman, C. (1999). *The answers are in the toolbox.* Washington, DC: U.S. Department of Education.

Pascarella, E. T., & Terenzini, P. T. (1991). *How college affects students.* San Francisco: Jossey-Bass.

U.S. Department of Education, National Center for Education Statistics. (1995). *Descriptive summary of 1989–90 beginning postsecondary students: 5 years later with an essay on postsecondary persistence and attainment.* Washington, DC: Government Printing Office.

U.S. Department of Education, National Center for Education Statistics. (2002). *Profile of undergraduate students in U.S. postsecondary institutions: 1999–2000.* Washington, DC: Government Printing Office.

2

"Decided," "Undecided," and "In Transition": Implications for Academic Advisement, Career Counseling, and Student Retention

JOE CUSEO
Marymount College

INTRODUCTION

The objective of this chapter is twofold: (a) to critically review research on how students' process of decision making with respect to selecting college majors and careers relates to their persistence in college, and (b) to tease out practical implications of this research for improving the academic advisement, long-range planning, and retention of first-year students.

The majority of new students entering higher education leave their initial college of choice without completing a degree (Tinto, 1993), and national attrition rates have been increasing since the early 1980s at two-year and four-year institutions, both public and private (Postsecondary Education Opportunity, 2002). At all types of higher education institutions, including highly selective colleges and universities, the most critical period or stage of vulnerability for student attrition continues to be the first year of college ("Learning Slope," 1991). More than half of all students who withdraw from college do so during their first year (Consortium for Student Retention Data Exchange, 1999), resulting in a first-year attrition rate of more than 25% at four-year institutions, and approximately 50% at two-year institutions (ACT, 2003).

Retention research suggests that student commitment to educational and career goals is perhaps the strongest factor associated with persistence to degree completion (Wyckoff, 1999). Given the increasing trend of new students to report that their number-one goal for attending college is "preparing for an occupation" (Astin, Parrot, Korn, & Sax, 1997), it becomes understandable that difficulty finding or committing to long-term goals will increase their risk for attrition. Furthermore, if students develop a viable plan for identifying a college major and related career that is compatible with their abilities, interests and values, then their overall level of satisfaction with college should increase. In turn, student retention at their chosen college should increase, because there is a well-established empirical relationship between students' level of *satisfaction* with the postsecondary institution they are attending and their rate of *retention* at that institution (Noel, Levitz, & Saluri, 1985), that is, college satisfaction is a "primary predictor" of student persistence (Noel & Levitz, 1995).

"DECIDED" AND "UNDECIDED" STUDENTS: MYTHS AND REALITIES

A commonly held assumption in higher education is that students who are *undecided* about a college major are at greater risk for *attrition* than students with a declared major. As Strommer (1997) notes, "Being undeclared is generally presumed to be an aberrant condition that needs fixing" (p. 72). However, this prevalent belief is not well supported by empirical evidence. For example, Lewallen (1993) gathered data on a representative national sample of more than 18,000 first-year students from over 400 colleges and universities, while controlling for confounding variables known to affect student retention (e.g., academic preparedness and socioeconomic status). He discovered that knowledge of whether students were decided or undecided did not have any significant effect on predicting or explaining their retention. In a subsequent study, Lewallen (1995) examined a national sample of over 20,000 decided and undecided students at six different types of postsecondary institutions, and he found that undecided students actually displayed higher levels of academic achievement (average GPA) and were more likely to persist to graduation than decided students.

The mistaken belief that undecided students are necessarily "at risk" students may have evolved from a misinterpretation of early research on student retention, which indicated that students who have low aspirations or lack commitment to educational and occupational goals are more likely to leave college (e.g., Astin, 1975; Noel et al., 1985). Over time, these findings may have metamorphosed into a common conception that undecided (undeclared) students are *uncommitted* students who lack long-term academic plans, career goals, or sense of direction; thus, they are at risk for attrition. In fact, the term "undeclared" has acquired such a negative connotation that a TV sitcom about college students was created with that very name. (Although I have never seen a single episode of the sitcom, "Undeclared," I would still be willing to bet that it focused on college students who were academically clueless and directionless "party animals.")

The prevalent belief that being "undecided" equates with being "at risk" may also have evolved from an erroneous overgeneralization emanating from research findings which indicate that *prolonged* indecisiveness is empirically associated with increased risk for attrition (Janasiewicz, 1987; Raimst, 1981). However, the assumption that undecided students are *indecisive* students and prone to decisional procrastination is both groundless and gratuitous. Students may be undecided for a variety of reasons, many of which are psychologically healthy, and which have nothing to do with absence of direction, lack of goal orientation, or propensity for procrastination. As Virginia Gordon (1984) points out, "There are as many reasons for being undecided as there are students" (p. 75). For instance, students may be undecided because they have diverse interests and are excited about multiple fields of study. Their indecision may simply reflect a high level of motivation for learning and active involvement in the productive process of critically evaluating and prioritizing their varied academic interests. Other undecided students may simply be deliberate, reflective thinkers, whose decision-making style predisposes them to gathering more information (e.g., by gaining first-hand experience with different academic disciplines) before making any long-term commitments. Empirical support for this contention is provided by a 25-year longitudinal study conducted at Ohio State University, involving over 19,000 students who were undecided about a major or career at college entry. Only 22% of these students indicated that they were "completely undecided," 31% said they were "tentatively decided," and 43% had "several ideas but were not ready to decide" (Gordon & Steele, 2003).

While the foregoing types of students have been generically categorized as "undecided," their healthy suspension of judgment and mature decision-making process suggests that the term "exploratory" or "investigative" would be a more accurate classificatory label. As J. R. R. Tolkein succinctly states in his influential trilogy, *Lord of the Rings:* "All who wander are not lost." (Fittingly, the National Academic Advising Association has established the Commission for "Undecided/Exploratory" Students, a.k.a., CUES, to provide a national forum for discussion of issues relating to this student subpopulation.)

In contrast, some decided and declared students may be at greater risk for attrition than undecided students. James Powell, former president of Oberlin and Reed College, once said: "The kids who worry me are the ones who are so darn sure they know what they're going to be doing" (quoted in Pope, 1990, p. 180). These students might indeed be a legitimate source of concern (and potential attrition) because they may have made a decision that is (a) *premature*—reflecting lack of careful planning and forethought; (b) *unrealistic*—resulting from lack of self-knowledge (e.g., accurate awareness of personal aptitudes), or (c) *uninformed*—resting on insufficient knowledge about the relationship between academic majors and future careers.

Furthermore, students' early decisions may be driven entirely by *extrinsic* factors (e.g., pleasing parents or maximizing income) rather than by careful introspection and choice of a major or career that is congruent with their *intrinsic* interests, abilities, and values. Upcraft, Finney, and Garland (1984) point out that early decisions about majors and careers may result from "students [being] pushed into careers by their families, while others have picked one just to relieve their anxiety about not having a career choice. Still others may have picked popular or lucrative careers, knowing nothing of what they're really like or what it takes to prepare for them" (p. 18).

Major Changers

Students who *change majors* have also been classified under the generic rubric, "undecided," and they, too, are commonly deemed to be at risk for attrition. However, research has not demonstrated that risk for college withdrawal is associated with doubt or indecision about an initial major and eventual change of that major. In fact, some studies demonstrate that students who change majors actually display higher rates of retention (persistence to graduation) than non-changers. For instance, research reported by Micceri (2002), based on student tracking of major changers in the Florida State University System, revealed that students who change majors at least once during their college experience proceed to graduate at a rate ranging between 70%–85%, while students who hold on to their original major display a retention rate of 45%–50%. These findings replicate earlier research conducted by Anderson, Creamer, and Cross (1989), who found that major changers attempt and complete more credit hours than "decided" students. These findings suggest that changing decisions about a major is not necessarily a negative phenomenon; instead, it may represent personal maturation and progression to an advanced developmental stage in college students' decision-making process. As Tinto (1993) notes, "Movements from varying degrees of certainty to uncertainty and back again may in fact be quite characteristic of the longitudinal process of goal clarification which occurs during the college years. Not only should we not be surprised by such movements, we should expect, indeed hope, that they occur" (p. 41).

Naturally, there is a downside to changing majors, if the change takes place at a late juncture in the college experience. This can result in delayed time to graduation because of the need to complete additional courses required by the newly chosen major. So, while changing majors may contribute positively to the outcome of *persistence* to graduation, it may adversely affect the outcome of *time to* graduation — if the change occurs after a sizable number of credit hours have been accumulated in a previous major.

Shadow Majors

"Shadow" majors may be defined as students who are decided on a major, but have not yet been accepted or admitted to the major of their choice. Certain majors, because of their popularity, are oversubscribed or "impacted" (e.g., business, engineering, pre-med, and allied health sciences), so departments may attempt to control their enrollment by limiting access only to students who have achieved superior grades in highly competitive ("killer") prerequisite courses, or by admitting only students who have achieved a certain grade point average in all pre-major courses. In effect, shadow majors are students who have already met the university's admissions standards, but have yet to meet the standards of "second-tier" admission into their intended field of study. These students may eventually transition into their major of choice, or they may be shut out of their intended major if they fail to meet the specific standards imposed by its department. When the latter happens, these already "decided" majors often resist the prospect of changing majors, because "they may feel they are letting someone down or shattering a lifelong dream" (Gordon & Steele, 1992, p. 24). As a result, they may end up "drifting along without an academic home, semester after semester, making 'satisfactory progress' — but not toward a degree" (Strommer, 1993, p. 14).

Although there is little empirical evidence available on the retention rate of shadow majors who have been denied entry into their "decided" field of study, it is reasonable to expect that they may be at risk for attrition due to loss of their long-term goal and, perhaps, loss of commitment to the process (higher education) which represented their path to that goal. Even if rejected shadow majors eventually accept the reality of their rejection, proceed to an alternative major, and persist to graduation, their delayed change to an alternative major may delay their graduation because of the need to fulfill additional courses required by their late choice of a new major.

IMPLICATIONS FOR FUTURE RESEARCH AND ASSESSMENT

The foregoing research reviewed in this chapter suggests that historic interest in the question of *whether* students are decided or undecided about a major may be less important than questions about *when* and *how* students decide on a major. Looking toward future research and assessment on the academic decision-making process, it appears as if not much more is to be gained from the traditional approach of categorizing students as either "decided" or "undecided" and computing correlations between this dichotomous variable and student retention. As Lewallen (1994) notes, "Because few differences have been found [between decided and undecided students], it appears that undecided students represent more a microcosm of the college population than a highly distinguishable group" (p. 12). It may now be time to engage in research on the *process* of how students go about deciding on a major (or deciding to remain "undecided") and move toward longitudinal assessment of *when* students reach these decisions during their college experience. Admittedly, this is a challenging task that will require the use of more time-consuming, labor-intensive *qualitative* research methods, such as: (a) focus group interviews with decided and undecided students at different stages of the college experience, and

(b) narrative analysis of advisors' notes (written or electronic) on their meetings with advisees — to detect thematic patterns in how, why, and when students reach final decisions about college majors — in order to assess relationships between different patterns of student decision making and student retention. A good illustration of the type of useful information that may be generated by such qualitative assessment is a study conducted at a large research university that involved personal interviews with 16 "advanced" undecided students — that is, students who had completed more than one third of the minimum number of units needed for graduation. These in-depth interviews revealed that a major roadblock for most undecided students with advanced class standing was an unrealistic view about the long-term consequences of committing to a major. Namely, these students believed that selecting a major should "give them answers to all of the questions about what they want to do with their lives [and would] send them down an unchangeable career path, one they would be committed [to] for life" (Hagstrom, Skovholt, & Rivers, 1997, p. 29).

Another potentially fertile area for future research is assessment of whether different institutional attitudes and policies toward undecided students affect their decision-making process and persistence to graduation. National survey research suggests that there is appreciable variability in terms of how colleges and universities approach student decision making about a college major. Some institutions require or strongly encourage first-year students to declare a major, some discourage it, and others take a laissez-faire approach (Policy Center on The First Year of College Year, 2003). Lewallen (1995) notes that variations in institutional attitude toward undecided students can have significant impact on their initial decision-making processes and their subsequent experiences: "Some institutions are extremely supportive; others are indifferent or even nonsupportive. These approaches appear to have the potential to profoundly influence a student's willingness to declare being undecided. Additionally, these approaches have the potential to influence the college achievement and experiences of undecided students" (pp. 28–29).

IMPLICATIONS FOR COLLEGE
PRACTICES AND POLICIES

When establishing college policies and advising practices that impact undecided students, it may be necessary for decision makers and advisors to remain cognizant of the following research findings:

1. Three of every four students are uncertain or tentative about their career choice at college entry (Frost, 1991; Titley & Titley, 1980).
2. Among first-year students who enter college with a major in mind, less than 10% feel they know "a great deal about their intended major" (Lemoine, cited in Erickson & Strommer, 1991).
3. Uncertainty among new students frequently increases rather than decreases during their first two years of college (Tinto, 1993).
4. Over two thirds of entering students change their major during their first year (Kramer, Higley, & Olsen, 1993).
5. Between 50% and 75% of all students who enter college with a declared major change their mind at least once before they graduate (Foote, 1980; Gordon, 1984; Noel, 1985).
6. Only one senior out of three will major in the same field they preferred as a freshman (Willingham, 1985).

These high levels of student uncertainty and propensity for changing educational plans have been reported at all institutional types, including selective private universities (Marchese, 1992), large research universities ("What We Know About First-Year Students," 1996; "What Do I Want to Be," 1997), and small liberal arts colleges (Santovec, 1996).

Such findings strongly suggest that final decisions about majors and careers do *not* occur *before* students enter college; rather, students make these decisions *during* the college experience. Thus, it is not accurate to assume that students who enter college with "declared" majors are truly "decided" majors; instead, it is probably more accurate to conclude that 75% of all students entering college are actually undecided about their academic and career plans, and at least half of all students with declared majors are "prematurely decided" majors—who will eventually change their minds. In his doctoral dissertation, Lewallen (1992) notes the implications of these findings for postsecondary institutions: "Clearly, the time has come to formally recognize in our policies and practices that the majority of entering students are in an undecided mode. Being undecided is not the exception, but rather the norm" (p. 110). The fact that such large numbers of students change their initially chosen major—coupled with research findings indicating that students who change majors are as likely, or more likely, to attain good grades and persist to graduation—serve to support institutional policies that encourage students to postpone initial decisions about an academic major until they gain more self-knowledge and more personal experience with the college curriculum.

The extant research literature also suggests that students are more prone to making impulsive or premature decisions about their major than they are to procrastinate indefinitely about these decisions. Farvell and Rigley (1994) note that "the well-intentioned question asking, 'What are you going to major in at college?' asked frequently enough by family and by advisers can lead students to believe they are somehow deficient because they have not yet chosen an academic major" (p. 37). Unfortunately, some institutions may be exacerbating this propensity for premature or impulsive decision making by urging or requiring new students to declare a major at college entry or during the first year of college. For instance, Gordon (1995) notes that "Many institutions allow entering students to specify on an admissions form if they are undecided about an academic program. Others do not recognize 'undecidedness' as a condition of enrollment" (p. 93).

A recent national survey of nearly 1,000 institutions conducted by the Policy Center on The First Year of College (2003) revealed that approximately 44% of colleges and universities either strongly encourage or require first-year students to select a major. By electing not to declare a major, undecided students may be left "homeless," — that is, left without an academic department, organizational niche, or administrative division that they can call their own. Such institutional practice may discourage first-year students to remain undecided, and tacitly encourage them to make hasty decisions in order to meet institutional expectations that they should be "decided" and housed in an academic department. As Frost (1991) notes, "In institutions that urge all freshmen to declare a major, undecided students might be reluctant to identify themselves and remain underserved. If college is to encourage students to develop the capacity to judge wisely, then perhaps freshmen should defer selecting a major until later in their college careers" (p. 32). Erickson and Strommer (1991) concur: "We would do well to treat each one of our entering freshmen as an undecided student. Institutions that extend substantial career/life planning and academic services to all freshmen can expect to achieve significant improvements in retention rates" (p. 74). Thus, policymakers need to remain cognizant of the fact that beginning college students need adequate "incubation" time for their major and career plans to crystallize.

When formulating institutional polices and practices about undecided students, decision makers also need to remain mindful of the purpose of *general education,* and the important role it plays in facilitating and informing student decisions about academic majors by introducing new students to a breadth of academic disciplines and a variety of potential majors, many of which they never encountered, or even heard of, prior to college. As Gordon and Steele (2003) point out, "Exploration through coursework is perhaps the most basic and important advising tool" (p. 30). Expecting students to reach final decisions about college majors before having sufficient experience (or any experience) with the process of general education, and the courses that comprise the liberal arts curriculum, may be viewed as devaluation of one of the major missions of higher education. It may also be seen as a disturbing disservice to a critical component of the college experience — one that provides the formative foundation and transferable skills which are essential for success in any college major and any career. Virginia Gordon argues that the first year, in particular, is a "critical time [for students] to learn how to gather information about their academic strengths and limitations and how they can incorporate these strengths into various major and occupational alternatives. They can experience the thrill of discovery and hone the skills of critical thinking and information management. The first year in college should be the time when students begin to lay the foundation for a lifetime of career choice and maintenance" (Gordon, 1995, p. 99).

Predictably, liberal arts colleges are the most likely to value the general education experience by encouraging students to *postpone* selection of a major until the sophomore year. In contrast, two-year colleges are the postsecondary institutions that are most likely to "strongly encourage" or "require" major selection in the first year (Policy Center on the First Year of College, 2003). The latter finding is a disturbing one, because two-year colleges are the very institutions that enroll the highest percentage of academically underprepared, underexperienced (first-generation), and underrepresented (minority) students (Striplin, 1999). From the community colleges' perspective, it is understandable why students are encouraged to make early decisions about a field of interest, because entering students often must decide between embarking on either a vocational-track or transfer-track curriculum. Moreover, if community college students intend to transfer successfully to baccalaureate-granting institutions, it may be necessary for them to complete all pre-major requirements (in addition to their developmental course work and general education requirements) to qualify for admission, particularly if they are applying for admission to popular universities or to academic majors that are oversubscribed or "impacted." For example, the University of California system now expects all two-year college graduates to complete 60 transferable units, including all areas of its general education curriculum and all pre-major courses in the student's chosen field of study. For majors that require completion of numerous pre-major courses prior to transfer (e.g., business, engineering, and health sciences), this policy essentially forces full-time, continuously enrolled, community college students to select a major and begin their sequence of pre-major coursework during the *first term* of college—if they expect to transfer to a four-year university in a reasonable period of time. The ugly irony associated with this policy is that it exerts the most academic decision-making pressure on students in community colleges, which enroll the highest percentages of academically underprepared and economically disadvantaged students (Cohen & Brawer, 2002; Roueche & Roueche, 1993). Rendon (1994) points out the danger of such policies for underrepresented students: "Minorities often exhibit a naiveté about the costs and benefits of the higher education system, and may find out they are committing themselves to goals they don't fully understand" (p. 30).

Institutional policies that "push" students into making early or premature commitments to an academic specialization also fail to acknowledge (a) the reality of academic uncertainty that exists among the majority of first-year students, and (b) the process of self-discovery that is so essential to personal development during the formative years of college. As Tinto (1993) observes, "The regrettable fact is that some institutions do not see student uncertainty in this [exploratory] light. They prefer to treat it as a deficiency in student development rather than as an expected part of that complex process of personal growth. The implications of such views for policy are not trivial" (p. 41).

Research and theory on the cognitive and psychosocial development of college students strongly suggests that the majority of first-year students have not yet reached a stage of intellectual maturity at which they are most capable of making well-reasoned educational and occupational decisions. For instance, Perry (1970, 1998) discovered through in-depth interviews with college students during different years in the undergraduate experience that first-year students are at a "basic duality" stage of cognitive development, during which the world is seen in dual terms—right or wrong, with correct answers being absolute and known by authorities. Multiple viewpoints, diversity of opinions, and different theoretical perspectives are seen as bothersome or confusing. Typically, it is during the sophomore year when students begin to appreciate relativistic thinking, that is, that multiple factors and perspectives need to be weighed in order to understand an issue, phenomenon, or decision. During the second year of college, students begin to understand that the uncertainty and potential chaos associated with relativistic thinking may be managed by making well-reasoned decisions and commitments.

Perry's findings are reinforced by the work of Baxter-Magolda (1992), who conducted open-ended interviews with students from the first to the final year of college. She reports that sophomores are at a stage of "transitional knowing," transitioning from the absolute thinking of the first year to the independent and contextual thinking that peaks during the junior and senior years of college.

Boston and DuVivier (cited in Evenbeck, Boston, DuVivier, & Hallberg, 2000), conducted focus-group interviews with students at Purdue University and found that sophomores reported moving from being defined in the eyes of their parents to deciding what was best for themselves. They felt that the first year of college provided them with the opportunity for self-analysis, from which emerged a sense of commitment to self-determination. The outcome of this developmental process often resulted in a change of plans about their academic major or a renewed commitment to their original goal.

These findings on the maturation of students' decision-making processes are consistent with Chickering's developmental theory of college student identity (Chickering, 1969; Chickering & Reisser, 1993), which postulates that the developmental tasks encountered in the first year of college center around developing intellectual, physical, and social competence, along with emotional independence. Chickering argues that higher education forces first-year students to make these decisions before they have developed the personal identity on which sound decisions are based. He contends that development of personal identity, long-term educational plans, and career purpose arises later in the undergraduate experience for the majority of college students.

Chickering's theory is supported by the empirical work of P. D. Gardner (2000), whose surveys of students at different stages of the college experience revealed that their conversations during the first year most often focused on college courses, personal problems, and campus issues. In contrast, sophomores reported spending significantly less time on these issues and substantially more time on career and major concerns.

STRATEGIES FOR ENHANCING THE QUALITY OF FIRST-YEAR STUDENTS' MAJOR/CAREER PLANNING AND DECISION MAKING

1. **Provide strong *incentives* for *first-year students to meet regularly* with their advisors.** At the very least, students should be required to see an

advisor in order to register for courses. At some four-year colleges and many community colleges, students can register for classes without ever seeing an academic advisor (e.g., via electronic or telephonic registration). Leaving first-year students on their own to design an educational plan and to select courses relevant to that plan, means that students completely bypass the advising process, along with its retention-promoting potential. This is a risky procedure to employ with any undergraduate student, but it is a especially risky for first-year students, who lack experience with higher education and familiarity with the college curriculum.

Strong incentives should also be provided (e.g., priority registration) for students who meet with advisors at times other than the hurried and harried period of course registration. Meetings need to take place at times when advisors have sufficient time to interact with students as persons — rather than "process" them as registrants, and when advisors have the opportunity to explore or clarify students' broader, long-term educational plans — rather than focusing narrowly, myopically, and episodically on the imminent, deadline-driven task of class scheduling.

2. Identify *highly effective advisors* and *"front-load"* them — that is, position them at the front (start) of the college experience to work with first-year students.   In a landmark report on the quality of undergraduate education issued by the National Institute of Education (1984), its panel of distinguished scholars' first recommendation for improving undergraduate education was "front-loading," which they define as the reallocation of faculty and other institutional resources to better serve first-year students. Delivery of high-quality developmental advising during the first semester of college is one way to implement the principle of front-loading and promote student persistence to graduation. The value of front-loading effective advisors to promote the retention of first-year students is noted by Noel (1985), who argues that "the critical time in establishing the kind of one-to-one contacts between students and their teachers and advisers that contribute to student success and satisfaction occurs during the first few weeks of the freshman year" (p. 20).

Moreover, front-loading our most effective and committed advisors to work with first-year students can be expected to result in their making more thoughtful, more accurate *initial* choices about majors and careers. This would serve not only to promote student retention, but it may also reduce the probability of premature decision making, which can eventuate in changing of majors at later stages in the college experience. Prolonged indecisiveness and late changing of majors can result in delayed progress toward degree completion by necessitating completion of additional courses to fulfill specific degree requirements for a newly chosen major. This may be one factor contributing to the extended length of time it now takes college students to complete their graduation requirements (U.S. Bureau of the Census, 1994); the number of students taking five or more years to graduate from college doubled between the early 1980s and 1990s (Kramer, 1993). Data collected by the U.S. Department of Education indicate that, for the student cohort who entered college in 1995 with the intention of earning a bachelor's degree, only 37% completed that degree within four years, while 63% took six years (Arenson, 2003). Intrusive and proactive delivery of high-quality advising during the first year of college may be expected to reduce delays in graduation, as well as the cost of college education, due to late major-changing stemming from an unwise or unrealistic choice of an initial major.

3. Promote early academic and career planning by infusing it into the first-year curriculum. This may be accomplished by adding a course to the curriculum that is devoted exclusively to the topic of academic and career planning, or by including the topic as an integral component of a first-year seminar. In such courses, students can engage in classroom activities or complete course assignments that involve long-term *educational and career* planning, serving to *connect* their *present* college experience with their *future* goals and aspirations. For instance, an assignment could be created that asks first-year students to develop an *undergraduate* plan, which includes courses in general education and pre-major courses in an academic field that the student intends to major in or is considering as a possible choice. This assignment could also include tentative *post-baccalaureate* plans for graduate school, professional school, or immediate career entry, which encourage students to (a) identify potential positions, (b) construct a skeletal or model resume that would prepare them for entry into such positions, and (c) initiate a personal *portfolio*—a collection of materials that illustrates student competencies or achievements, and demonstrates educational or personal development—for example: written work, artistic products, research projects, letters of recommendation, co-curricular accomplishments, personal awards, and certificates of achievement.

Another advantage of promoting early academic and career planning within the context of a first-term course is that it allows for *continuity of contact* between the course instructor and new students *throughout their initial term* of college enrollment. This continuous contact enables the instructor to closely monitor the progress of new students during their critical first semester, and allows sufficient time for bonding to take place between students and teacher. If it can be arranged for new students' *academic advisors* to serve as *course instructors* in a first-year seminar, then the course can serve as a conduit for providing close and continuous contact between student and advisor during the critical first term of the college experience. Presently, 20% of institutions offering first-year seminars have arranged for students to be placed into sections of the course taught by their academic advisors (National Resource Center for the First-Year Experience, 2002), thus ensuring regular advisor–advisee contact during the critical first term.

Research conducted at North Dakota State University indicates that, if new students' academic advisors also serve as their first-year seminar instructors, students make significantly more *out-of-class* contact with their academic advisor during their first term than students whose advisors do not co-serve as first-year seminar instructors (Soldner, in Barefoot, Warnock, Dickinson, Richardson, & Roberts, 1998).

4. *Integrate* the Offices of *Academic Advisement* and *Career Counseling*. New students need support to integrate the tasks of selecting an academic major and planning for a future career. As Tinto (1993) emphatically states, "It is part of the educational mandate of institutions of higher education to assist maturing youth in coming to grips with the important question of adult careers" (p. 41). Yet, according to a national report released by the Wingspread Group (1993), few campuses have created one-stop "success centers" where students can receive integrated assistance, such as integrated assistance from academic advisement and career development services.

5. Establish an *Office, Center,* or *Organizational Unit* for the Advisement of *Undecided (Exploratory) Students*. In their 25-year longitudinal study of nearly 20,000 first-year students, Gordon and Steele (2003) discovered that 85% of undecided students at college entry report being "somewhat anxious" or "very anxious" about choosing a major, and approximately 50% of "completely decided" students indicated that they were "very anxious." These findings suggest that new students need a safe and supportive sanctuary to engage in the academic exploration and decision-making process. At many colleges, academic advising is handled by discipline-based academic departments, which either leaves undecided students without a designated home or arbitrarily remands them for assignment to an academic department that may have little or no relation to their eventual field of interest. Such an assignment is not likely to provide undecided students with the support structure needed to reflectively investigate their academic and career options (Hart, 1995).

It may be that some institutions pressure first-year students, either tacitly or explicitly, into making an early commitment to a major, simply for the self-serving and institutionally convenient purpose of channeling them into academic departments—where they are advised by discipline-based faculty advisors. Habley (1994) observers that "Some faculty-only systems virtually ignore the developmental needs of undecided students either by assigning them at random to faculty members throughout the campus, or by using undecided students to level the advising load of faculty in departments with fewer majors" (p. 19). Unfortunately, many faculty advisors do not have the time, interest, or expertise to facilitate the process of major and career exploration. (I say this as a faculty member who values academic advising and enjoys advising first-year students. Nevertheless, it must be said because graduate education does not adequately prepare faculty for their role as advisors, and their home institutions often compound the problem by failing to systematically orient, develop, and reward faculty for engaging in the type of high-quality developmental advising that enables students to arrive at mature, thoughtful decisions about their majors and careers.) As Hart (1995) observes, "Entering students often do not have a real area of study in mind. This suggests that entering college students, at a minimum, should have ready access to persons trained as career counseling and advising generalists rather than only to discipline-based faculty. Expecting teaching faculty to meet the unique advising needs of entering students, given other expectations and demands on their time, is unrealistic" (pp. 76, 81).

A good illustration of an organizational unit that has been intentionally designed to support undecided students is Kent State University's Undergraduate Studies (US) unit, which houses a Student Advising Center (SAC) created for undeclared majors—who are referred to as "exploratory majors." SAC houses a computer lab equipped with career interest assessments and inventories, and a team of eight full-time advisors specifically trained to guide "exploratory" students (Kuhn, Howard, & Matyas, 1996). Similarly, Pace University has created an "Office of Transitional Advising" specifically for "undecided majors," which serves as a resource center for students who (a) have not yet declared a major, (b) want to change majors, and (c) need to leave a major because of academic reasons and find another one. Among the services provided by this office are: (a) connecting students with faculty, staff, and student liaisons, (b) providing student opportunities to observe classes that will expose them to different fields of study, (c) delivering workshops on academic goal clarification, (d) providing guidance on the relationships between academic majors and careers, and (e) making referrals to university programs, services, campus events, and student clubs (Schmid, 2001).

6. Create *Experiential* Learning Opportunities for First- and Second-Year Students to Promote Early Awareness of the *Realities* of Work in Different Careers. This may be accomplished by such practices as having students: (a) *interview* professionals in different career positions, (b) *shadow* different career professionals during a "typical" workday, and (c) *volunteer* or engage in *service learning* in different settings. As J. N. Gardner (2002) argues, "The working relationship among service-learning programs and units responsible for providing career planning needs to be strengthened and made more intentional" (p. 147).

Guest panelists may also be invited into the classroom to share their experiences (e.g., in freshman seminars or career-planning courses). Potential invitees include: (a) college seniors majoring in different academic fields, (b) alumni who graduated with different college majors, (c) faculty representing different academic disciplines, and (d) trustee members or other working professionals representing different careers.

These human resources may also be invited to a central place on campus, as part of an integrated "major and career fair." Assignments could be crafted in freshman seminars, career planning courses, or other first-year courses, which reward students for participating in and reflecting on this event.

CONCLUSION

Research reviewed in this chapter strongly suggests that *intentionally* designed interventions are needed to improve the effectiveness of first-year students' academic decision making and career planning. These institutional interventions will likely have the most salutary impact if their delivery is *intrusive*—that is, if the college *initiates* supportive action by *reaching out* to new students and bringing support to them, rather than passively offering programs and hoping that students will come to take advantage of them on their own accord.

Intrusive delivery is perhaps most effectively achieved when support is channeled through the curriculum, via courses that encourage and reward students to engage in meaningful academic and career planning. The practice of offering programmatic support in the form of a *graded, credit-bearing* course has the advantage of promoting the program's *credibility* in the eyes of students. The program's content will more likely be seen as central to a college education and comparable in importance to content covered in other courses that comprise the college curriculum. Furthermore, when programmatic support is delivered through a course in the curriculum, the course grade can serve as a strong motivational *incentive* for elevating students' *level of effort and depth of involvement* with respect to the program's content, as well as elevating *instructor expectations* of the amount of time and energy that students should devote to its content. Both of these consequences should serve to magnify the program's potential for exerting positive effects on student learning, development, and success.

Support programs are also more likely to have significant impact when their delivery is *proactive,* that is, when *early* and *preventative* action is taken that addresses students' needs in an *anticipatory* fashion—before they eventuate in problems that require reactive intervention. It is evident from research reviewed in this chapter that first-year students need support in the area of academic and career decision making. Moreover, providing programmatic support in the *first term* of college may impact students' level of involvement with the support program during their remaining years in college. It is reasonable to hypothesize that a proactively delivered, academic decision-making and career-planning program experienced by students during their first term on campus will serve to stimulate subsequent student involvement with the program, enabling it to exert recurrent and cumulative effects on student development throughout the undergraduate experience.

Lastly, an academic decision-making and career-planning program that is delivered intrusively and proactively to first-year students may be expected to produce bi-directional benefits for the institution and its students. It should benefit the *institution* by promoting student retention and satisfaction with the college, and it should benefit *students* by increasing the likelihood that they will pursue an academic specialization and career path that is both personally meaningful and self-fulfilling.

REFERENCES

ACT. (2003, February). *National college dropout and graduation rates, 2002*. Retrieved February 14, 2003, from http:www.act.org/news

Anderson, B. C., Creamer, D. G., & Cross, L. H. (1989). Undecided, multiple change, and decided students: How different are they? *NACADA Journal, 9*(1), 46–50.

Arenson, K. W. (2003, April 13). The longtime student. *The New York Times.* Retrieved May 26, 2003 from http://www.nytimes.com

Astin, A. W. (1975). *Preventing students from dropping out.* San Francisco: Jossey-Bass.

Astin, A. W., Parrot, S., Korn, W., & Sax, L. (1997). *The American freshman—Thirty year trends, 1966–1996.* Los Angeles: Higher Education Research Institute.

Barefoot, B. O., Warnock, C. L., Dickinson, M. P., Richardson, S. E., & Roberts, M. R. (Eds.). (1998). *Exploring the evidence: Vol. 2. Reporting outcomes of first-year seminars.* (Monograph No. 29). Columbia, SC: National Resource Center for The First-Year Experience and Students in Transition, University of South Carolina.

Baxter-Magolda, M. B. (1992). *Knowing and reasoning in college: Gender-related patterns in students' intellectual development.* San Francisco: Jossey-Bass.

Chickering, A. W. (1969). *Education and identity.* San Francisco: Jossey-Bass.

Chickering, A. W., & Reisser, L. (1993). *Education and identity* (2nd ed.). San Francisco: Jossey-Bass.

Cohen, A. M., & Brawer, F. B. (2002). *The American community college* (4th ed.). San Francisco: Jossey-Bass.

Consortium for Student Retention Data Exchange. (1999). *Executive summary 1998–1999 CSRDE report: The retention and graduation rates in 269 colleges and universities.* Norman, OK: Center for Institutional Data Exchange and Analysis, University of Oklahoma.

Erickson, B. L., & Strommer, D. W. (1991). *Teaching college freshmen.* San Francisco: Jossey-Bass.

Evenbeck, S. E., Boston, M., DuVivier, R. S., & Hallberg, K. (2000). Institutional approaches to helping sophomores. In L. A. Schreiner & J. Pattengale (Eds.), *Visible solution for invisible students: Helping sophomores succeed* (Monograph No. 31, pp. 79–88). Columbia, SC: University of South Carolina, National Resource Center for the First-Year Experience and Students in Transition.

Farvell, R. K., & Rigley, D. (1994). Essential resources for advising undecided students. In V. N. Gordon (Ed.), *Issues in advising the undecided student* (Monograph No. 15, pp. 37–48). Columbia, SC: University of South Carolina, National Resource Center for the Freshman Year Experience.

Foote, B. (1980). Determined- and undetermined-major students: How different are they? *Journal of College Student Personnel, 21*(1), 29–34.

Frost, S. H. (1991). *Academic advising for student success: A system of shared responsibility.* ASHE-ERIC Higher Education Report No. 3. Washington, DC: The George Washington School of Education and Human Development.

Gardner, J. N. (2002). What, so what, now what: Reflections, findings, conclusions, and recommendations on service learning and the first-year experience. In E. Zlotkowski (Ed.), *Service-learning and the first-year experience: Preparing students for personal success and civic responsibility* (Monograph No. 34, pp. 141–150). Columbia, SC: University of South Carolina, National Resource Center for the First-Year Experience and Students in Transition.

Gardner, P. D. (2000). From drift to engagement: Finding purpose and making career connections in the sophomore year. In L. A. Schreiner & J. Pattengale (Eds.), *Visible solution for invisible students: Helping sophomores succeed* (Monograph No. 31, pp. 67–78).

Columbia, SC: University of South Carolina, National Resource Center for the First-Year Experience and Students in Transition.

Gordon, V. N. (1984). *The undecided college student: An academic and career advising challenge.* Springfield, IL: Thomas.

Gordon, V. N. (1995). Advising first-year undecided students. In M. L. Upcraft & G. L. Kramer (Eds.), *First-year academic advising: Patterns in the present, pathways to the future* (Monograph No. 18, pp. 93–100). Columbia, SC: University of South Carolina, National Resource Center for the First-Year Experience & Student in Transition.

Gordon, V. N., & Steele, G. E. (1992). Advising major-changers: Students in transition. *NACADA Journal, 12,* 22–27.

Gordon, V. N., & Steele, G. E. (2003). Undecided first-year students: A 25-year longitudinal study. *Journal of the First-Year Experience, 15*(1), 19–38.

Habley, W. R. (1994). Administrative approaches to advising undecided students. In V. N. Gordon (Ed.), *Issues in advising the undecided student* (Monograph No. 15, pp. 17–24). Columbia, SC: University of South Carolina, National Resource Center for the Freshman Year Experience.

Hagstrom, S. J., Skovholt, T. S., & Rivers, D. A. (1997). The advanced undecided college student: A qualitative study. *NACADA Journal, 17*(2), 23–30.

Hart, D. (1995). Reach-out advising strategies for first-year students. In M. L. Upcraft & G. L. Kramer (Eds.), *First-year academic advising: Patterns in the present, pathways to the future* (Monograph No. 18, pp. 75–82). Columbia, SC: University of South Carolina, National Resource Center for the First-Year Experience & Student in Transition.

Janasiewicz, B. (1987). Campus leaving behavior. *National Academic Advising Association Journal, 7,* 23–30.

Kramer, M. (1993). Lengthening of time to degree. *Change, 25*(3), 5–7.

Kramer, G. L., Higley, B., & Olsen, D. (1993, Winter). Changes in academic emphasis among undergraduate students. *College and University,* 88–98.

Kuhn, T., Howard, C., & Matyas, J. (1996, October). *Choice vs. responsibility: The mandatory advising dilemma.* Paper presented at the Second National Conference on Students in Transition, San Antonio, TX.

Learning Slope. (1991). *Policy Perspectives, 4*(1), 1A–8A. Pew Higher Education Research Program.

Lewallen, W. C. (1992). Persistence of the "undecided": The characteristics and college persistence of students undecided about academic major or career choice. *Dissertation Abstracts International, 53,* 12A, 4226. (University Microfilms No. 93-10950)

Lewallen, W. C. (1993). The impact of being "undecided" on college student persistence. *Journal of College Student Development, 34,* 103–112.

Lewallen, W. C. (1994). A profile of undecided college students. In V. N. Gordon (Ed.), *Issues in advising the undecided student* (Monograph No. 15, pp. 5–16). Columbia, SC: University of South Carolina, National Resource Center for the Freshman Year Experience.

Lewallen, W. C. (1995). Students decided and undecided about career choice: A comparison of college achievement and student involvement. *NACADA Journal, 15*(1), 22–30.

Marchese, T. (1992). Assessing learning at Harvard: An interview with Richard J. Light. *AAHE Bulletin, 44*(6), 3–7.

Micceri, T. (2002, May 30). *Will changing your major double your graduation chances?* Invited paper posted on the First-Year Assessment Listserv, sponsored by the Policy

Center for the First Year of College. Retrieved May 30, 2002, from http://www.brevard.edu/fycindex.htm

National Institute of Education. (1984). *Involvement in learning*. Study Group on the Conditions of Excellence in Higher Education. Washington, DC: Author.

National Resource Center for the First-Year Experience. (2002). *2000 survey of first-year seminar programming: Continuing innovations in the collegiate curriculum* (Monograph No. 35). Columbia, SC: University of South Carolina, National Resource Center for the First-Year Experience and Students in Transition.

Noel, L. (1985). Increasing student retention: New challenges and potential. In L. Noel, R. Levitz, & D. Saluri (Eds.), *Increasing student retention* (pp. 1–27). San Francisco: Jossey-Bass.

Noel, L., & Levitz, R. (1995). New strategies for difficult times. *Recruitment & Retention in Higher Education, 9*(7), 4–7.

Noel, L., Levitz, R., & Saluri, D. (Eds.). (1985). *Increasing student retention: New challenges and potential.* San Francisco: Jossey-Bass.

Perry, W. G. (1970). *Forms of intellectual and ethical development in the college years.* New York: Holt, Rinehart & Winston.

Perry, W. G. (1998). *Forms of intellectual and ethical development in the college years.* San Francisco: Jossey-Bass.

Policy Center on the First Year of College (2003). Second national survey of first-year academic practices, 2002. Retrieved from http://www.brevard.edu/fyc/survey2002/findings.htm

Postsecondary Education Opportunity. (2002, March). Institutional graduation rates by control, academic selectivity and degree level, 1983–2002. *The Environmental Scanning Research Letter of Opportunity for Postsecondary Education, 1–16.*

Pope, L. (1990). *Looking beyond the ivy league.* New York: Penguin Press.

Raimst, L. (1981). *College student attrition and retention* (College Board Rep. No. 81-1). New York: College Entrance Examination Board.

Rendon, L. I. (1994). Validating culturally diverse students: Toward a new model of learning and student development. *Innovative Higher Education, 19*(1), 23–32.

Roueche, S. D., & Roueche, J. E. (1993). *Between a rock and a hard place: The at-risk student in the open-door college.* Washington, DC: The Community College Press.

Santovec, M. L. (1996). Alpha gives undecided students a sense of identity. In M. L. Santovec (Ed.), *Making more changes: Editor's choice* (pp. 88–90). Madison, WI: Magna Publications.

Schmid, S. (2001). *Office for undeclared majors.* E-mail message to First-Year Assessment List [FYA-LIST@VM.SC.EDU], May 11, 2001.

Striplin, J. J. (1999, June). Facilitating transfer for first-generation community college students. *Digest.* Los Angeles: University of California at Los Angeles. (ERIC Document Reproduction Service No. EDO-JC-99-05)

Strommer, D. W. (1993). Not quite good enough: Drifting about in higher education. *AAHE Bulletin, 45*(10), 14–15.

Strommer, D. W. (1997). Review of "The undecided college student: An academic and career advising challenge" by Virginia N. Gordon (1995). *NACADA Journal, 17*(1), 72–73.

Tinto, V. (1993). *Leaving college: Rethinking the causes and cures for student attrition* (2nd ed.). Chicago: University of Chicago Press.

Titley, R., & Titley, B. (1980). Initial choice of college major: Are only the "undecided" undecided? *Journal of College Student personnel, 21*(4), 293–298.

Upcraft, M. L., Finney, J. E., & Garland, P. (1984). Orientation: A context. In M. L. Upcraft
(Ed.), *Orienting students to college* (pp. 5–25). San Francisco: Jossey-Bass.

U.S. Bureau of the Census. (1994). *Statistical abstract of the United States: 1994* (114th ed.).
Washington, DC: U.S. Government Printing Office.

What Do I Want To Be . . .? (1997, Winter). *LAS News* (College of Liberal Arts and Sciences
Newsletter, p. 12). Urbana-Champaign: University of Illinois.

What We Know About First-Year Students. (1996). In J. N. Gardner & A. J. Jewler, *Your college experience: Instructor's resource manual* (p. G-90). Belmont, CA: Wadsworth.

Willingham, W. W. (1985). *Success in college: The role of personal qualities and academic ability.* New York: College Entrance Examination Board.

Wingspread Group. (1993). *An American imperative: Higher expectations for higher education.* Racine, WI: The Johnson Foundation.

Wyckoff, S. C. (1999). The academic advising process in higher education: History, research,
and improvement. *Recruitment & Retention in Higher Education, 13*(1), pp. 1–3.

II

Diversity and the First Year of College

3

First-Year Students: Embracing Their Diversity, Enhancing Our Practice

RAECHELE L. POPE
TERESA A. MIKLITSCH
MATTHEW J. WEIGAND
The State University of New York at Buffalo

The transition from high school to college for many traditional-aged students involves leaving home, saying goodbye to friends, family, and loved ones, and setting up residence on a college campus. For others the transition means, at the very least, venturing temporarily outside of their familiar community of family and friends while commuting to college. For first-year students this ritual will likely be repeated for many semesters to come. It is a time of excitement and anxiety, an experience of new beginnings and an end to the practices and traditions of the past twelve years. While in college, students have the opportunity to choose their courses, their professors, if and when they attend class, when and where to eat, where to live and with whom, and a new lifestyle where limited parental control exists except in the attitudes and values instilled over their lifetime.

The first year of college involves many new experiences, and first-year students have many opportunities to try new behaviors and embrace new attitudes and beliefs.

College faculty and university professionals are integral partners with first-year students in these opportunities. Building bridges between first-year students and the campus community is crucial because initial encounters between first-year students and other students, faculty, student affairs and university personnel often set the tone for how well or how soon first-year students adjust to their new environment. The cognitive, behavioral, and affective development of traditional-age first-year students is at a unique stage of formation as they experience the challenges and opportunities that college has to offer. It is essential therefore for higher education faculty and staff members to understand the nature of this development and the characteristics and experiences of these first-year students. It is equally important to fully appreciate how diverse the campus student body has become and how not all first-year students experience the college classroom or campus community in the same way.

DIVERSITY DEMOGRAPHICS IN HIGHER EDUCATION

The racial, ethnic, gender, and sexual-orientation composition of college students is more diverse today than it was twenty years ago. Demographic data (Chronicle of Higher Education, 2003) and trends (Chronicle of Higher Education, 2003; Keller, 2001; Skrentny, 2001) provide some glimpse into this ever-evolving reality. Female students comprise more than 56% of the student population (Chronicle of Higher Education, 2003). The ages of college students have fluctuated, with 18–22-year-olds currently encompassing 44% of the overall student population—significantly fewer than twenty years ago (Chronicle of Higher Education, 2003). According to the Chronicle of Higher Education (2003), the number of undergraduate Asian and Hispanic students has more than doubled since 1980. The percentage of Hispanic undergraduate students has increased from 4.14% in 1980 to 9.56% in 1999; and the Asian student percentage has increased from 2.38% in 1980 to 6.18% in 1999 (Chronicle of Higher Education, 2003). Recent census data has confirmed that Hispanics have become the largest population of color (U.S. Government, 2003) and have exceeded the growth of the current and projected White (Non-Hispanic) population (Clemetson, 2003). The proportions of undergraduate Black and Native American collegians have grown at less dramatic levels from 9.73% to 11.60% and from .74% to 1.05% for these respective student populations (Chronicle of Higher Education, 2003). College enrollment data also have revealed that White undergraduate students comprised 69.36% of the total collegiate population in 1999, which is 11.64% fewer than in 1980 (Chronicle of Higher Education, 2003). Finally, the presence of increasing numbers of international students, representing a myriad of cultures, also adds to the emerging diversity of campus populations.

This demographic data is critical in portraying a vivid picture of college students today and in understanding that there is no such thing as a "typical" American college student. The multicultural nature of the contemporary student population mandates that college and university professionals acknowledge and address this reality. Such diversity calls for innovative campus-wide practices as educators and practitioners design programs and offer services to meet the needs of an ever-changing student population. These efforts are more likely to be successful when the campus community embraces and promotes diversity as a stated mission of the institution (Pope, 1995).

The purpose of this chapter is to focus on the importance of addressing diversity issues within first-year programs and practices. Typically, research and practice addressing the issues and concerns of first-year students depict these students as a homogeneous group with similar needs, goals, and experiences. Research within student development has increasingly highlighted the unique experiences of students of color and how their identity, relationships, and attitudes often differ from those of White students. Higher education professionals committed to the success of first-year students need further education about how to address the unique concerns and issues of students of color. In addition, it is vital for all first-year students to be educated about the value of diversity. Teaching first-year students the attitudes and skills necessary to form meaningful relationships with individuals who may be culturally different from them will prepare them to enter the workforce after college and make important contributions as citizens. Such emphasis on cultural competence can become integrated into all relevant programs and services using models and frameworks already developed (see Pope, Reynolds, & Mueller, 2004).

The Multicultural Change Intervention Matrix (MCIM) is just one example of a multicultural framework that can be easily incorporated into current practice. This matrix, based on the multicultural organization development (MCOD) literature and created by Pope (1995), can be utilized to develop and assess the multicultural strategies and interventions on campus. The MCIM identified two major dimensions to any multicultural change effort. The first concentrates on the possible targets of the interventions, specifically whether they are focused on individuals, groups, or the institution itself. The second dimension describes two discrete levels of intervention: first-order and second-order change. These levels highlight the difference between important yet superficial change and deep, structural change. While both levels of change are essential to creating a multicultural campus, second-order change is more focused on organizational transformation in which the core values and practices of the institution are redefined and altered.

The Multicultural Change Intervention Matrix provides six distinct cells or types of intervention that can assist campus administrators and faculty in creating a systemic and systematic approach to addressing multicultural issues within their institution. The tools and strategies of MCOD allow administrators to plan for change and the meaningful inclusion of multicultural issues into all aspects of an organization, including the mission statement, key policies, recruitment and retention of a diverse staff, staff training, programs and services, physical environment, and assessment/ evaluation approaches (Pope, 1995; Pope et al., 2004).

IMPACT OF DIVERSITY
ON HIGHER EDUCATION

Diversity enhances the educational endeavor and enterprise as delineated in the American Council on Education/American Association of University Professor's Diversity Report (1998). This Diversity Report provides a comprehensive assessment of diversity, particularly as it impacts current classroom settings (ACE/AAUP, 1998). A majority of the faculty surveyed believed that their institutions valued racial and ethnic diversity; that diversity enhanced the learning experience and intellectual development of students; that diversity augmented interactions within and outside of the classroom, thereby benefiting student and faculty members; that diversity was a critical component of the institution's missions; and that diversity promoted positive educational outcomes. Patricia Gurin's expert legal testimony in the University of Michigan 6th Circuit Federal Appeals Court case also presented compelling data regarding the value of diverse student populations and environments (Gurin, 1998; and see Nagda, Gurin, & Johnson, chapter 4, this volume). The Civil Rights Project's research on the impact of diversity on collegians' educational outcomes and the campus community reinforced the argument that "diversity is indeed a central and compelling interest of the college" (Orfield, 2001, p. 5).

Research has increasingly demonstrated how campus climate plays a significant role in affecting student experiences and outcomes. Understanding university environments therefore remains essential in addressing how students develop during and as a result of their college years (Astin, 1993; Harris & Nettles, 1996; Kuh, 2000; Lee, 2002). Initially, studies of campus climate did not explore issues of diversity; more recently, research has been used to better understand the unique experiences of college students of color. This research, while still in its early stages, highlights essential concerns that can uniquely affect the experiences of first-year students of color. It is important to emphasize, however, that research on the role of diversity in educating students has not focused mainly on first-year students but rather has examined students at all levels of higher education.

Ancis, Sedlacek, and Mohr (2000) examined student perceptions of campus cultural climate by race, specifically the multidimensional perceptions and experiences of the cultural climate and students' racial-ethnic identity development. Their findings confirmed previous research that "African Americans consistently reported more negative experiences compared with Asian American, Latino/a, and White students. . . . Asian American and Latino/a students also reported experiences of stereotyping and prejudice in the form of limited respect and unfair treatment by faculty, teaching assistants, and students; and pressure to conform to stereotypes" (Ancis et al., 2000, p. 183).

Antonio (2001) examined diversity and its influence on friendship groups at UCLA. Antonio's findings indicated that participation in cultural awareness workshops and/or ethnic/women's studies programs resulted in a positive effect on interracial interactions, overall cultural awareness, and commitment to racial understanding. While participation in ethnic-oriented student organizations yielded no effect on interracial interaction, cultural awareness or commitment to racial understanding; involvement in Greek organizations and commuting did have a negative effect on these three relational variables. Racially diverse friendships were correlated with enhanced cultural awareness and racial understanding. Conversely, two of the friendship group characteristics, academic ability and materialism, were negatively correlated with interracial interaction and increased cultural awareness (Antonio, 2001).

Renn (1998, 2000), utilizing Root's (1996) model of biracial identity development, explored patterns of situational identity among biracial and multiracial college students. Renn's qualitative research reinforced the notion that students of color experience the campus climate in a variety of ways, from identification with a separate cultural space for students of color, including multiracial students, to experiences of either fluid or rigid relationships with other students from other cultures. Root's situational identity model appropriately defined the complex and organic nature of these students' experiences of the campus climate.

Adjustment to college is a time of learning, of growing, of making connections, of building relationships, and of navigating the campus with all its complexities. The development of students, in the first years of college, is most often encompassed in the universal experiences of identity development, managing interpersonal relationships, experiencing cultural differences, and solving problems. Given that many students of color experience the campus climate in ways that are different from those of their White counterparts (Ancis et al., 2002; Helm, Sedlacek, & Prieto, 1998; Pewewardy & Frey, 2002) and coupled with the normative transitional process and issues, it is likely that students of color experience additional stressors as first-year students. As universities continue to search for programs and services that increase retention and create diverse communities, students and the campus-wide community can only benefit from a growing awareness of this unique first-year experience for students of color as well as understanding the impact that multiculturalism has on all first-year students.

FIRST-YEAR COLLEGE STUDENTS

The higher education and specifically the college student affairs community has seen a proliferation of literature on first-year students and an increase in the number of programs targeting first-year students in the past two decades. This explosion is due in part to the increasing evidence that student success is largely determined during the freshman year (Noel, Levitz, & Saluri, 1985). That is, success in the first year of college is crucial to college success in general. As a result, and in efforts to wisely invest increasingly scarce resources, many colleges and universities have begun to "front-load" the college experience for students, offering more support in the first year (Noel et al., 1985; Upcraft & Gardner, 1989; Wolfe, 1993).

Given this context, it is imperative to understand how institutions of higher education can promote success in the first year of college. College student success has been defined and measured in a number of ways. Many researchers and scholars have used *persistence* (often to the sophomore year) as a measure of first-year college student success, while others use *graduation rates* as a measure of student success. Some view first-year student success in more *developmental* terms. Consider the following excerpt from Upcraft and Gardner's (1989) *The Freshman Year Experience:*

> We believe freshmen succeed when they make progress toward fulfilling their educational and personal goals: (1) developing academic and intellectual competence; (2) establishing and maintaining interpersonal relationships; (3) developing an identity; (4) deciding on a career and lifestyle; (5) maintaining personal health and wellness; and (6) developing an integrated philosophy of life (Upcraft, 1984). This definition transcends the racial, ethnic, gender, and age diversity of freshmen; it describes their basic commonalities. (p. 2)

No matter how success is defined or measured, the literature consistently describes specific factors that contribute to first-year college student success. Perhaps most important are *involvement* and *academic and social integration* of students in college as factors for success (Astin, 1993; Tinto, 1993). Astin described involvement as the investment of psychological and physical energy in the college experience, specifically in people or activities. Research has consistently supported the notion that the level of student development and learning is proportional to the quality and quantity of involvement in college (Astin, 1993; Pascarella & Terenzini, 1991).

Tinto (1993) suggested that as students try to achieve academic and social integration, they experience stages that are characterized by "separation," "transition," and "incorporation." These stages involve dealing with separation from familiar surroundings and home life, transition that is characterized by adjusting to campus life and forming new relationships with students, staff, and faculty, and finally, exploring the new dimensions of their lives and integrating with campus norms (Pope, Ecklund, Miklitsch, & Suresh, in press). Tinto further stated that every campus has multiple communities and that any one of those communities could be a means for students to become integrated into campus life.

Some universities have the resources to provide unique programs and services that offer diverse student populations the means to facilitate their transition to higher education and enhance their experiences within the first year. In order to help first-year students build meaningful connections with their campus community, it is important to explore their attitudes concerning their social and academic experiences (Franklin, Cranston, Perry, Purtle, & Robertson, 2002). Strategies employed by colleges and universities aimed at helping first-year students persist, learn, and develop must therefore focus on helping students adjust and involving them in their college experience (Levitz & Noel, 1989). Making connections and interacting with faculty, staff, and/or peers are critical to the development and satisfaction of students (Astin, 1993; Pascarella & Terenzini, 1991). Sax, Gilmartin, Keup, DiCrisi, and Bryant (2000) noted the important effect that faculty members, parents, and especially peers have on first-year students' decisions to persist or withdraw from college. Levitz and Noel (1989) indicated that first-year students who can name a campus-affiliated person they can rely on for help are more than twice as likely to return for the sophomore year as those who cannot. Astin (1993) further concluded, "The student's peer group is the single most potent source of influence on growth and development during the undergraduate years" (p. 398). Thus, for students to succeed, the first year must be structured in a way that encourages high-quality, frequent interactions between first-year students and faculty, staff, and peers. Effective orientation programs, first-year seminars, small classes, living-learning communities, early intervention programs, and peer mentoring programs are examples of strategies that colleges and universities can implement to help ensure first-year student success.

First-Year Students of Color

For students of color, the challenges of succeeding in the first year of college may be different and perhaps magnified (Pounds, 1989). Smedley, Myers, and Harrell (1993) cited studies suggesting that factors associated with college adjustment and performance may affect students of color and White students differently. Further, Schwitzer, Griffin, Ancis, and Thomas (1999) reported that students of color often felt underrepresented in their first year of college, which was a new experience since many reported that they felt supported in high school and their home communities. Sedlacek (1987) found that African American students experience greater estrangement from the campus community, and Patterson, Sedlacek, and Perry (1984) found that African American students experience heightened discomfort in interactions with faculty and peers. Finally, students of color are often first-generation college students and may lack a well-developed understanding of the college experience (Justiz & Rendón, 1989; Pounds, 1989). It is essential, then, for campuses to attend specifically to the needs of first-year students of color, ensuring successful adjustment and integration into the institution.

One important strategy for ensuring the success of first-year students of color is to broaden their access to racially/ethnically similar role models (Schwitzer et al., 1999; Justiz & Rendón, 1989; Pounds, 1989) by hiring faculty of color and encouraging them to advise students of color students and student groups, effectively recruiting prospective students of color, and training upper-class students of color to provide peer mentoring and support. Colleges and universities can also assist first-year students of color by providing programs and services (such as orientation, academic support services, and residence hall arrangements) designed to specifically meet their needs, actively supporting and advising cultural clubs and organizations on campus, and providing proactive advisement and feedback to students throughout their first year. Pope (1998, 2000) and others such as Evans, Forney, and Guido-DiBrito (1998), Jordan-Cox (1987), and McEwen, Kodama, Alvarez, Lee, and Liang (2002) have emphasized how the developmental needs of college students of color are unique and require deliberate consideration in the design and implementation of programs and services.

Implications of Student Development Theory for First-Year Students

As campuses and first-year college students become more and more diverse, higher education professionals are increasingly called upon to design and implement multicultural programs and services (Stabb, Harris, & Talley, 1995). Further, specific campus professionals, such as student affairs professionals, have begun to embrace their responsibility to better understand diverse student groups (McEwen & Roper, 1994). Although the Dynamic Model of Student Affairs Competence proposed by Pope et al. (2004) emphasized multicultural awareness, knowledge, and skills as core competencies for all student affairs professionals, all higher education professionals can adopt these competencies. An understanding of student development theory as it applies to students of color is a central component to helping first-year students of color successfully integrate into the campus community.

Early student development theories, such as Chickering's (1969) theory of psychosocial development, were criticized for insufficiently explaining the growth and development of students of color—primarily because the participants in early research were mostly White males from middle-class backgrounds (Evans et al., 1998). More recently, some student development theories have been updated and expanded, and new theories have emerged that take into consideration the development of diverse student groups. For example, Chickering and Reisser (1993) updated Chickering's original theory, adding complexity to vectors such as "developing identity" in an attempt to be more responsive to differences in identity development based on such demographics as ethnic and racial background.

A brief review of student development theory and literature as it applies to students of color may be necessary to fully appreciate the challenges that exist in making student development theories relevant and useful for all students. However, before proceeding, it is important to note, "Whereas theories attempt to describe universal phenomena, students are unique individuals" (Evans et al., 1998, p. 29). Higher education professionals must be cautioned against ignoring within-group and individual differences when interpreting and applying student development theories to students of color.

Miller and Winston (1990) urged educators to consider the importance of sociocultural influences when examining psychosocial development of college students, and they describe a number of studies to illustrate their point. An important study by Nettles and Johnson (1987) found that peer group relationships in college were significant in the socialization of White students, while overall integration with the institution seems more central to the socialization of Black students. Asian American students sometimes have difficulty integrating into the college community with their non-Asian counterparts due to comparatively high degrees of devotion to their family, restraint of emotional expression, and so on. Many Hispanic students face the challenge of choosing between "*assimilation,* relinquishing their cultural identity, or *integration,* becoming an integral part of the larger society while maintaining their cultural identity" (Miller & Winston, 1990, p. 108). Finally, the authors suggest that many Native American students experience difficulty in developing relationships on campus due to a cultural distrust toward non-Indians.

Although research on student development for students of color is in its initial stages, and evidence regarding significant developmental differences among racial groups may only be partially established, race and culture clearly add another dimension that must be considered (Stikes, 1984). Racial and ethnic identity development of students of color is an example of an additional variable that warrants further study. Student development theories that fail to do so ignore the cultural context in which students of color exist, and are inherently less accurate (Jones, 1990). For example, researchers have suggested that African American college students attend to developing their racial and ethnic identity, perhaps delaying other aspects of development (Taub & McEwen, 1992; Evans et al., 1998).

Racial identity theory offers some understanding of how students view themselves, others—both racially similar and racially different—and the world around them (Helms, 1990; Pope, 1998, 2000). It is a lens through which students view the world, affecting their understanding and interpretation of their environment. It is important that higher education professionals—especially those who work with first-year students—have at least a rudimentary understanding of the developmental challenges that students of color may face and the social and cultural variables that influence their college experience. Unfortunately, few resources or studies are available to help higher education professionals and faculty apply what is known about racial identity theory to their work (Evans et al., 1998). Valuing the experiences, backgrounds, and perspectives of students of color is a critical first step.

Tatum (1992) suggested that faculty must gain a better understanding of their own racial identity as well as that of their students in order to create welcoming, productive classroom environments. Tatum suggested that "establishing clear guidelines for discussion" and creating "opportunities for self-generated knowledge" (p. 18) were important suggestions for creating safe atmospheres on campus. Hardiman and Jackson (1992) concurred, urging higher education administrators to actively help facilitate student development (including racial identity development) despite the challenges that may arise. Administrators must allow students of color to express their evolving views, as they progress through stages of racial identity development, without fear of retribution from others on campus (Hardiman & Jackson, 1992).

Most importantly, higher education professionals must move beyond one-size-fits-all programs, services, and pedagogies. Orientation programs for first-year students provide a useful example. In writing about the Council for the Advancement of Standards in Higher Education, Miller (1997) stated, "Student orientation programs must be available to all students new to the institution . . . with specific attention given to the special needs of sub-groups (e.g., traditionally underrepresented students. . . .) (p. 133). It is equally important to take into consideration individual campus environments, as differential perceptions and experiences among students of color may exist based on different environments (Patterson et al., 1984). Gonzales, Hill-Traynham, and Jacobs (2000) illustrated this point when writing in the National Orientation Directors Association's *Orientation Planning Manual:*

> Ethnic and gender minority students may have strong needs for an extended program to build support networks and a community environment. . . . While separate and extended programs can provide additional intensity, some find that [students of color] are better served within the general

programs because of limited interest or resources, and, in the case of separate programs, a negative effect of not participating in the regular program.
The determination is an institutional decision. (p. 26)

First-year students are diverse—and first-year students of color are
diverse—and must not be treated as a homogeneous group. Reynolds and
Pope (1991) critiqued the tendency to address development and identity
one-dimensionally. They urged scholars to incorporate students' multiple
identities, such as race, gender, religion, and sexual orientation, when examining student development and oppression. Cokley's (2001) research,
which found differences among Black students in the impact that racial
identity had on academic psychosocial development based on gender, is an
important illustration of that notion. For Black females, he found a correlation between the centrality of race to their identity and positive academic
self-concept and intrinsic motivation. However, he found no statistically
significant relationship between racial identity and either academic self-
concept or intrinsic motivation for Black males (Cokley, 2001).

Even as more is learned about the development of specific groups of
students of color, there is still considerable variability in individual circumstances based on membership in other groups (such as being gay or
lesbian) and on individual backgrounds and experiences. It is crucial for
higher education professionals to understand a broad range of student development theories, while remaining cognizant of individual differences,
in order to best serve all first-year college students.

MULTICULTURAL COMPETENCE
AND BEST PRACTICES
IN FIRST-YEAR PROGRAMS

The Policy Center on the First Year of College identified the benchmarks
for effective support programs for first-year students based on a qualitative field study of 150 institutions of higher education (Cutright, 2002).
Several themes emerged that lend contextual perspective to the first-year
experience. First, new and expanded programs are proliferating; second,
most first-year student courses are embedded within a specific discipline
or college; third, integration and multiple strategies yielded the most positive first-year experiences; fourth, learning communities are central to this
mission; fifth, teaching and learning need to be re-evaluated; and sixth,
academic–student affairs partnerships generate a cross-sectional approach

to program development aimed at improving the first-year experience (Cutright, 2002). The mission of educators and practitioners in higher education is to understand this first-year experience more fully and deeply and to provide programs that will service our university first-year population in the most effective and supportive manner. While the literature on first-year programs and practices has not specifically addressed the issue of multicultural sensitivity, the broader student affairs and higher education literature has begun to explore this issue more thoroughly.

Based on extensive research in the field of counseling, Pope and Reynolds (1997) developed a conceptual framework of core competencies for the student affairs profession that incorporated multicultural competence as one of the necessary competencies for effective student affairs work. Pope et al. (2004) and others (Ebbers & Henry, 1990; Pope & Reynolds, 1997; Talbot, 1996), have highlighted the importance of higher education professionals being prepared to address multicultural issues and develop the necessary awareness, knowledge, and skills to work effectively with culturally diverse populations. The research by Pope and Mueller (2000) builds on the earlier research of Pascarella and Terenzini (1991) which, when identifying key policy areas in higher education, suggested that the experiences of diverse communities and "institutional tolerance for individual student differences" be a central policy and practice within higher education (Pascarella & Terenzini, 1991, p. 636).

Through incorporation of multicultural competence in all aspects of first-year programs and services, higher education professionals will be better prepared to address the increasingly complex reality of college and university life. Pope et al. (2004) offer a dynamic model in which they suggest that multicultural competence be integrated into all core aspects of working in higher education (Administration and Management, Helping and Advising, Assessment and Research, Teaching and Training, Ethics and Professional Standards, and Theory and Translation). In addition, they recommend that Multicultural Awareness, Knowledge, and Skills be viewed as a separate and essential competency by itself through which higher education professionals develop specific and specialized attitudes and skills to address the dynamic nature of multicultural issues and diverse populations on campus.

When applied to the operational policies, procedures, and practices of first-year programs, multicultural competence can enhance and strengthen the ability of higher education professionals to provide services that are effective and culturally relevant. For example, within the realm of helping and advising skills, it is important to develop an awareness of how culture affects communication style and interpersonal skills. How a higher educational professional advises and assists a student from another cultural background with possibly different expectations about asking for help, working with authorities, and nonverbal communication significantly affects how their efforts will be received and interpreted. It is important that professionals be aware of their own biases and any assumptions that make them less empathic and supportive of the unique needs of students. Ultimately, working with students with unique concerns and experiences, such as those with learning disabilities or whose native language is not English, may ultimately require specific attitudes, knowledge, and skills that many professionals do not have. Seeking out additional training to become more aware and sensitive to the concerns of specific student populations is often necessary since higher education and student affairs administration preparation programs may not adequately prepare professionals to address multicultural issues (Fried & Forrest, 1993; Talbot, 1997).

Another central aspect of first-year programs is teaching and training, where there is much that can be done to integrate multicultural issues and concerns. Whether it is in how professional and student staff members are trained or in the development of specific course work or learning communities for first-year students, it is important that multicultural concerns be addressed. First-year students and their families may have unique issues and concerns that need to be explored during orientation and other programs, and staff members need to be prepared to address those issues.

College and university professionals need to be educated about the issues related to the first-year experience for all students, and in particular to the unique experience of first-year students of color and other unique and underserved groups. College and university professionals should be encouraged to receive training to augment their multicultural awareness, knowledge and skills in order to understand the college experience for students of color. Within this context, university personnel would be introduced to cultural constructs, racial identity development, and to the worldviews of the diverse students they teach and serve. Training programs that address discrimination and prejudicial practices need to be developed so the campus is prepared to respond to any campus incidents so that every member of the campus community comprehends the subtle and/or overt forms of racism and appreciates the importance of diversity issues. Students should also be encouraged to receive training in the areas of multicultural awareness, knowledge and skills; these educational efforts create multicultural sensitivity to the unique needs and concerns of all students.

Academic courses and other educational interventions have the power to expose students to diverse cultures and ways of looking at the world that will challenge and enrich their assumptions and life experiences. Learning communities that engender interactions between faculty and students, within and outside of the classroom, create an environment where all members of the campus community thrive, and diversity issues need to be addressed within those academic interactions and programs. Courses and workshops that identify and honor diverse races/ethnicities can be offered as a means to educate others to the traditions and heritages of a variety of groups. When creating courses for first-year programs, instructors need to examine their texts, the examples they use in class, and the classroom environment to ensure that they are unbiased, representative, and relevant to all students.

Administration and management of first-year programs is another example of an area needing additional assistance in incorporating multicultural issues, concerns, and realities. The culture of first-year students is centered within the larger university environment—it is the locus of their common living and learning experiences. First-year programs can play an important role in assisting in the creation of social networks in the first year of college. Social integration has a significant impact on the academic success, persistence, and individual adjustment of first-year students (Brooks & DuBois, 1995; Kenny & Stryker, 1996; Wolfe, 1993). Higher education professionals need to provide opportunities for interracial interactions and interpersonal relationships between all members of the campus. First-year programs can assist by empowering student organizations to reflect the values and experiences of diverse student bodies through support mechanisms, such as faculty advisors, student government funds, and meeting spaces. In everything they do, first-year and orientation programs need to be welcoming and inclusive of all students, their families, and their communities of origin.

As part of administrative responsibilities within first-year programs, there are some specific areas needing attention. Updating current materials used, such as forms, campus publications, communications, and surveys so that they reflect diversity issues is a simple yet often overlooked way to demonstrate sensitivity. Just as institutions need to hire underrepresented faculty and staff for many students of color who will view professionals of color as potential role models, advisors and advocates, first-year programs need to ensure that staff members that work directly with first-year students are representative and diverse. Finally, higher education professionals need to evaluate diversity aspects of first-year programs and services and assess relevant outcomes in order to have an understanding of the programs' abilities to meet the needs of all students.

Multicultural competence needs to be included in all aspects of first-year programs, including how they are administered and managed (e.g., who they hire, how resources are allocated), what theories are used (e.g., do they address the realities of particular student groups like students of color or lesbian, gay, bisexual, and transgender students), and how the programs and services are evaluated (e.g., do program evaluations ask about cultural sensitivity; is campus climate assessed around diversity issues?). Multicultural competence in higher education is in its infancy stage and there is much that needs to be done in applying it to various functional areas within colleges and universities. Rather than relying on the campus professionals who emphasize multicultural work, it is vital that every member of the campus community take responsibility for integrating multicultural issues into every aspect of their work.

Diverse student bodies require higher education professionals, services, and programs that are geared toward a multicultural university environment and healthy psychosocial development (Malaney, 1998; Mueller & Pope, 2001; NASPA, 2002; Pope, 2000; Pope & Reynolds, 1997; Pope et al., 2004; Sue & Sue, 1999; Tanaka, 2002). Professionals who work in first-year programs and are committed to using educational programs as a means to transform how students perceive differences and interact with others can have a powerful influence not only on their institutional climate but also on the future expectations and experiences of their students. It is important that higher education professionals embrace the value that multiculturalism has on the individual lives of students as well as the enhanced atmosphere of the institution and become an advocate for the inclusion of diversity into all aspects of the institution.

SUMMARY

Students of color in the first year of college encounter many of the same stressors that White students face; however, their unique concerns are often not acknowledged or identified until they leave the institution or until later in their education. When students experience transitions from familiar cultures to new college environments, higher education professionals need to expand the awareness, knowledge, and skills in the students' lives and their lens—how they are viewed and experience the campus environment. In this chapter we outlined some of the challenges and issues that both

White students and students of color experience during the first critical months of their collegiate education. As higher education professionals we must, perhaps now more than ever, construct communities that embrace diversity; promote multiculturalism in our classrooms and in our offices; and develop programs, policies, strategies, and interventions that enhance diversity.

REFERENCES

American Council on Education/American Association of University Professors. (2000). *Does diversity make a difference? Three research studies on diversity in college classrooms.* Retrieved September 6, 2002, from http://www.acenet.edu/programs/omhe/diversity.cfm.

Ancis, J. R., Sedlacek, W. E., & Mohr, J. J. (2000). Student perceptions of campus cultural climate by race. *Journal of Counseling and Development, 78*(2), 180–185.

Antonio, A. L. (2001). Diversity and the influence of friendship groups in college [electronic version]. *The Review of Higher Education, 25*(1), 63–89.

Astin, A. W. (1993). *What matters in college? Four critical years revisited.* San Francisco: Jossey-Bass.

Brooks, J. H., & DuBois, D. L. (1995). Individual and environmental predictors of adjustment during the first year of college. *Journal of College Student Development, 34*(4), 347–360.

Chickering, A. W. (1969). *Education and identity.* San Francisco: Jossey-Bass.

Chickering, A. W., & Reisser, L. (1993). *Education and identity* (2nd ed.). San Francisco: Jossey-Bass.

Chronicle of Higher Education. (2003, August 30). Almanac 2003–04. *The Chronicle of Higher Education, 49*(1). Washington, DC: Author.

Clemetson, L. (2003, January 22). Hispanics now largest minority, census shows [electronic version]. *The New York Times.* Retrieved January 22, 2003, from http://college4.nytimes.com/guests/articles/2003/01/22/969333.xml

Cokley, K. O. (2001). Gender differences among African American students in the impact of racial identity on academic psychosocial development. *Journal of College Student Development, 42,* 480–487.

Cutright, M. (2002). What are research universities doing for first-year students? *About Campus, 7*(4), 16–20.

Ebbers, L. H., & Henry, S. L. (1990). Cultural competence: A new challenge to student affairs professionals. *NASPA Journal, 27,* 319–323.

Evans, N. J., Forney, D. S., & Guido-DiBrito, F. (1998). *Student development in college: Theory, research, and practice.* San Francisco: Jossey-Bass.

Franklin, K. K., Cranston, V., Perry, S. N., Purtle, D. K., & Robertson, B. E. (2002). Conversations with metropolitan university first-year students. *Journal of the First-Year Experience & Students in Transition, 14*(2), 57–88.

Fried, J., & Forrest, C. (1993). *Multicultural perspectives and practices in student affairs preparation programs.* Unpublished manuscript.

Gonzales, T. V., Hill-Traynham, P. S., & Jacobs, B. C. (2000). Developing effective orientation programs for special populations. In M. J. Fabich (Ed.), *Orientation planning manual* (pp. 26–33). Pullman, WA: National Orientation Directors Association.

Gurin, P. Y. (1998). Expert witness report of Patricia Y. Gurin. In *Gratz v. Bollinger., No. 97-75321 (E.D. Michigan); In Grutter v. Bollinger., No. 97-75928 (E.D. Michigan)*. Ann Arbor, MI: The University of Michigan, December 15, 1998. Retrieved September 6, 2002, from http://www.umich.edu/~urel/admissions/legal/expert/gurintoc.html.

Hardiman, R., & Jackson, B. W. (1992). Racial identity development: Understanding racial dynamics in college classrooms and on college campuses. In M. Adams (Ed.), *Promoting diversity in college classrooms: Innovative responses for the curriculum, faculty, and institutions* (New Directions for Teaching and Learning, No. 52, pp. 21–37). San Francisco: Jossey-Bass.

Harris, S. M., & Nettles, M. T. (1996). Ensuring campus climates that embrace diversity. In L. I. Rendon, R. O. Hope, & Associates, *Educating a new majority: Transforming America's educational system for diversity* (pp. 330–371). San Francisco: Jossey-Bass.

Helm, E. G., Sedlacek, W. E., & Prieto, D. O. (1998). The relationship between attitudes toward diversity and overall satisfaction of university students by race. *Journal of College Counseling, 1*(2), 111–120.

Helms, J. E. (1990). *Black and white racial identity: Theory, research, and practice*. Westport, CT: Praeger Publishers.

Jones, W. T. (1990). Perspectives on ethnicity. In L. V. Moore (Ed.), *Evolving theoretical perspectives on students* (pp. 59–72). San Francisco: Jossey-Bass.

Jordan-Cox, C. A. (1987). Psychosocial development of students in traditionally Black institutions. *Journal of College Student Development, 28,* 504–512.

Justiz, M. J., & Rendón, L. I. (1989). Hispanic students. In M. L. Upcraft & J. N. Gardner (Eds.), *The freshman year experience: Helping students survive and succeed in college* (pp. 261–276). San Francisco: Jossey-Bass.

Keller, G. (2001). The new demographics of higher education. *The Review of Higher Education, 24*(3), 219–235.

Kenny, M. E., & Stryker, S. (1996). Social network characteristics and college adjustment among racially and ethnically diverse first-year students. *Journal of College Student Development, 37*(6), 649–658.

Kuh, G. D. (2000). Understanding campus environments. In J. J. Barr (Ed.), *The handbook of student affairs administrators* (2nd ed., pp. 50–72). San Francisco: Jossey-Bass.

Lee, W. Y. (2002). Culture and institutional climate: Influences on diversity in higher education. *The Review of Higher Education, 25*(3), 359–368.

Levitz, R., & Noel, L. (1989). Connecting students to institutions: Keys to retention and success. In M. L. Upcraft & J. N. Gardner (Eds.), *The freshman year experience: Helping students survive and succeed in college* (pp. 65–81). San Francisco: Jossey-Bass.

Malaney, G. D. (1998, March). *Student satisfaction with campus services: Comparisons among racial/ethnic groups*. Paper presented at the annual meeting of the National Association of Student Personnel Administrators, Philadelphia, PA (ERIC Document Reproduction Service No. ED 429496)

McEwen, M. K., Kodama, C. M., Alvarez, A. N., Lee, S., & Liang, C. T. H. (2002). *Working with Asian American college students* (New Directions for Student Services, No. 97, pp. 1–104). San Francisco: Jossey-Bass.

McEwen, M. K., & Roper, L. D. (1994). Incorporating multiculturalism into student affairs preparation programs: Suggestions from the literature. *Journal of College Student Development, 35,* 46–53.

Miller, T. K. (1997). *CAS: The book of professional standards for higher education.* Washington, DC: Council for the Advancement of Standards in Higher Education.

Miller, T. K., & Winston, R. B. (1990). Assessing development from a psychosocial perspective. In D. Creamer (Ed.), *College student development: Theory and practice for the 1990s* (pp. 99–126). Alexandria, VA: American College Personnel Association.

Mueller, J. A., & Pope, R. L. (2001). The relationship between multicultural competence and White racial consciousness among student affairs practitioners. *Journal of College Student Development, 42,* 133–144.

National Association of Student Personnel Administrators [NASPA]. (2002). *Principles of good practice for student affairs* [Electronic version]. Retrieved August 19, 2002, from http://www.naspa.org/resource/principles.cfm.

Nettles M. T., & Johnson, N. A. (1987). Race, sex, and other factors as determinants of college students' socialization. *Journal of College Student Personnel, 28,* 512–524.

Noel, L., Levitz, R., & Saluri, D. (Eds.). (1985). *Increasing student retention: Effective programs and practices for reducing the dropout rate.* San Francisco: Jossey-Bass.

Orfield, G. (Ed.). (2001). *Diversity challenged: Evidence of the impact of affirmative action.* Boston: Harvard Education Publishing Group.

Pascarella, E. T., & Terenzini, P. T. (1991). *How college affects students: Findings and insights from twenty years of research.* San Francisco: Jossey-Bass.

Patterson, A. M., Sedlacek, W. E., & Perry, F. W. (1984). Perceptions of Black and Hispanics in two campus environments. *Journal of College Student Personnel, 25,* 513–518.

Pewewardy, C., & Frey, B. (2002). Surveying the landscape: Perceptions of multicultural support services and racial climate at a predominantly White university. *Journal of Negro Education, 71*(1–2), 77–95.

Pope, R. L. (1998). The relationship between psychosocial development and racial identity of Black college students. *Journal of College Student Development, 39*(3), 273–282.

Pope, R. L. (2000). The relationship between psychosocial development and racial identity of college students of color. *Journal of College Student Development, 41,* 302–312.

Pope, R. L., Ecklund, T. R., Miklitsch, T., & Suresh, R. (2004). Enhancing the first-year experience for multiracial students. In L. I. Rendón, M. Garc, & D. Person (Eds.), *Transforming the first year of college for students of color.* Columbia, SC: National Resource Center for the First Year Experience and Students in Transition.

Pope, R. L., & Mueller, J. A. (2000). Development and initial validation of the multicultural competence in student affairs-preliminary 2 scale. *Journal of College Student Development, 41*(6), 599–607.

Pope, R. L., & Reynolds, A. L. (1997). Student affairs core competencies: Integrating multicultural awareness, knowledge, and skills. *Journal of College Student Development, 38,* 266–277.

Pope, R. L., Reynolds, A. L., & Mueller, J. A. (2004). *Multicultural competence in student affairs.* San Francisco: Jossey-Bass.

Pounds, A. W. (1989). Black students. In M. L. Upcraft & J. N. Gardner (Eds.), *The freshman year experience: Helping students survive and succeed in college* (pp. 277–286). San Francisco: Jossey-Bass.

Renn, K. A. (1998, April). *Check all that apply: The experience of biracial and multiracial college students.* Paper presented at the annual meeting of the Association for the Study of

Higher Education (ASHE), Miami, FL. (ERIC Document Reproduction Service No. ED 427602)

Renn, K. A. (2000). Patterns of situational identity among biracial and multiracial college students. *The Review of Higher Education, 23*(4), 399–420.

Reynolds, A. L., & Pope, R. L. (1991). The complexity of diversity: Exploring multiple oppressions. *Journal of Counseling and Development, 70*, 174–180.

Root, M. P. P. (Ed.). (1996). *The multiracial experience: Racial borders as the new frontier.* Thousand Oaks, CA: Sage.

Sax, L. J., Gilmartin, S. K., Keup, J. R., DiCrisi III, F. A., & Bryant, A. N. (2000). *Designing an assessment of the first year of college: Results from the 1999–2000 YFCY pilot study.* Los Angeles: University of California Los Angeles, Higher Education Research Institute.

Schwitzer, A., Griffin, O. T., Ancis, J. R., & Thomas, C. R. (1999). Social adjustment experiences of African American college students. *Journal of Counseling and Development, 77*, 189–197.

Sedlacek, W. E. (1987). Black students on white campuses: 20 years of research. *Journal of College Student Personnel, 28*, 484–495.

Skrentny, J. D. (2001, February 16). Affirmative action and new demographic realities [Electronic version]. *The Chronicle of Higher Education: The Chronicle Review*, p. B7. Retrieved February 20, 2001, from http://chronicle.com.

Smedley, B. D., Myers, H. F., & Harrell, S. P. (1993). Minority-status stresses and the college adjustment of ethnic minority freshmen. *Journal of Higher Education, 64*(4), 434–452.

Stabb, S. D., Harris, S. M., & Talley, J. E. (1995). *Multicultural needs assessment for college and university student populations.* Springfield, IL: Charles C. Thomas.

Stikes, C. S. (1984). *Black students in higher education.* Carbondale, IL: Southern Illinois University Press.

Sue, D. W., Carter, R. T., Casas, J. M., Fouad, N. A., Ivey, A. E., Jensen, M., LaFromboise, T., Manese, J. E., Ponterotto, J. G., & Vasquez-Nutthall, E. (1998). *Multicultural counseling competencies: Individual and organizational development.* Thousand Oaks, CA: Sage.

Sue, D. W., & Sue, D. (1999). *Counseling the culturally different* (3rd ed.). New York: John Wiley & Sons, Inc.

Talbot, D. M. (1996). Multiculturalism. In S. R. Komives & D. B. Woodard (Eds.), *Student services: A handbook for the professional* (3rd ed., pp. 380–396). San Francisco: Jossey-Bass.

Talbot, D. M. (1997). Student affairs graduate faculty members' knowledge, comfort, and behaviors regarding issues of diversity. *Journal of College Student Development, 38*, 278–287.

Tanaka, G. (2002). Higher education's self-reflexive turn: Toward an intercultural theory of student development. *The Journal of Higher Education, 73*(2), 263–296.

Tatum, B. D. (1992). Talking about race, learning about racism: The application of racial identity development theory in the classroom. *Harvard Educational Review, 62*, 1–24.

Taub, D. J., & McEwen, M. K. (1992). The relationship of racial identity attitudes to autonomy and mature interpersonal relationships in black and white undergraduate women. *Journal of College Student Development, 33*, 439–446.

Tinto, V. (1993). *Leaving college: Rethinking the causes and cures of student attrition* (2nd ed.). Chicago: The University of Chicago Press.

U.S. Government Census Bureau. (2003). *National population trends* [Electronic version].

Retrieved February 10, 2003, from http://www.census.gov/population/pop-profile/adobe/1_ps.pdf.

Upcraft, M. L. (1984). Orienting students to college. *New directions for student services* (Vol. 25). San Francisco: Jossey-Bass.

Upcraft, M. L., & Gardner, J. N. (1989). *The freshman year experience: Helping students survive and succeed in college.* San Francisco: Jossey-Bass.

Wolfe, J. S. (1993). Institutional integration, academic success, and persistence of first-year commuter and resident students. *Journal of College Student Development, 34,* 321–326.

4

Living, Doing and Thinking Diversity: How Does Pre-College Diversity Experience Affect First-Year Students' Engagement With College Diversity?

BIREN (RATNESH) A. NAGDA
University of Washington

PATRICIA GURIN
University of Michigan

SHAWNTI M. JOHNSON
University of Washington

Learning communities have emerged as an important developmental experience in students' transition into college. One definition of a learning community emphasizes that it provides academic content, social relationships among students, and a shared physical space (Brower & Dettinger,

1998). Learning communities are thought to foster learning engagement, cognitive flexibility, and integration into the larger college life. Because colleges today are enrolling an increasingly diverse racial/ethnic student population, one can no longer presume racial/ethnic homogeneity or like-mindedness among community members. Nor can one assume similarity in student views about themselves and the world, or that meaningful communication and building relationships among diverse community members will be easy or natural. Educators and researchers are, therefore, now considering previously unexamined aspects of learning communities: *Who* are the students in such a community? *What* pre-college experiences affect members' participation in the learning community? *How* do we foster positive and meaningful social relationships in a learning community comprised of students from different racial and ethnic backgrounds?

We focus in this chapter on pre-college experiences with racial and ethnic diversity. We are interested in their impact on first-year students' decisions to participate in a diverse learning community, and on self- and societal perspectives that students bring to this community. We define *diverse learning communities* as comprising racial/ethnic heterogeneity among participating students as well as intentional learning structures that provide an intellectual understanding of race and ethnicity in the context of relational engagement that facilitates meaningful and substantive interactions among the participating students. Like other programs directed to assisting student involvement and integration into college life, diverse learning communities offer important educational benefits, such as cognitive development, intellectual engagement, and institutional commitment. We posit that relationships and experiences with diverse peers are an important promoter of these benefits in diverse learning communities, and thus we need to know about how pre-college experiences with diversity affect taking part in a diverse learning community during college.

In this chapter we give an overview of what is known about the impact of experience with diversity during the college years and then focus on an understudied issue — what predisposes students to have experiences with diversity, such as choosing to participate in a diverse learning community? How influential are pre-college diversity experiences? Are students with the most diversity experience before coming to college predisposed in their thinking about self and society to better fit into a diverse learning community? Program staff and faculty need answers to these questions in order to both support and challenge students so that they maximally benefit from a diverse learning community in their transition into college.

We investigated these questions by comparing two groups of first-year students at the University of Michigan: an experimental group (students who participated in a diverse learning community during their first year of college) and a comparison group (matched on gender, race/ethnicity, pre-college home residency within Michigan or out-of-state, and campus residence hall). That study is described in this chapter. We end this chapter with a discussion of our findings and their implications for developing diverse learning communities.

THE RATIONALE FOR THE EDUCATIONAL IMPACT OF DIVERSITY

Why is experience with diversity important in fostering educational benefits? We have argued elsewhere (Gurin, 1999; Gurin, Dey, Hurtado, & Gurin, 2002; Gurin, Nagda, & Lopez, 2004) that, for most students who enroll in the nation's selective institutions, ethnic and racial diversity provides the conditions that cognitive developmentalists agree are critical for active involvement with learning and thinking. To recap our argument, we begin with the observation, now widely accepted in social and cognitive psychology, that the thinking of most people, most of the time, is automatic, preconscious, mindless, implicit, inactive, and effortless. The terms differ depending on the particular theorist, but whatever the term, much research has shown that active thinking and engagement in learning should not be taken for granted (Bargh, 1997).

One of the early studies that set the stage for research on thinking—a study of what Langer (1978) calls "mindless" thinking—argues that mindlessness occurs because previous learning has become so routine that thinking is unnecessary. As in carrying out such automatic tasks as driving a car, we rely on scripts or schemas that are activated and operate automatically instead of thinking in a minded or active way about how to carry out these tasks. One of our tasks as educators is to interrupt these automatic processes and facilitate active thinking in our students. Higher education needs to find ways to produce the more active, less automatic mode of thinking among students. Langer further argues that minded, active thinking helps people develop new ideas and new ways of processing information, ways that may have been available to them previously but were simply not often used. In several experimental studies, she showed that such thinking increases alertness and greater mental activity—surely something all college teachers strive for in classrooms. Finally, she suggests three situations that foster minded and active thinking: (a) novel situations for which people have no script or with which they have had no past experience; (b) situations that are not entirely novel but are not entirely familiar either, and demand more than people's scripts allow them to grasp; and (c) situations that are disruptively different from one's past experiences. In novel, or somewhat unfamiliar and discrepant situations, people have to think about what is going on and struggle to make sense of the situation.[1]

This struggle is what most first-year students face when they make the transition from home to college, especially when they enroll in residential colleges rather than commuter colleges while continuing to live in their comfortable, familiar home environments, and when the college environment is different from their home environments in important ways. The importance of discrepancy and discontinuity is the critical issue, according to Diane Ruble, in the early stages of a transition (Ruble, 1994). She has written on many different kinds of transitions (to junior high, marriage, parenthood). She ties developmental change to moments of transition (Ruble, 1994; Ruble & Goodnow, 1998; Ruble & Seidman, 1996) because they present situations about which individuals have little knowledge and in which they will experience uncertainty.

The early phase of a transition, which Ruble (1994) calls the phase of *construction*, is an especially active influence on thinking. People have to seek information in order to make sense of their new situations. They are likely to undergo cognitive growth unless they are able to retreat to a familiar, certain, comfortable world. Applied to higher education, the period of construction is represented by the first year of college and perhaps even only the very first few weeks of college (Fenzel & Hessler, 2001). In this period, classroom and social relationships that challenge rather than replicate the relationships, ideas, and experiences students bring with them from their home environments are especially important in fostering cognitive and emotional growth.

These conditions—discrepancy from the home environment, discontinuity, unfamiliarity, uncertainty—are exactly what racially and ethnically diverse learning environments provide for students coming to college from racially segregated environments or even diverse environments where thinking and talking about diversity were not the norm. As we will see later, a sizeable majority of the white students, and approximately a third

---

[1] Many cognitive-developmental theories concur that to grow cognitively, we need to be in such situations that lead to a state of uncertainty, and even possibly anxiety (Acredolo & O'Connor, 1991; Berlyne, 1970; Doise & Palmonari, 1984; Piaget, 1971, 1985; Ruble, 1994).

to more than half of the students of color (depending on the particular arena of diversity) in the study described in this chapter came to the University of Michigan from racial/ethnic environments that mirrored their own race/ethnicity. Thus, the university's diversity provided at least some of the unfamiliarity, discrepancy, and uncertainty that are needed to promote active, conscious, and effortful thinking, as well as other aspects of personal development.

Diverse learning communities also promote preparation for participation and leadership in a diverse democracy, especially social identity development, perspective taking, understanding others and the role of social structures in people's lives, and perception of commonalities and not merely differences between racial/ethnic groups. Diverse learning communities present a challenge, however, to the conceptualization of a community as a warm, fuzzy place of like-minded, similar others. The compatibility of diversity, community, and democracy is not self-evident, however. Indeed, how to achieve unity, despite or because of difference, has been a central theme in democratic theory ever since the ancient Greeks. In her 1992 book, *Fear of Diversity*, University of Michigan political scientist Arlene Saxonhouse details the debates that took place in ancient Greece about the impact of diversity on capacity for democracy. She argues that it was only Aristotle who advanced a political theory in which democracy and unity in the public world would be achieved through difference. In contrast, common conceptions of democracy in the United States do not treat difference and conflict as congenial to unity, either. Instead, lay understandings of democracy and citizenship in general take one of two forms: (a) a liberal, individualist conception in which citizens, out of their individual self-interests, participate through voting for public servants to represent them or participate through other highly individual ways, and (b) a direct participatory conception, in which people from similar backgrounds who are familiar with each other come together, sharing a common, overarching identity, to debate the common good, as in the New England town meeting. Both of these conceptions attribute privilege to individuals rather than groups, and value similarities rather than differences. Moreover, neither is a sufficient model for democracy in the United States today (or for that matter for democracies in the increasingly heterogeneous societies all over the world).

We argue that today's college students need to learn how difference *can* be congenial with democracy. They need to participate in educational environments, such as diverse learning communities, that help them develop skills and sentiments that will be necessary for the fulfillment of democratic ideals in an increasingly heterogeneous society, domestically and globally. We also argue that some students may be more prepared and predisposed to take part in such communities, and make use of racial/ethnic diversity in others ways, because of their prior experiences with diversity (Hurtado, Engberg, Ponjuan, & Landreman, 2003). They may already be ready to delve into the explicit and substantive content and peer experiences that these communities offer. For others who are encountering diversity for the first time, these diverse learning communities offer great opportunities for growth because they are so different from these students' pre-college lives. At the same time, diverse learning communities may present a major challenge for the students who have lived and interacted with peers in racially/ethnically homogeneous environments as well as for the faculty teaching in these learning communities. Diverse learning communities, as we have defined them, incorporate not only demographic diversity among their participants, but also an explicit learning of intergroup issues and relationship building across differences. Even the students who have had the most experience living in ethnically/racially diverse environments may not have learned how to discuss racial issues and learn from racial/ethnic diversity. Race is often a topic, like religion, that students avoid talking about because it is so fraught with emotion and possibilities for interpersonal misunderstandings. Diverse learning communities, therefore, offer novel and discrepant experiences for almost all students.

THE PROGRAM ON INTERGROUP RELATIONS: A DIVERSE LEARNING COMMUNITY FOR THE TRANSITION TO COLLEGE

Learning communities have become widely recognized in their capacity to provide academic and social integration into college. Such communities have taken different forms—living-learning centers, first-year interest groups, integrated course and learning offerings, and undergraduate research opportunities. Within these learning communities, however, the issues of diversity and democracy are not always explicit or even implicit. We focus here on a particular diverse learning community in the Program on Intergroup Relations (IGR) at the University of Michigan, and how it enhances students' learning about diversity and social justice. While similar to other learning communities in its emphasis on building community among peers in a living-learning environment, IGR is focused on the issues of intergroup relations, conflict, and community. IGR is based on the understanding that substantive learning about diversity and social justice must involve systematic instruction, critical social analysis of everyday life, meaningful relations, and dialogue among diverse peers—all conditions for transformative learning deemed crucial for the development of an ethos of social responsibility for the common good (Daloz, 2000). Our students are engaged in developing what Richard Guarasci, President of Wagner College, calls the democratic arts: "voice, critical judgment, empathy, reciprocity, commitment and action" (Guarasci, 2001, p. 11).

Programmatically, the Program on Intergroup Relations offers a series of courses and seminars on intergroup relations, social conflict, and social change for students across the four years of college. The program specially emphasizes first-year seminars and intergroup dialogues for students making the transition from high school to college. Students take an introductory course on "Intergroup Relations and Conflict" that (a) introduces students to the historical, conceptual, and empirical roots of social differences and social inequalities, (b) provides opportunities for constructive engagement with diverse peers and different perspectives, and (c) fosters learning through both content—lectures, readings, presentations, videos—and active learning—experiential activities, reflective journal writing, and intergroup dialogues (Nagda, Gurin, & Lopez, 2003; Sfeir-Younis, 1993). Content and active learning strategies are now common in many learning communities; what sets IGR apart is the use of intergroup dialogues. They were developed specifically by the Program on Intergroup Relations to advance the ideals of transformative, diverse learning communities. Intergroup dialogues are facilitated, small group environments bringing together students from two or more social identity groups in a co-learning environment. These identity groups, usually characterized by historical and structural power inequalities and conflicts, are defined along racial, ethnic, gender, sexual orientation, religion, class and other social identities. For example, intergroup dialogue offerings usually include people of color and white people; women and men; gay, lesbian, bisexual and heterosexual people; and Jews and Christians. The dialogues are facilitated by trained students—either undergraduate or graduate—who use a developmental curriculum that engages students in reflecting on social identity, understanding systems of inequalities and their impact on intergroup relations, discussing controversial topics (such as Affirmative Action, sexual harassment on campus), and exploring possibilities of collaborative action to promote more equal relations (Zúñiga, Nagda, & Sevig, 2002).

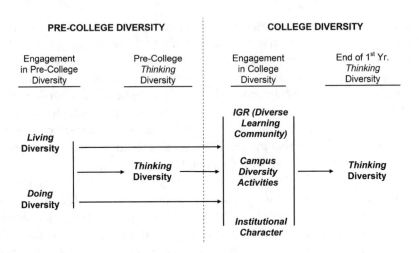

FIG. 4.1.   Conceptual model of pre-college and college diversity experiences on students' *thinking* diversity.

CONCEPTUAL MODEL OF EXPERIENCE
WITH DIVERSITY

Figure 4.1 shows a conceptual framework for research on pre-college and college diversity experiences and students' *thinking diversity*. In this section, we first review the research evidence for the impact of college experiences with diversity. We then move to the focus of this chapter — analyzing how pre-college diversity experience affects whether or not students actually participate in the many opportunities colleges and universities now offer for them to interact with and learn from diverse peers.

Previous Research on the Impact
of Diversity Experience

Our prior work has examined the impact of experience with diversity across three levels: multiple institutions, using the database made available by the Cooperative Institutional Research Program at UCLA (Gurin, 1999; Gurin et al., 2002); a single institution, specifically the Michigan Student Study (MSS) that examined the cohort of students entering the University of Michigan in 1990 and then followed them through to the end of their senior year in 1994 (Gurin, 1999; Gurin et al., 2004; Matlock, Gurin, &

Wade-Golden, 2001); and the same curricular program at the Program on Intergroup Relations as was used in the study presented in this chapter. It was evaluated with a pre–post, participant/comparison group design in which the participants and non-participants were matched on in/out-of-state pre-college residency, gender, race/ethnicity, and campus residency (Gurin, 1999; Gurin et al., 2002; Gurin et al., 2004; Lopez, Gurin, & Nagda, 1998). Subsequent analyses were conducted to evaluate the impact of the program pedagogy, using pre–post design (Lopez et al., 1998; Nagda et al., 2003). These studies, and many others summarized in amicus briefs from social scientists and educational researchers[2] to the Supreme Court in the recent Affirmative Action legal cases (*Grutter v. Bollinger* and *Gratz & Hamacher v. Bollinger;* see Brief of the APA, 2003, and Brief of the NEA, 2003, respectively), show that actual experience with diversity in classrooms and in the informal campus world fosters engagement in learning and thinking (Gurin, 1999; Kuh, 2001; Maruyama & Moreno, 2000; Orfield & Whitla, 2001), consideration of multiple perspectives (Gurin et al., 2002; Orfield & Whitla, 2001), reduction of unconscious prejudice (Blair, 2002; Blascovich, Wyer, Swart, & Kibler, 1997; Dovidio & Gaertner, 2000; Dovidio, Kawakami, & Gaertner, 2002), preparation for citizenship (Bowen & Bok, 1998; Gurin et al., 2002), greater comfort with diversity, and increased contact across race and ethnicity (Duncan, Boisjoly, Levy, Kremer, & Eccles, 2003). These varied studies nearly always show similar effects for both white students and students of color (for summaries of the diversity evidence, see Chang, Hakuta, & Jones, 2002; Hurtado, 2001; Milem & Hakuta, 2000; Orfield & Kurlaender, 2001).

In this chapter we are focusing again on the study of the Program on Intergroup Relations at the University of Michigan to examine what predisposes students to participate in a diverse learning community as they make the transition to college. We know from past research that the program has positive effects on students both at the end of their first year in college and at the end of the senior year, after controlling for possible predisposing orientations the participants bring to college. In studies that allowed us to use entrance measures of outcomes as controls for selectivity, we found that participants (as compared to matched non-participants) endorsed more structural attributions for racial/ethnic inequality (Lopez et al., 1998). They also thought more structurally in analyzing vignettes depicting intergroup conflicts of the type that arise on diverse campuses (e.g., language

---

[2] See especially the amicus briefs of the American Educational Research Association, the American Psychological Association, and the National Education Association.

disputes, disagreements about what constitutes sexual harassment, rights of organizations to post announcements for gay-lesbian programs, and racist graffiti in residence halls). When these kinds of conflicts are posed to students, the students in the Program on Intergroup Relations more frequently than the matched comparison students endorsed such structural causes as failures in university policies and practices, societal inequalities, and differences in cultural socialization of various groups of students on the campus. The students from the Program on Intergroup Relations also more frequently were motivated to take the perspectives of other students. They also more frequently believed that difference and democracy can be compatible, and reported a greater sense of commonality in life values with racial/ethnic groups other than their own. Furthermore, the participating students had more positive evaluations of conflict, as indicated for example in greater agreement/disagreement that "conflict and disagreements in classroom discussion enrich the learning process" (and three other similar statements, some phrased negatively such as "I learned that conflict rarely has constructive consequences."). They exhibited greater mutuality in learning about both their own identity groups and other groups as reflected in learning about the history and experiences of other groups as well as about their own group, and participating in activities of other groups as well as activities of their own groups. They also showed greater interest in politics than did the matched comparison students (Gurin et al., 2004; Nagda et al., 2003).

We also know something about the processes that occur in the program's major first-year course that account for its effects. We examined the impact of its content — reflected in readings and lectures — and its active learning pedagogy — reflected in exercises and reflective journals. We found that both content and active learning positively influenced structural attributions and causality. However, *only* active learning pedagogy was related to endorsement of actions to intervene in the intergroup conflict. Therefore, active involvement of students in the learning process through experiential activities and reflections through writing influenced both their cognitive capacities for structural causation and their action strategies (Lopez et al., 1998; Nagda et al., 2003). Engaged learning — the extent to which students apply principles and concepts outside of the class, discuss material from the class with peers outside of the class, and think about course material on their own — was particularly influential in fostering students' democratic sentiments and citizenship engagement that were affected by being in the Program on Intergroup Relations' first-year course (Nagda et al., 2003).

These studies revealed important short- and long-term effects of participation in diverse learning community. They have not focused, however, on what experiences and beliefs students bring to these learning communities—their pre-college diversity experiences, cognitive orientations, and democratic sentiments.

Pre-College Diversity Experience

In this study, we distinguished two types of pre-college experience with racial/ethnic diversity. *Living diversity* is reflected in the ethnic/racial heterogeneity/homogeneity in the neighborhoods in which the students grew up, and in the high schools they attended. *Doing diversity*, in contrast, involves more than the demographic composition of a place and implies actual interaction across race/ethnicity. We looked at two types of *doing diversity*, the racial/ethnic characteristics of the students' six best friends prior to enrolling in college, and whether or not the students have traveled, lived, and/or attended an educational program in another country, outside of the United States and Canada. We use the word "implies" because the students themselves were not asked how much interaction across race/ethnicity they experienced in these two types of *doing diversity*.

We asked in this study if *living diversity* and *doing diversity* have different import for choosing to participate in a diverse living community. We also asked if students' diversity perspectives and orientations, what we are calling *thinking diversity*, may predispose participation. We looked at five aspects of *thinking diversity*: (a) social identity, (b) democratic citizenship commitments, (c) cognitive orientations toward diversity, (d) political and societal perspectives, and (e) support for university diversity policies.

Based on the conceptual framework presented in Fig. 4.1, we address three questions in this study:

1. Do pre-college experiences of *living* and *doing diversity* lead students to choose to participate in the first-year course of the Program on Intergroup Relations?

2. Are pre-college *living* and *doing diversity* experiences correlated with *thinking diversity* when students enter the University of Michigan?

3. Does pre-college *thinking diversity* predict participation in the first-year course of the Program on Intergroup Relations?

WHAT DID WE DO?

Participants and Design

Participants in the study were part of a longitudinal study at the University of Michigan. An experimental-control design was used to assess the impact of participation in the Program on Intergroup Relations as first-year students. All participants completed two entrance surveys, one given to all students entering the University of Michigan (see Matlock et al., 2001, for a description of MSS), and one given at the beginning of the introductory IGR course. They also answered two post-surveys, one given to all students in MSS at the end of the first year and one given at the end of the IGR course. Control subjects were matched for gender, race/ethnicity, in-state versus out-of-state pre-college residency, and campus residency to the participants, and also answered all of these questionnaires. Altogether 174 students (87 participants and 87 non-participants) were in the first-year study. In each group, there were 60 women (69%) and 27 men (31%), and 25 (29%) students of color and 62 (71%) white students.

Measures

Pre-College Diversity Experiences

1. Living Diversity. Students answered a question about the racial/ethnic composition of their three pre-college environments. "How would you describe the racial composition of the following: (a) The neighborhood where you grew up; (b) The high school you attended; and (c) Your place of worship?" The response scale was: 1 = All or nearly all white; 2 = Mostly white; 3 = Half white and half people of color; 4 = Mostly people of color; 5 = All or nearly all people of color. The response scale was reversed for students of color such that higher scores for both white students and students of color would indicate environments that were more different in relation to their own racial/ethnic background.

Neighborhood and high school diversity were highly correlated (.724 for white students and .694 for students of color), as one would expect in light of widespread racial/ethnic residential segregation in the United States (Farley, 1996; Massey, 2003; Sugrue, 1999; Tienda & Cortes, 2003). Religious settings are also among the most racially/ethnically segregated settings in the United States. Diversity of religious settings was also correlated with neighborhood (.708 for white students, and .559 for students of color) and high school diversity (.600 for white students, and .470 for students of color). We formed a scale of pre-college *living diversity* that was the average of students' responses on these three items (Cronbach's $\alpha = .817$).

2. Doing Diversity.

a. *Friendship Diversity*—Students were given the following statement: "We are interested in the social network you had before coming to the University of Michigan. First you should think of your six closest friends. For each friend, you should indicate his or her race or ethnicity." Other questions asked about friend's gender, religion, social class background, whether attending the University of Michigan, and their educational goals in relation to the respondents. Responses to this question were then coded for several dimensions of the student's network, including the racial/ethnic background of the friends as the same or different from the respondent. Possible range: 0 = no friends of different race/ethnicity to 6 = all 6 friends of different race/ethnicity than respondent.

b. *International Experiences*—Students were asked if they had ever spent any time outside the United States and Canada: (1 = no, 2 = yes):
    i. On some type of exchange program.
    ii. As a resident of another country.
    Unlike measures of *living diversity*, the two types of *doing diversity* were not significantly correlated (.126 for white students and –.067 for students of color). The two scores were combined into a *Doing Diversity* index.

3. Thinking Diversity.
Students' *thinking diversity*, often conceived as learning outcomes, has been the focus of much previous research. We conceptualized *thinking diversity* in five categories:

a. **Social identity** included cognitive centrality of race and common fate of race (Gurin & Markus, 1988).

b. **Democratic citizenship commitments** included openness to diversity (Matlock et al., 2001), perspective taking (Davis, 1983), commonality of values with white people, commonality of values with people of color, and anticipated post-college citizenship commitments (Matlock et al., 2001).

c. *Cognitive orientations* included intellectual exchange (Matlock et al., 2001), active thinking, and socio-historical thinking (Fletcher, Danilovics, Fernandez, Peterson, & Reeder, 1986).

d. **Political and societal perspectives** included political ideology, structural attributions for racial/ethnic inequality (Gurin, Miller, & Gurin, 1980), structural attributions for poverty, and attributions for wealth (Feagin, 1972).

e. **Support for University diversity policies** included students' support for Affirmative Action, race/ethnicity course requirement, and college social responsibility (Matlock et al., 2001).

WHAT DID WE FIND?

Question 1: Does pre-college experience with diversity lead students to choose to participate in the first-year course of the Program on Intergroup Relations?

Descriptive statistics showed that most white students experienced mostly or all-white pre-college settings in neighborhoods (86%), places of worship (97%) and high schools (75%). In their friendship networks, 75% of the white students did not have any friends of color. Just a little less than a quarter of the white students had one or two friends of different race/ethnicity and about 2% reported that they had more than three friends of a different race/ethnicity. Looking at international experiences, 24% of the white students reported participating in an exchange program or residing outside the United States or Canada.

Students of color showed more variability in their pre-college settings. Just over a third of students of color came from neighborhoods that were at least half people of color, while 65% lived in mostly or all white neighborhoods. Sixty-one percent of students of color attended places of worship that were at least half people of color. Over 44% students of color went to high schools that were at least half people of color while about 56% went to mostly or all-white high schools. Examining their pre-college friendship networks, we found that 38% of students of color did not have friends of a race or ethnicity different from their own. About a quarter of students of color had one or two friends of different race/ethnicity, while 38% had three or more friends of a different race/ethnicity. Finally, over a third (36%) of students of color had participated in some form of international experience.

These descriptive statistics show that white students and students of color entered the University of Michigan with different pre-college experiences with diversity. More students of color, compared to white students, came from more diverse settings, had more diverse friendship networks, and participated more in international experiences before coming to college.

However, the different aspects of pre-college *living* and *doing diversity* experience did not predict which students chose to participate in the IGR. Independent samples' *t*-test analyses comparing course participants and non-participants, conducted separately for white students and for students of color, showed no significant differences between participants and non-participants. Two important results emerged from these analyses: (a) white students and students of color, as we have already noted, differed in how much experience with diversity they had previously had, but (b) within each group, pre-college experiences with diversity were not related to whether or not the students chose to participate in IGR. In fact, within the racial groups, participants and non-participants were remarkably similar in the degree of diversity they had experienced through their neighborhoods, high schools, places of worship, friendships, and international experiences.

Question 2: Is pre-college experience correlated with *thinking diversity* (as reflected in the orientations students hold when they enter the University of Michigan?

We examined the relationship between pre-college diversity and indicators of *thinking diversity* in regression analyses in which the summary measure of *living diversity* (neighborhood, high school, and worship) and the summary measure of *doing diversity* (number of six best friends of a racial/ethnic background different from the student and international experience) were used as predictors of *thinking diversity,* along with gender as a control variable. We again conducted these analyses separately for white students and for students of color. Table 4.1 shows the results.

Looking first at white students, we found that *doing diversity* was far more influential than *living diversity.* The only four statistically significant effects of *living diversity* show that white students who were in the most diverse settings prior to coming to college thought more frequently about their racial identity. They also thought more structurally about racial inequality, and attributed poverty to structural causes (e.g., lack of jobs and

TABLE 4.1
The Influence of Pre-College Diversity Experience on *Thinking* Diversity
Orientations (Regression Analyses Reporting *b* co-efficients)

	White Students			Students of Color		
	Living Diversity	Doing Diversity	R^2	Living Diversity	Doing Diversity	R^2
Social identity						
Centrality of race/ethnicity	.205*	−.052	.038	.477*	−.751***	.327
Race/ethnic common fate	.094	−.048	.008	−.307	−.031	.106
Democratic citizenship commitments						
Openness to diversity	−.081	.274**	.169	−.147	.019	.175
Perspective taking	−.017	.161	.025	−.057	−.099	.021
Commonalities with students of color	.072	.195+	.060	.112	.158	.185
Commonalities with white students	—	—	—	.120	−.101	.148
Post-college citizenship commitments	−.086	.340**	.139	.124	−.312	.075
Cognitive orientation						
Intellectual exchange	.042	.186	.109	.126	−.340	.072
Active thinking	−.152	.214*	.050	.376+	−.269	.073
Socio-historical thinking	−.021	.185+	.034	.275	−.208	.060
Political and societal perspectives						
Political ideology	.046	.125	.147	.039	−.134	.021
Structural thinking about racial inequality	.246*	.052	.072	.244	−.586**	.215
Structural attributions for poverty	.212*	−.062	.042	−.476*	.317	.141
Structural attributions for wealth	.063	.205*	.078	.276	−.563**	.289
University diversity policies						
Affirmative Action	.293**	.076	.109	.221	−.496*	.151
R & E requirement	−.114	.260**	.064	.149	−.084	.026
College responsible to address injustice	.122	.008	.082	.002	−.141	.050

+$p < .10$. *$p < .05$. **$p < .01$. ***$p < .001$.

good schooling). They also held more positive views of Affirmative Action by agreeing more strongly that "different admissions criteria with respect to SAT and ACT score may be justified for some students of color" (as well as three other indicators of approval of Affirmative Action).

Doing diversity, in contrast, among white students was significantly related to 7 of the 17 measures of *thinking diversity.* White students who came to college with the most prior diversity experience through friends and international exposure were the most open to diversity, as indicated by choosing Michigan because of its "racially and ethnically diverse student body," "the chance to meet people who are different from them in background and values," and by valuing "getting to know people from backgrounds different" from their own, "learning about cultures different" from their own, and "learning about the world and gaining knowledge and skills to make the world a better place." They more often viewed themselves as someone "who prefers experiences that are new and different instead of familiar and predictable" and someone "who is eager to try new experiences." They believed that they had more commonality with groups of color (African American, Asian American, Latino/a, and Native American) in terms of life values involving family and work. They more frequently anticipated being active politically after college, for example, "working to correct social and economic inequalities," "influencing the political structure," "helping my group or community," and "helping to promote racial/cultural understanding." All of these differences are important aspects of preparation for citizenship in a diverse democracy.

The white students with the most experience in *doing diversity* before coming to college also differed from other white students on several measures of *thinking* orientations. They had higher scores on a sub-scale of the Fletcher et al.'s (1986) *attributional complexity* scale that indicates a preference for "complex rather than simple explanations for people's behaviors," liking to "analyze the reasons or causes for people's behaviors," not taking "people's behavior at face value" but rather thinking about "the inner causes for their behavior," and enjoying "getting into discussions where the causes for people's behavior are being talked over." We think of this as active or complex thinking. They also had higher scores on another sub-scale of the Fletcher et al. (1986) measure, a preference for finding causation for people's behaviors in socio-historical phenomena.

Finally, white students who had the most diverse friends and international experiences more frequently attributed the causes of wealth to such structural factors as family inheritance. These students also entered college more frequently agreeing that "colleges and universities should have a requirement for graduation that students take at least one course on the role of race and ethnicity in society."

For students of color, the analyses of the influence of pre-college diversity on *thinking diversity* resulted in seven significant relations. In contrast to white students, for whom all the significant relations were aligned positively with increasing diversity, students of color showed more complex relationships. Two of the significant *living diversity* results showed a positive relationship with diversity, while one showed a positive result for racial/ethnic homogeneity (not diversity). All four significant *doing diversity* results showed a positive relationship with greater racial/ethnic homogeneity or solidarity rather than diversity.

Students of color who had been in the most diverse settings before coming to the University of Michigan thought more frequently about their racial/ethnic identities, but it was the students of color whose friends were the *least* diverse who thought the *most* frequently about their racial/ethnic identities. Thus, both diversity and solidarity were important for racial identity. These two findings, more than any other, show the complexity in what diversity meant to students of color.

A second positive effect of *living diversity* for students of color is that those students who had been in the most diverse neighborhoods, high schools, and places of worship had significantly higher scores on the measure of active, complex thinking. Students of color who had lived in the *least* diverse neighborhoods tended to have more *structural* attributions for poverty.

Doing diversity was negatively related to thinking structurally about racial/ethnic inequality and the causes for wealth in our society as well as to approval of Affirmative Action. Students of color who had the fewest diverse friends and had not had international experiences tended to think more structurally about racial/ethnic inequality and wealth, and they more frequently approved of university Affirmative Action policies. Once again we see how much more complex the impact of diversity is for students of color, as compared to white students for whom all associations between pre-college diversity experience and *thinking diversity* were positive.

Question 3: Do these entrance orientations toward diversity predict participation in the first-year course of the Program on Intergroup Relations?

The answer to this question is "Yes," especially for white students. Table 4.2 shows that white students participating in the course were more open to diversity and more of them had experienced group-based prejudice in

TABLE 4.2
Thinking Diversity at Entrance to College
and Pre-Disposition to Program Participation (Mean Scores)

	White Students		Students of Color	
	Participants	Non-participants	Participants	Non-participants
Social identity				
Centrality	1.84	1.62	1.95	2.29
Common fate	2.58	2.62	2.81	3.17
Democratic citizenship commitments				
Openness to diversity	3.77	3.43*	4.24	3.75[+]
Perspective taking	3.58	3.52	4.00	3.78
Commonalities with students of color	2.57	2.55	—	—
Commonalities with white students	—	—	2.24	2.46
Post-college commitments	3.32	2.77*	4.12	3.69
Cognitive orientations				
Intellectual exchange	3.88	3.45	4.38	4.06
Active thinking	4.02	3.70*	3.89	3.82
Socio-historical thinking	3.18	3.01	3.43	3.13
Political and societal perspectives				
Political ideology	5.13	4.07***	4.36	5.13
Structural thinking about racial inequality	2.67	2.71	2.91	2.96
Structural attributions for poverty	2.15	2.12	2.34	2.41
Structural attributions for wealth	1.96	1.93	2.05	2.05
University diversity policies				
Affirmative Action	2.15	2.03	2.76	2.47[++]
R & E requirement	2.94	2.52**	3.29	2.92
College respond to injustice	2.85	2.77	3.10	3.29

[++]$p = .08.$ [+]$p = .06.$ *$p < .05.$ ***$p < .001.$

the form of personal hostility or discrimination. Compared to non-participants, participating white students were more liberal politically, had more social activist post-college commitments, were more motivated to think actively and complexly about behavior, and more strongly endorsed university policies to require a course examining the role of race and ethnicity in the United States as a graduation requirement.

The differences between participating and non-participating students of color were less marked. They differed on only two measures. Students of color participating in the course were more open to diversity, and they more strongly (nearly statistically significantly) endorsed university policies supporting Affirmative Action as compared to non-participating students of color.

WHAT DOES THIS MEAN?

We investigated the influence of pre-college diversity experiences — *living* and *doing diversity* — on students' *thinking diversity* and their predisposition to participate in a diverse learning community during their first year in college. We conceptualized these three types of diversity within an overall theoretical framework of discrepancy, arguing that diverse learning communities are disruptively different environments for many students entering college from widespread residential segregation in the United States. We previously argued that this discrepancy is what makes experience with diversity during the college years causally significant for student development. In this chapter we examined whether or not discrepancy between the racial/ethnic characteristics of the pre-college background and the diverse learning community affected the likelihood that students would participate in the community, and in what ways this pre-college diversity experience played a role in the attitudes, cognitions, and societal commitments that students brought to such a community. We looked at how such influences might be similar and/or different depending on students' racial/ethnic background. The limitations of this study — self-reported measures, one program at one institution, and small sample size, especially for students of color — mean that our results can only be taken as suggestive. For purposes of suggesting how pre-college diversity may affect students in diverse learning communities, our study is exploratory and needs to be corroborated by further research. These caveats notwithstanding, the study makes important conceptual and empirical contributions. Most importantly, our study shows once again that race matters. Diverse learning communities must address the implications of similar and different pre-college diversity experiences of white students and students of color. We discuss next four underlying tensions that our results raise, and then elaborate on their programmatic implications.

Discrepancy: An Issue or Not for Diverse Learning Communities?

The results provide a complicated picture of discrepancy. On the one hand, pre-college diversity was not a factor in explaining which students chose to participate in the diverse learning community that we studied. On the other hand, pre-college diversity was a factor in the attitudes and cognitions that students brought to the University and that, especially for white students, *were related to the decision to participate.* The white participants entered the program with predisposing orientations—what we are calling *thinking diversity*—that were basically aligned with the intellectual thrust of the IGR: to explore the experiences and perspectives of diverse students, to analyze inequality and learn how economic and social constraints influence inequality, to think actively about the self and society, and to develop commitments for citizenship in a diverse democracy. The white students for whom the IGR was the most different and who might need the most support in its intellectual challenge were those whose attitudes, many of which *were influenced by their pre-college experience with* diversity, did not match the program very well.

The issue of discrepancy is less straightforward for the students of color. On average, they had more experience with diversity before coming to college, although how much experience they had did not predict whether or not they chose to participate in the IGR. Their pre-college diversity experiences, moreover, were less influential in how they thought about diversity, as compared to the white students. Finally, there is clear evidence here that *both* diversity and racial solidarity played a role for students of color.

Staff and faculty of diverse learning communities must have a nuanced understanding of how pre-college diversity may affect white students and students of color somewhat differently. Whether or not a discrepancy exists, it is important to encourage students to actively reflect on their pre-college socialization through readings and pedagogical tools, such as an initial or early paper that asks students to describe their pre-college environments and reflect on how *they* think their experiences in these environments have prepared them for the educational challenge of interacting with diverse peers.

Living, Doing and Thinking Diversity: Disparate or Connected?

We found that *living* and *doing diversity* affected only some *thinking diversity* orientations. These aspects of diversity were sometimes interrelated and sometimes separate, and the patterns were not the same for white students as for students of color. Thus, we cannot assume that diversity experience necessarily translates to pro-diversity attitudes and values for all students. Harold Saunders, in *A Public Peace Process: Sustained Dialogue to Transform Racial and Ethnic Conflicts,* notes a parallel dilemma from interracial conflicts in communities:

In 1972, a group of citizens in a southern US city formed an organization to improve race relations. In 1994, one of its officers reflected to me that, after two decades, a number of integrated civic committees had done much good work, close working relationships had been formed and trust had been built, but that "in fundamental ways, the underlying relationships between the races have changed little." She concluded, "I guess we followed the strategy of doing work together but not talking about the deeper relationships." (Saunders, 1999, p. 1)

Thus, while interracial/ethnic living and doing activities together may be positive, *talking about race and ethnicity* is important for integrating *living, doing* and *thinking diversity*. Without talking, students may not develop a deeper personal and broader contextual understanding of what racial/ethnic diversity really means. We return to this issue in discussing the processes that we believe are fundamental for effective diverse learning communities.

Racial/Ethnic Diversity and Solidarity: Competing or Co-Influential?

Perhaps the most striking finding of this study is the differential influences of racial/ethnic diversity and solidarity for white students and students of color. *Living* and *doing diversity* were related positively to *thinking diversity* for white students; there were no negative relationships between either pre-college *living* or *doing diversity,* and how white students thought about diversity when they entered college. White students coming from pre-college settings that were more racially/ethnically diverse or had more diverse friends and international experiences were more likely to have more diversity-oriented thinking. *Doing diversity* had the most consistent relationships with the orientations that students brought to college. Hurtado and colleagues (2003) report a similar finding: participation in a wide range of pre-college diversity activities were related to democratic sentiments — the ability to see multiple perspectives, acceptance of conflict as a normal feature of social life, and valuing engagement in social action — that were measured during the first year of college. We also found that several of the orientations we are calling *thinking diversity* distinguished white participants from non-participants in the IGR. Moreover, most of these orientations were correlated with *living* or *doing* pre-college diversity experiences, *even though these diversity experiences themselves did not predict participation in the IGR.*

    In contrast, the relationship between pre-college diversity experience and *thinking diversity* was more complex for students of color. Both racial/

ethnic diversity and racial/ethnic solidarity experiences were related to *thinking diversity* for them. In addition, there were only two areas—openness to diversity and support for Affirmative Action—that differentiated participating students of color from non-participants.

The importance of the *joint* influence of diversity and solidarity experiences for students of color is very poorly understood by most white students and critics of diversity who often point to what they call "balkanized campuses" as evidence that diversity does not foster a positive educational environment. What they fail to apprehend, or perhaps comprehend, is that on predominantly white campuses, students of color spend most of their time interacting with white students—in classes, organizations, residence halls. At some time during their days they seek out students of their own identity groups who share common backgrounds and some common experiences at college in what they call "safe havens." Ethnic studies, racial solidarity groups, and cultural events focused on particular groups play an important but not exclusive role for most of Michigan's students of color (Matlock et al., 2001).

The applicable lesson from these findings is threefold:

- Diverse learning communities can build on the positive predisposition of white students, but also challenge them to further hone the orientations they already bring to the diverse learning community and develop greater understanding of race and ethnicity.
- Students of color will benefit from both in-group bonding and cross-group relationship building because both solidarity and diversity in the pre-college experiences are important for them.
- All students need to develop a contextual understanding of the differences between solidarity and inter-racial/ethnic spaces.

Conceptions of Diversity: Structural or Relational?

Sociologist Troy Duster (Duster, 1993), in his research on students' desires and hopes for diversity at University of California, Berkeley, noted divergent conceptions of diversity across race and ethnic groups. Students of color appeared to be much more structurally focused in their desire for university-sponsored programs to promote access for underrepresented minorities and equal opportunities on the campus for all students. White students, on the other hand, desired more informal interracial contact and friendships, especially with African American students. The Michigan Student Study (Matlock et al., 2001) has found much the same distinction between structural and relational orientations of white students and students of color. Students of color focus more on the institutional responsiveness and commitment to greater inclusiveness; white students focus more on personal relationships across race and ethnicity. Both groups value friendships across race/ethnicity, but the emphasis on having personal relationships is greater among white students than others. Furthermore, students of color more frequently advance a structural analysis of the wider society as well as of the racial environment of the university in comparison with white students.

In examining *thinking diversity* more closely, it is possible to group these orientations broadly into structural and relational categories. Structural orientations include social identity, political and societal perspectives, and university diversity policies. Relational orientations include democratic citizenship commitments and cognitive orientations (because they have to do in some way with exchange and causal analysis of *individual behavior*). All of the significant influences of *living* and *doing diversity* on *thinking diversity* for students of color involved structural orientations. For white students, both structural and relational orientations were influenced by pre-college diversity. What seemed to matter for white students, however, was the type of diversity. Broadly speaking, *doing diversity* mostly influenced relational diversity orientations, while *living diversity* mostly influenced structural orientations. As was noted in the results, *doing diversity* had more significant influences in comparison with *living diversity*.

Learning communities, by their very nature, try to build relational ties among students. The challenge of our findings, for diverse learning communities, is to foster a socio-structural analysis such that the relations of diversity and solidarity are understood in a larger context of structural racial and ethnic inequalities. For example, students coming from homogeneous pre-college environments may be able to locate their experiences in the context of residential and educational segregation.

WHAT DO WE DO?
PROGRAMMATIC IMPLICATIONS

These four issues — discrepancy; interrelationships of *living, doing,* and *thinking diversity;* diversity and solidarity; and structural and relational orientations of the students — have important implications for designing diverse learning communities. The pedagogical philosophy of the Program on Intergroup Relations diverse learning community addresses all of them by:

- Fostering *living, doing,* and *thinking* at the same time.
- Challenging students to understand structural causes of inequality.
- Providing separate as well as integrated spaces.
- Most importantly, engaging students in explicitly *talking with each other* about diversity, and building cross-race/ethnic relationships.

Talking about difference and commonality, social structure, friendships and relationships, past experiences, and future visions is the critical feature of this diverse learning community. Yet, it is a different kind of talking that we are concerned with, namely *dialoguing* about and across differences. Dialoguing involves more than a simple conversation; it requires both talking and listening. Intergroup dialogue then becomes a nexus for talking, as a student noted, "about issues that most people choose to avoid." It involves a sustained and informed discussion about social group identities, similarities and differences in socialization experiences, and intergroup conflicts. Of course, the students in this diverse living-learning community also live with each other. They do activities and think together in both curricular and co-curricular aspects of the community. It is this *integration,* however, of *living, doing, thinking* and *dialoguing about diversity* that marks the Program on Intergroup Relations' success in *learning about diversity.* Talking and dialoguing about the deeper issues of race and ethnicity in a structured curricular and co-curricular setting provides a learning process in which *living, doing,* and *thinking diversity* can be brought together.

What is the nature of such an integrating diversity learning experience? To understand more clearly how this learning process impacts students, we read through students' final papers in which they described their learning in the first course of the diverse learning community. As Langer (1978) suggested, for many students, the diverse learning community provided a completely novel experience, especially in its diverse demographic composition. For other students, the diversity itself was not very different from their pre-college experience. For *most* students, however, it was the learning engagement that was markedly different from previous experience. We identified four such learning engagement processes and spaces that were pivotal in students' learning: (a) reflective, (b) dialogic, (c) contextualizing, and (d) re-thinking and connecting reflection to action.

Reflective Processes

Reflective processes in dialogue refer to the encouragement and challenge given to students to more deeply understand the meaning of their own pre-college diversity experiences. The white students who came to this diverse learning community with orientations that predisposed them to its goals still needed to be challenged to develop a more critical and reflective analysis of their previous experiences with diversity and of their attitudes toward inequality and social justice. Students wrote about the importance of reflection in trying to understand the meaning of their pre-college lives and the challenge of the diverse learning community, something they had not explicitly done before:

> I have always been interested in the kinds of issues that we discussed, probably a product of the environment in which I grew up. I was lucky enough to have a family and past educational experience that helped shape the perspective I have, although I'm not exactly sure what that perspective is all about. (White student)

Reflective processes counter the tendency to take experiences and attitudes for granted without understanding either their source or their meaning in the students' lives. The diverse learning community provided a supportive, yet challenging, space to examine exactly these kinds of socialization experiences:

> Many times throughout this course I would ponder on one of our discussions or lectures and it really opened my eyes to what I really believed. I was very uncomfortable with those feelings throughout the term, but I realized that what was happening was that I was gaining truth and knowledge. Changing your beliefs is not only hard, but it leaves you with a sense of insecurity. (White student)

The challenge and learning from reflective processes were not exclusive to white students; students of color also wrote about questioning their own supposed open-mindedness to diversity:

> One thing this journey has definitely taught me about myself is that I am more close-minded than I wish to be. I tend to view myself as an individual who is open minded with views that do not constrict anyone. By the end of this course I realized that to be such an individual is close to impossible. I have been programmed since birth by parents, relatives, neighbors, teachers, television, and a million more sources as these. This class has made me more aware of issues, which has taught me to make more of an effort to understand people who do things to hurt others. (Student of color)

Through such self-reflection, students engaged in thinking differently from Langer's (1978) nonreflective, "mindless" thinking; students became more "mindful" as they questioned, examined, and understood the sources of their views on diversity and different "others."

Dialogic Processes

Reflective processes by themselves, however, are not enough to encourage more democratic participation, and connectedness to the diverse, common good. Understanding this, many students wrote about the importance of talking face-to-face:

> Communication gives the parties involved a chance to hear each other's side and, then, hopefully understand where each other is coming from. This is where the dialogue groups have proven to be of assistance. They helped to combine two different groups of people so as to open up, bring out, clarify and pose possible solutions to the thoughts, feelings, attitudes and even misconceptions about one group over the other that are often the sources of conflict. . . . Another important aspect of dialogue groups has to do with the fact that many people don't realize the extent to which stereotypes, family and environment play in developing false perceptions of the "other." (Student of color)

Dialogue, a bridge to understanding and appreciating differences, as the student noted, counters debate-oriented ways of communicating that often aim at proving one right perspective. While dialogue promotes personal and social inquiry, debate stifles it. "Only dialogue, which requires critical thinking, is also capable of generating critical thinking" (Freire, 1970/2000, p. 92).

Sometimes diversity programs are premised on a common but often unstated assumption that interaction with diverse peers works the same for all people. This study has emphasized the important difference of solidarity spaces in which students of color can feel safe. Intergroup dialogue, as a sustained process occurring over a period of time, offers both diversity and solidarity spaces. While the term *intergroup* connotes an interracial/interethnic public space and defines the focus of the dialogue, the dialogues also incorporate conversations that take place within racial/ethnic identity groups as well as across groups (see Zúñiga et al., 2002). Solidarity spaces need not be seen as ends unto themselves, but rather as connected and complementary to interracial/ethnic spaces. For example, in identity caucus groups, students of color are able to examine questions that may be difficult to discuss openly right away in mixed groups:

I learned something new about my own group, which pertains to our ethnic identification. From the main consensus of blacks in the class we would like to be called African Americans. This amazed me, because in most of my papers I identify us as blacks and not African Americans. So therefore I had to get use to calling my group as such. (Student of color)

After the caucus meeting, the in-group discussion is shared in the larger, mixed group to foster fuller dialogue and understanding by members of the other group. In this instance, it was greater understanding by the white students of the meaning and impact of both solidarity and diversity for students of color. A white student shares her corresponding learning:

Another lesson I learned was that African Americans do not wish to be called "Black" by white people. At first I thought this was ridiculous, but after I heard a few of their statements, I understood the reason for this preference. One of the African American students said that the word "Black" has many negative connotations. We thought of examples: "Black hole," "Black widow," . . . I found that the word white, contrarily has positive connotations: "snow white," "virgin white," "pure white" . . . It seems to me that the word "black" in the English language has come to represent things that are evil, bad and dirty. Conversely, "white" has been utilized to represent all that is good and clean.

It is worth underscoring here that this white student did not stop simply t understanding the perspectives of the African American students, an important part of the dialogue itself, but extended her learning by questioning and contextualizing the label "white," which she knew was attached to her own identity, at least as others saw her. The dialogic and reflective processes come together so that learning about the "other" and about the "self" are conjoined.

We see a similar joint solidarity-diversity and reflective-dialogic process unfold in students' discussions specifically about issues of solidarity, perceived exclusion and unquestioned self-segregation:

We talked about things such as what about the other group makes us mad. . . . I realized that we hold just about every white person in one way or another responsible for what happened to our ancestors whether or not they actually took part in it or not. The white group said ironically that they get upset when we exclude them. The exclusion is seen by us all sticking together and hanging out together with usually no white people with us. I found this comment extremely confusing. I asked: How do they think we feel when we look around, especially on this campus, and we see an abundance of white people not really interacting with many of the Black students on campus? (Student of color)

A white student reported on the same dialogic exchange:

> I had always assumed that African American students had no desire to mix with students of other ethnic groups, but I soon found out that they do not try to segregate themselves at all. They just spend time with each other in order to unite. It is interesting that although many whites do not mix with members of other racial groups, they are never accused of segregating themselves. (White student)

Although we cannot claim that every intergroup dialogue is able to achieve such a level of dialogic understanding, we know that achieving a balance of solidarity-diversity spaces can be fruitful.

As these excerpts from student papers reveal, open discussion of solidarity-diversity can be productive in bringing forward often unexamined assumptions about exclusion and inclusion. Such a dialogue can engender a greater understanding on the part of white students about the importance of solidarity spaces for students of color on predominantly white campuses, as well as the privileged solidarity meaning that the total campus has for white students. Dialogue brings about *critical analysis*. Conversely, for the students of color, an openness to such understanding on the part of white students may reflect their own growing sense of trust, or at least lessened perceived threat:

> In discussions on such topics as racism and discrimination, I did not feel the usual "distance" I sometimes experience with mixed groups, [that is a group of] whites and people of color. (Student of color)

Dialogic processes encourage deeper relationship building as well as critical inquiry. They provide norms for interactions that may indeed be dramatically different from the "race-avoidant" or polite conversations that are more the rule than the exception in larger society.

Contextualizing Processes

How do students make sense of their reflections and dialogues as part of a larger social structure? Similar to the learning about the differential societal valuing of "black" and "white" group labels, many students wrote about expanding a more reflective stance toward their attitudes in order to understand how social positions—including their own place in the social structure—have affected them:

> I lived in a sheltered environment in high school, where nothing really struck me. It did not strike me as odd that although about 60% of my school

were Latinos, only about 4% of our school's governing power/leaders were of this ethnicity. The rest were Caucasians. The issues are not raised. Actually, they are not even issues. Out of the top 10% of the students in my graduating class with the highest GPA's (25 students), I can think of only two that were not white. (White student)

With a growing sense of trust and commitment to dialogue, it is in face-to-face encounters that students are able to confront their own societally influenced, non-reflective thinking and break down stereotypes about others that they have been socialized to accept:

When we were writing down stereotypes of African Americans, we realized that maybe we never gave second thought to them but just kind of inherited our ideas. . . . For example, I really did believe that most African Americans were born terrific athletes. This brought about some laughter because one member said that everyone always picked him in phys[ical] ed[ucation] to be on their team and he would let them down. This story perfectly depicted society's expectations that emerge from overly exaggerated stereotypes. (White student)

In addition to thinking about contextualizing as an examination of structural influences, students compared and contrasted their experiences across racial/ethnic lines in the dialogue groups to their current social context—residence halls and campus life. For example, students of color noticed a difference in their perceptions of white students as a result of the dialogues. One student of color described a divergence of her own racial attitudes compared to that of a friend, also a student of color, who was not participating in the interracial/ethnic learning:

Besides talking with the group about the issues, I spoke with a friend of mine about them. I did not really enjoy our conversation. I wanted to talk to someone besides the people in my group, to hear their opinion about the issues. Since he was a person of color as well I felt as though he would be able to share some of the same feelings about the dominant groups. Unfortunately we differed because he had very negative feelings about the topics. I got the impression that he held a lot of prejudices even though he said he did not. My friend said that he "hates white people because they try to dominate people of color." I, on the other hand, felt differently. Perhaps it was because of my experiences and my participation in the dialogue group. I now realize that one should not blame all white people for the mistakes and prejudiced acts that white people have made. Unfortunately, my friend has yet to learn this. (Student of color)

Both students of color and white students recognized that intergroup dialogue provides counterspaces that are indeed different from what is generally available in their campus worlds. That is, there is little access to structured interracial/interethnic interaction to foster meaningful contact. Even worse, most *living* and/or *doing diversity* experiences on campus, in the absence of facilitated learning processes, foster more hostile and estranged intergroup relations:

> I came to this university with an open mind, ready to interact with a variety of people and learn from our difference. I was very disheartened by my experiences in the dorm and acquired a bitter attitude. I am referring to a large percentage of the African-American women that I lived with. I am not, however, considering the other wide diversity of people that I was exposed to my freshman year and had positive experiences with. I now realize how strange it is that I dwelled on the bad experience (not to mention that I focused on African Americans). I think that this is due to the fact that before I came to this university, everything was black and white (literally). Other types of subordinated groups were not apparent to me. I am not saying that I was not exposed to other subordinated groups, but rather, I did not consider them as subordinated. I try to think back and decide what exactly my perception was, but my previous mindset has been replaced. I am much more confident now, feeling that I have an understanding (if there is such a thing) of people and their oppression, dominance, [and] motives. . . . This class has helped me immensely to regain my faith in the future. (White student)

Through her experiences in the learning community, she not only broadened her previously narrow definition of diversity, she also contextualized it in dominant–subordinate power relations and felt a renewed faith in diversity.

Re-Thinking and Connecting Reflection to Action

As intimated in the preceding student's paper, reflection and dialogue provide a bridge to the final dialogic learning process — rethinking and reappraising one's roles in race/ethnic relations, and in systems of racism and ethnocentrism. We found ample evidence of students rethinking and connecting their new understanding to a new, or renewed, desire and agency for confronting and combating prejudiced and racist ways of being:

> I can understand how if you grow up in the same area and with the same people all your life, you're bound to take on some of their attitudes and

beliefs, but we have to learn to take control of and be responsible for absorbing the positive ideas and letting go of the negative ones. (Student of color)

I always considered myself open-minded and therefore, in no way responsible for society's discrimination. I soon learned that by remaining silent in the presence of discrimination, even if it was only verbal comments, I too must accept some blame. (White student)

Another student shared her own awakening to the common realizations that came from dialoguing and appreciating change:

[This class] has opened my eyes to myself and to other people. I have learned that change is a slow process that involves many minds. I realize that each person must care enough to contribute. By contribution, I mean becoming educated, reading about the issues, discussing the issues, and getting other people thinking. (Student of color)

All of the learning processes we have described here — reflective, dialogic, contextualizing, and rethinking and connecting reflection to action — are much more complex, of course, than our excerpts of students' narratives may convey. We cited earlier the work of social and cognitive psychologists who identified the conditions of discrepancy from the home environment, discontinuity, unfamiliarity, and uncertainty as important in fostering cognitive and emotional growth. Our findings and discussion of students' narratives move us to consider the important processes that facilitate learning. We have purposefully not spelled out a list of recommendations or specific practices for other programs. Instead, by illuminating the dilemmas posed by our findings and conveying the students' learning in their own voices here, we hope to elucidate ways in which participants — both students of color and white students — make sense of and integrate their experiences in this diverse learning community. What emerges as a critically important consideration for program staff and faculty is the understanding that diverse learning communities can provide not only new and unfamiliar environments, but also learning processes that enable students to make sense of the discontinuities and engage effectively about and across racial/ethnic differences. Specific practices for fostering appropriate learning conditions for such communities, developing instructor and facilitation competencies, and actively engaging students are well described in resources for social justice education (Adams, Bell, & Griffin, 1997; Arnold, Burke, James, D'Arcy, & Thomas, 1991) and intergroup dialogues (Schoem & Hurtado, 2001; Zúñiga et al., 2002). These pedagogical resources are immensely helpful in their discussion of the theoretical and conceptual dimensions of learning in diverse situations that inform their practice recommendations.

CONCLUSION

Gordon Allport (1954), renowned social psychologist, wrote in his seminal book *The Nature of Prejudice:* "It is not the mere fact of living together that is decisive. It is the form of resulting communications that matter" (p. 272). Allport was addressing tensions in intergroup living, and the necessity of connective ties across differences in the interest of forging community and positive intergroup relations. Paulo Freire (1970/2000), renowned educator, brings this very idea home to education and diversity in his seminal book, *Pedagogy of the Oppressed:* "Without dialogue there is no communication, and without communication there can be no education" (pp. 92–93). Freire was emphasizing the generative power of dialogue as a way of actively engaging learners in critically thinking about the world through the lens of their lived experiences and countering dominant–subordinate relations. Our program, current study and lessons from students have benefited greatly from both Allport's and Freire's wisdom in thinking about how to create and understand diverse learning communities that matter. We have stressed the critical importance of *talking and dialoguing* for integrating *living, doing,* and *thinking diversity.* We end, hoping that the broad movement toward learning communities in our higher education institutions will incorporate the educational potential of diversity by:

- Seeing it as an *educational focus* and not just a question of demographic composition.
- Emphasizing that *learning about and through diversity* is an integrative process involving different aspects of students' lived experiences, learning needs, and styles.
- Conceiving of *community as inherently connected to diversity* in forging a "commons" that recognizes and honors difference, and fosters critical thinking about social injustices.

REFERENCES

Acredolo, C., & O'Connor, J. (1991). On the difficulty of detecting cognitive uncertainty. *Human Development, 34,* 204–223.

Adams, M., Bell, L. A., & Griffin, P. (1997). *Teaching for diversity and social justice: A source-book for teachers and trainers*. London: Routledge.

Allport, G. (1954). *The nature of prejudice*. Cambridge, MA: Addison-Wesley.

Arnold, R., Burke, B., James, C., D'Arcy, M., & Thomas, B. (1991). *Educating for a change*. Toronto, Ontario: Between the Lines and the Doris Marshall Institute for Education and Action.

Bargh, J. A. (1997). The automaticity of everyday life. *Advances in Social Cognition, 10*, 2–48.

Berlyne, D. E. (1970). Children's Reasoning and thinking. In P. H. Mussen (Ed.), *Carmichael's manual of child psychology* (Vol. 1, pp. 939–981). New York: Wiley.

Blair, I. V. (2002). The malleability of automatic stereotypes and prejudice. *Personality & Social Psychology Review, 6*(3), 242–261.

Blascovich, J., Wyer, N., Swart, L., & Kibler, J. L. (1997). Racism and racial categorization. *Journal of Personality & Social Psychology, 72*(6), 1364–1372.

Bowen, W. G., & Bok, D. (1998). *The shape of the river: Long-term consequences of considering race in college and university admissions*. Princeton, NJ: Princeton University Press.

Brief of the American Psychological Association as *Amici Curiae* in Support of Respondents. (2003). *Grutter v. Bollinger, et al.*, No. 02-241; *Gratz v. Bollinger, et al.*, No. 02-516.

Brief of National Education Association, et. al. (2003). *Amici Curiae* in Support of Respondents. *Grutter v. Bollinger, et al.*, No. 02-241; *Gratz v. Bollinger, et al.*, No. 02-516.

Brower, A. M., & Dettinger, K. M. (1998). What "is" a learning community? Toward a comprehensive model. *About Campus, 3*(5), 15–22.

Chang, M. J., Hakuta, K., & Jones, J. (2002). *Compelling interest: Examining the evidence on racial dynamics in colleges and universities*. Palo Alto, CA: Stanford University Press.

Daloz, L. A. P. (2000). Transformative learning for the common good. In J. Mezirow & Associates (Eds.), *Learning as transformation: Critical perspectives on a theory in progress* (pp. 103–123). San Francisco, CA: Jossey-Bass.

Davis, M. (1983). Measuring individual differences in empathy: Evidence for a multidimensional approach. *Journal of Personality and Social Psychology, 44*, 113–126.

Doise, W., & Palmonari, A. (Eds.). (1984). *Social interaction in individual development*. New York: Cambridge University Press.

Dovidio J. F., & Gaertner, S. L. (2000). Aversive racism and selection decisions: 1989 and 1999. *Psychological Science, 11*(4), 315–319.

Dovidio, J., Kawakami, K., & Gaertner, S. L. (2002). Implicit and explicit prejudice and interracial interactions, *Journal of Personality and Social Psychology, 82*(1), 62–68.

Duncan, G. J., Boisjoly, J., Levy, D. M., Kremer, M., & Eccles, J. (2003). Empathy or antipathy? The consequences of racially and socially diverse peers on attitudes and behaviors. Retrieved June 1, 2003, from http://www.jcpr.org/wp/Wpprofile.cfm

Duster, T. (1993). The diversity of California at Berkeley: An emerging reformulation of competence in an increasingly multicultural world. In B. W. Thompson & S. Tyagi (Eds.), *Beyond a dream deferred: Multicultural education and the politics of excellence* (pp. 238–255). Minneapolis: University of Minnesota Press.

Farley, R. (1996). *The new American reality: Who we are, where we are going*. New York: Russell Sage Foundation.

Feagin, J. R. (1972). Poverty: We still believe that God helps those who help themselves. *Psychology Today, 6*, 101–129.

Fenzel, L. M., & Hessler, S. P. (2001). *Predictors of adjustment of first-year students to college: The role of early involvement and type of residence*. Presentation at a Roundtable, The

Freshman Year: Transitions and Adjustments, American Educational Research Association, Seattle, WA.

Fletcher, G., Danilovics, P., Fernandez, G., Peterson, D., & Reeder, G. D. (1986). Attributional complexity: An individual difference. *Journal of Personality and Social Psychology, 51*, 875–884.

Freire, P. (2000). *Pedagogy of the oppressed.* New York: Continuum. (Original work published 1970)

Guarasci, R. (2001). Developing the democratic arts. *About Campus, 5*(6), 9–15.

Gurin, P. (1999). Selections from *The Compelling Need for Diversity in Higher Education,* expert reports in defense of the University of Michigan: Expert report of Patricia Gurin. In *Equity and Excellence in Education, 32*(2), 37–62.

Gurin, P., Dey, E. L., Hurtado, S., & Gurin, G. (2002). Diversity and higher education: Theory and impact on educational outcomes. *Harvard Educational Review, 72*(3), 330–366.

Gurin, P., & Markus, H. (1988). Group identity: The psychological mechanisms of durable salience. *Revue Internationale de Psycologie Sociale, 1*(2), 257–274.

Gurin, P., Miller, A. H., & Gurin, G. (1980). Stratum identification and consciousness. *Social Psychology Quarterly, 43*, 30–47.

Gurin, P., Nagda, B. A., & Lopez, G. E. (2004). The benefits of diversity in education for democratic citizenship. *Journal of Social Issues, 60*(1), 17–34.

Hurtado, S. (2001). Linking diversity with educational purpose: How the diversity impacts the classroom environment and student development. In G. Orfield (Ed.), *Diversity challenged: Legal crisis and new evidence* (pp. 187–203). Cambridge, MA: Harvard Publishing Group.

Hurtado, S., Engberg, M., Ponjuan, L., & Landreman, L. (2003). Students' precollege preparation for participation in a diverse democracy. *Research in Higher Education, 43*(2), 163–186.

Kuh, G. D. (2001). Assessing what really matters in students learning. *Change, 66,* 10–17.

Langer, E. J. (1978). Rethinking the role of thought in social interaction. In J. Harvey, W. Ickes, & R. Kiss (Eds.), *New directions in attribution research* (Vol. 3, pp. 35–38). Hillsdale, NJ: Lawrence Erlbaum Associates.

Lopez, G. E., Gurin, P., & Nagda, B. A. (1998). Education and understanding structural causes for group inequalities. *Journal of Political Psychology, 19*(2), 305–329.

Maruyama, G., & Moreno, J. F. (2000). University faculty views about the value of diversity on campus and in the classroom. In G. Maruyama, J. F. Moreno, R. H. Gudman, & P. Marin (Eds.), *Does diversity make a difference? Three research studies on diversity in college classrooms* (pp. 14–16). Washington, DC: American Council on Education & American Association of University Professors.

Massey, D. (2003). *The source of the river: The social origins of freshmen at America's selective colleges and universities.* Princeton, NJ: Princeton University Press.

Matlock, J., Gurin, G., & Wade-Golden, K. (2001). *The Michigan Student Study: Student's expectations of and experiences with racial/ethnic diversity.* Ann Arbor, MI: The University of Michigan Office of Academic Multicultural Initiatives.

Milem, J. F., & Hakuta, K. (2000). The benefits of racial and ethnic diversity in higher education. In D. Eilds (Ed.), *Minorities in higher education: Seventeenth annual status report.* Washington, DC: American Council on Education.

Nagda, B. A., Gurin, P., & Lopez, G. E. (2003). Transformative pedagogy for democracy and social justice. *Race Ethnicity & Education, 6*(2), 165–191.

Nagda, B. A., Kim, C. W., & Truelove, Y. (2004). Learning about difference, learning with others, learning to transgress. *Journal of Social Issues, 60*(1), 195–214.

Orfield, G., & Kurlaender, M. (Eds.). (2001). *Diversity challenged: Evidence on the impact of Affirmative Action.* Cambridge, MA: Harvard Publishing Group.

Orfield, G., & Whitla, D. (2001). Diversity and legal education: Student experiences in leading law schools. In G. Orfield & M. Kurlaender (Eds.), *Diversity challenged: Evidence on the impact of affirmative action* (pp. 143–174). Cambridge, MA: Harvard Publishing Group.

Piaget, J. (1971). The theory of stages in cognitive development. In D. R. Green, M. P. Ford, & G. B. Flamer (Eds.), *Measurement and Piaget* (pp. 1–111). New York: McGraw-Hill.

Piaget, J. (1985). *The equilibration of cognitive structures: The central problem of intellectual development.* Chicago, IL: University of Chicago Press. (Original work published 1975)

Ruble, D. N. (1994). Developmental changes in achievement evaluation: Motivational implications of self-other differences. *Child Development, 65,* 1095–1110.

Ruble, D. N., & Goodnow, J. (1998). Social development from a lifespan perspective. In D. Gilbert, S. Fiske, & G. Lindzey (Eds.), *Handbook of social psychology* (pp. 741–787). New York: McGraw Hill.

Ruble, D. N., & Seidman, E. (1996). Social transitions: Windows into social psychological processes. In E. T. Higgins & A. Kruglanski (Eds.), *Handbook of social processes* (pp. 830–856). New York: Guilford Press.

Saunders, H. H. (1999). *A public peace process: Sustained dialogue to transform racial and ethnic conflicts.* New York: St. Martin's Press.

Saxonhouse, A. (1992). *Fear of diversity: The birth of political science in ancient Greek thought.* Chicago, IL: University of Chicago Press.

Schoem, D., & Hurtado, S. (Eds.) (2001). *Intergroup dialogue: Deliberative democracy in school, college, community and workplace.* Ann Arbor, MI: University of Michigan Press.

Sfeir-Younis, L. F. (1993). Reflections on the teaching of multicultural courses. In D. Schoem, L. Frankel, X. Zúñiga, & E. Lewis (Eds.), *Multicultural teaching in the university* (pp. 61–75). Westport, CT: Praeger.

Sugrue, T. (1999). Expert report: *The Compelling Need for Diversity in Higher Education.* Prepared for *Gratz, et al. v. Bollinger, et al.* No. 97-75231 (E.D. Mich.) and *Grutter, et al. v. Bollinger, et al.* No. 97-75928 (E.D. Mich.).

Tienda, M., & Cortes, K. N. (2003). *College attendance and the Texas Top 10 Percent Law: Permanent contagion or transitory promise.* Unpublished manuscript, Princeton University.

Zúñiga, X., Nagda, B. A., & Sevig, T. D. (2002). Intergroup dialogues: An educational model for cultivating student engagement across differences. *Equity and Excellence in Education, 35*(1), 7–17.

III

Assessing First-Year Outcomes

5

Cognitive Impacts of the First Year of College

ERNEST T. PASCARELLA
The University of Iowa

The last four decades have witnessed the publication of a number of comprehensive syntheses of the evidence pertaining to the impact of college on students (e.g., Bowen, 1977; Feldman & Newcomb, 1969; Gardiner, 1994; Pascarella & Terenzini, 1991). A major, if unsurprising, conclusion from these research syntheses is that the college years are a time of substantial student growth and development, particularly in the areas of learning and cognition. Quite understandably, most of the studies that address how much students learn or develop cognitively during college are concerned with documenting the changes that occur from the time students enter an institution until the time they graduate. Yet, there is certainly evidence to suggest that the first year of college can be a time of potentially important changes in the ways students learn to think and what they come to know (e.g., Baxter Magolda, 1990; Facione, 1997; Heath, 1968; Osterlind, 1997; Pascarella, 1989; Pascarella, Bohr, Nora, & Terenzini, 1996; Upcraft, Gardner, & Associates, 1989). In this chapter, I selectively review the accumulated evidence on college student learning and cognitive development, with special reference to the first year of college. I also give particular attention to the research published since 1990.

Even if we confine our focus to the first year of college, the literature on the various impacts of postsecondary education on learning and cognitive development is extensive. To make some conceptual sense of this large body of evidence, I have organized this chapter around the following four questions:

1. What is the net, or unique, impact of the first year of college on learning and cognitive development? (Hereafter, I refer to this as the *net effects* question.)
2. Do different kinds of postsecondary institutions have a differential impact on learning and cognitive development in the first year of college? (Hereafter, this is termed the *between-college effects* question.)
3. What are the effects of different classroom and non-classroom experiences on learning and cognitive development in the first year of college? (Hereafter, this is called the *within-college effects* question.)
4. Do various classroom and non-classroom experiences have a differential impact on first-year learning and cognitive development for different kinds of students? (Hereafter, this is termed the *conditional effects* question.)

NET-EFFECTS OF THE FIRST YEAR OF COLLEGE

Because one cannot conduct randomized experiments in which individuals are "assigned" to different levels of formal education, estimating the net or unique impact of the first year of college on learning and cognitive development is a challenging task. Empirical attempts to meet this challenge usually involve the use of "statistical controls" to remove potential confounding influences from the relationship between extent of exposure to the first year of college and various measures of learning or cognition. Such studies exist in both cross-sectional (Flowers, Osterlind, Pascarella, & Pierson, 2001) and longitudinal (Pascarella, 1989; Pascarella, Bohr, et al., 1996) form; and while they do not permit the same degree of causal inference as experiments, they are useful in estimating the plausible cognitive effects of the first year of college. The weight of evidence from these investigations suggests that the first year of college has an important impact on standardized measures of both subject-matter acquisition and critical thinking skills that cannot be explained away by competing hypotheses.

The Flowers et al. (2001) study analyzed student samples from 56 four-year colleges (located in 16 states) to determine the differences between freshmen, sophomores, juniors, and seniors on the College Basic Academic Subjects Examination (CBASE). The CBASE is a standardized measure of content learning in college with four subscales: English, mathematics, science, and social studies. In the presence of statistical controls for student ACT/SAT scores, race, sex, college grades, credit hours taken, and the average ACT/SAT score of students at the institution attended, they found that sophomores had statistically significant advantages over freshmen in English (.50 of a standard deviation, or SD), mathematics (.44 SD), science (.44 SD), and social studies (.60 SD). The two studies by Pascarella and colleagues (Pascarella, 1989; Pascarella, Bohr, et al., 1996) followed two independent samples of students at 29 different institutions to estimate the net impact of the first year of college on critical thinking skills. Critical thinking was measured with the Watson Glaser Critical Thinking Appraisal or the Collegiate Assessment of Academic Proficiency Critical Thinking Test, and statistical controls were introduced for such influences as precollege critical thinking score, age, race, sex, academic motivation, socioeconomic status, and the like. In the presence of these controls, students with the most exposure to postsecondary education had a significant advantage in first-year growth in critical thinking skills over those with the least or no exposure to college (.41 to .44 SD).

The evidence on the net cognitive effects of college also suggests another trend. Specifically, the cognitive gains that occur in the first year of college along some dimensions may represent a substantial percentage, and perhaps even most, of the growth that happens from the freshman to the senior year. For example, Flowers et al. (2001) found that the net difference between freshman and sophomores was about 75% of the net freshman–senior difference on the CBASE English test, and about 85% of the net freshman–senior difference on the social studies test. In mathematics and science, the net freshman–sophomore differences were about equal to the net freshman–senior differences. Similarly, the net effect of the first year of college on critical thinking skills reported by Pascarella, Bohr, et al. (1996) was nearly 75% of the estimated net effect of the first three years of college on critical thinking (Doyle, Edison, & Pascarella, 1998).

Thus, while the body of evidence on the net effects of the first year of college is not extensive, it nevertheless suggests two important points. First, it would appear that the first year of postsecondary education can have an important net impact on how much students learn and the development of their critical thinking skills. Second, the growth in content learning and critical thinking skills that occurs during the first year of college may represent a substantial part of the total growth in those areas attributable to the entire undergraduate experience.

BETWEEN-COLLEGE EFFECTS
ON FIRST-YEAR COGNITIVE OUTCOMES

If the first year of college has an important influence on student learning and cognitive growth, does the magnitude of that effect depend on the type or characteristics of the college attended (e.g., student academic selectivity, size, two- versus four-year, racial or gender composition, and the like)? The answer appears to be "neither consistently nor to any great extent." Generally, the search for between-college effects has not been very productive in identifying specific institutional characteristics that consistently enhance student learning and cognitive growth (e.g., Anaya, 1996, 1999; Astin, 1968, 1993; Astin & Astin, 1993; Flowers et al., 2000; Hagedorn et al., 1999; Knox, Lindsay, & Kolb, 1992; Opp, 1991; Pascarella & Terenzini, 1991; Strauss & Volkwein, 2001; Terenzini, Springer, Yaeger, Pascarella, & Nora, 1994; Toutkoushian & Smart, 2001; Whitmire & Lawrence, 1996). (The one possible exception to this may be certain small, residential, highly selective, liberal arts colleges [Astin, 1999; Pascarella & Terenzini, 1991].) Similarly, evidence from the somewhat smaller body of research on between-college cognitive effects during the first year of college also tends to be equivocal. For example, when student precollege characteristics are taken into account, first-year gains in reading comprehension, mathematics, and critical thinking appear to occur equally at community colleges versus four-year colleges (Bohr et al., 1994; Pascarella, Bohr, Nora, & Terenzini, 1995a), and, for African American students, at historically Black versus predominantly White colleges (Bohr, Pascarella, Nora, & Terenzini, 1995).

The estimated effects of the academic selectivity of an institution's student body on first-year learning and cognitive growth is mixed. Hagedorn et al. (1999) uncovered a small but statistically significant net, positive effect of student body selectivity on first-year critical thinking gains, but it disappeared after the initial year of college. Conversely, Flowers et al. (2001) found that student-body academic selectivity had only a trivial and nonsignificant impact on freshman–sophomore differences in the CBASE English, mathematics, science, and social studies tests.

In addition to inconsistent findings, the research on between-college effects on learning and cognitive outcomes is characterized by the fact that, in the most internally valid studies, even the statistically significant effects tend to be quite small and often trivial in size. Of course, there may be some methodological and measurement explanations for this phenomenon (see, for example, Pascarella & Terenzini, 1991, pp. 80–83). However, there may also be a substantive explanation argued by Baird (1988, 1991) and Pace (1997) and supported empirically by Smart (1997) and Smart and Feldman (1998). Specifically, we find few major between-college influences because aggregation of characteristics at the institutional level (e.g., type, size, student-body selective, and the like) provides indices that are simply too remote from the intellectual and social experiences in college that shape individual learning and cognitive growth. I turn now to a selective synthesis of the impact of these within-college effects.

WITHIN-COLLEGE EFFECTS ON FIRST-YEAR COGNITIVE OUTCOMES

The literature on within-college effects on learning and cognitive development is massive, and consists of literally hundreds of studies. Because of this enormous body of literature, I have been selective in reviewing relevant evidence, focusing on four areas: class size, teacher behaviors, innovative instructional approaches, and social influences. Not all of the studies in these four areas are conducted solely with samples of students in their first year of college. Yet the findings would appear to be quite applicable to enhancing learning and general cognitive growth during students' initial exposure to postsecondary education.

Class Size

Class size has a considerable tradition as a "hot button" issue in education (e.g., Ehrenberg, Brewer, Gamoran, & Willms, 2001). It is one of the few educational variables that enters into political elections and budgetary considerations at multiple levels. At the postsecondary level, it may be one of the few variables of any discernible educational consequence that is part of the highly questionable annual "ranking" of colleges and universities by national news magazines and other publications. But what is the actual evidence with regard to the link between class size and student learning and cognitive growth? In a review of the evidence through the 1980s, we (Pascarella & Terenzini, 1991) concluded that small classes were more efficient than large classes when the goal of instruction was to influence affective change or higher order cognitive skills (e.g., critical thinking, evaluation, composition). This is probably attributable to the fact that small classes (e.g., 10–15 students) increase the probability of high-level discussion and analysis of ideas and issues between faculty and students, and among students themselves (Smith, 1977). There was little consistent evidence, however, to suggest that mastery of subject-matter content is accomplished any more effectively in small, discussion-oriented classes than in large lecture-oriented classes.

The literature from the decade of the 1990s and beyond suggests a modest revision in our 1991 conclusion that subject matter knowledge is acquired with equal proficiency in large as well as small classes. Interestingly, however, the strength of the conclusions one can make vary with the measure of learning used. When course grade or a common final examination is used as the dependent measure, the weight of evidence is reasonably clear that, other factors being equal, increasing class size has a negative influence on subject matter learning (Biner, Welsh, Barone, Summers, & Dean, 1997; Goldfinch, 1996; Keil & Partell, 1998; Raimondo, Esposito, & Gershenberg, 1990; Scheck, Kinicki, & Webster, 1994; Thompson, 1991). However, when a common standardized test was used as the dependent measure, the evidence is considerably less convincing. Both Zietz and Cochran (1997) and Becker and Powers (2001) found that class size negatively influenced achievement on the Test for Understanding of College Economics (TUCE). However, similar studies by Kennedy and Siegfried (1997) and Lopus and Maxwell (1995) found no net relationship between class size and TUCE scores.

Overall, the most recent research suggests that smaller classes may have modest positive effects on student learning, but the evidence is not totally convincing. Clearly, class size can influence the types of social and intellectual interactions that occur among faculty and students; but, irrespective of class size, the quality of instruction received probably has substantially greater consequences for what students learn.

Teacher/Instructional Behaviors

We know much about good teaching and student perceptions of the behaviors of effective teachers. Literally, hundreds of correlational investigations have been conducted to determine the extent to which student perceptions of teacher behaviors such as instructional clarity, expressiveness, rapport with students, feedback to students, and organization and structure are linked to various measures of course-related knowledge acquisition. Fortunately, there have been a number of excellent meta-analyses and narrative syntheses of this research (e.g., Cashin, 1999; d'Apollonia & Abrami, 1997; Feldman, 1997; Marsh & Dunkin, 1997). The bottom line from these reviews is that student perceptions of teacher behaviors are multidimensional, are reasonably reliable and stable, and have moderate positive correlations (e.g., .30 to .50) with various measures of course learning (e.g., course grade, course final examination).

To be sure, there is evidence to suggest that student perceptions of teaching are influenced by a number of course characteristics. These include expected or actual grade, academic discipline, class size, and grading leniency. Such extraneous influences may be troublesome when student perceptions of teaching are used in faculty promotion, tenure, or salary decisions. However, they probably have little impact on the extent to which student perceptions of teacher behaviors can enlighten us to teaching actions that, at least in the aggregate, enhance student learning (Aleamoni, 1999). Furthermore, the positive impacts of three dimensions that show some of the strongest positive links with student course learning in correlational studies—teacher clarity, teacher expressiveness/enthusiasm, and teacher/course organization—have been validated in experimental research (Hines, Cruickshank, & Kennedy, 1985; Schonwetter, Menec, & Perry, 1995; Schonwetter, Perry, & Struthers, 1994; Wood & Murray, 1999). Perhaps even more significantly, many of the constituent behaviors that comprise clarity (e.g., use of examples, identifying key points), expressiveness/enthusiasm (e.g., speaking emphatically, eye contact), and organization (e.g., providing class outline, using course objectives) may themselves be learnable by faculty (Weimer & Lenze, 1997).

Nearly the total body of research on teacher behaviors has focused on course-level learning. However, there is additional evidence to suggest that at least one dimension of effective teacher behavior—organization and preparation—may have positive impacts on more general academic competencies and skills not directly tied to a particular course. For example, in an 18-institution study, Pascarella, Edison, Nora, Hagedorn, and Braxton (1996) found that the more students reported that the overall instruction they received in college was well organized (e.g., course objectives are clear, class time is used effectively, presentation of material is well organized), the greater their first-year gains on standardized tests of reading comprehension, mathematics, and critical thinking. These associations could not be explained away by statistical controls for precollege test scores, race, academic motivation, full- or part-time enrollment, or patterns of course work taken. By facilitating the efficient acquisition of factual knowledge and definitions (Perry, 1991), well-organized teaching may permit greater instructional emphasis on more general and higher order cognitive skills.

Innovative Instructional Approaches

Teacher behaviors are only one of many classroom influences on student learning and cognitive growth in college. The literature of the last 20 years, and particularly the literature of the last decade, has also estimated the cognitive impacts of a number of innovative approaches to instruction. These instructional approaches vary substantially in both format and emphasis, but perhaps their major pedagogical features are the dramatically different roles assumed by teachers and students. In some approaches, such as learning for mastery, there is a great deal of teacher control over the presentation of material and the pace of instruction. Students are essentially recipients of subject matter content delivered by a faculty "expert." In other approaches, such as collaborative or constructivist learning, the instructor is more of a consultant or guide than an expert who conveys knowledge. Students work at various projects to "construct" knowledge and understanding, rather than passively receiving it from a faculty "expert." Despite these rather sharp pedagogical differences, each of these instructional approaches has been shown to significantly enhance student learning. I turn now to a brief review of the evidence on: learning for mastery, computer-based instruction, supplemental instruction, collaborative/cooperative learning, active learning, constructivist learning, and service learning.

Learning for Mastery. Learning for mastery or group-based mastery learning (Bloom, 1968; Guskey, 1985) requires students to demonstrate mastery of course content against an absolute criterion. In a mastery learning class, the teacher determines the pace of the original instruction and directs accompanying feedback and corrective procedures. Course content is divided into units, and students are required to demonstrate mastery of one unit before moving on to new content. Students who fail unit mastery tests usually receive individual or group tutorial help before moving on to new material or before being allowed to take the course final examination. Detailed discussions of the implementation of learning for mastery are provided in Bloom (1968), Guskey (1985), and Guskey and Pigott (1988).

The effects of learning for mastery in postsecondary instruction have been synthesized in two separate meta-analyses with about a 65% overlap in the studies reviewed (Guskey & Pigott, 1988; Kulik, Kulik, & Bangert-Drowns, 1990). Both meta-analyses considered only experimental or quasi-experimental studies, and the subject areas included algebra, history, education, biology, reading, psychology, and English. Mastery learning instruction had an average course achievement advantage over conventional (non-mastery) instruction of between .41 SD (Guskey & Pigott, 1988) and .68 SD (Kulik et al., 1990). It also appears that, in comparison to non-mastery instruction, students in mastery-taught classes spend more time on task or engaged in learning and that instructors in mastery-taught classes use class time more efficiently (Guskey & Pigott, 1988). These factors, along with the mastery criterion, may account for the impact of learning for mastery on knowledge acquisition.

Computer-Based Instruction.   It appears to be widely accepted that computers and related information technologies have the potential to fundamentally transform the nature of teaching and learning in postsecondary settings (e.g., Green, 1996; Kuh & Vesper, 1999). Not surprisingly, the last 15 years have witnessed the growth of an extensive body of inquiry on the use of computers and related technologies to assist or augment postsecondary instruction. In the early 1990s, a number of narrative or quantitative (meta-analytic) research reviews were produced suggesting that computer-based instruction leads to modest improvements in subject-matter acquisition with a decrease in instructional time (e.g., Kulik & Kulik, 1991; Liao & Bright, 1991; McComb, 1994).

The most comprehensive of these research syntheses is the meta-analysis of Kulik and Kulik (1991). They synthesized the results of 149 experimental and quasi-experimental studies conducted with college samples. The course content was in mathematics, science, social science, reading and language, and vocational training. The studies were classified in three groups: computer-assisted instruction (CAI), where the computer provides (a) drill-and-practice exercises, but not new material, or (b) tutorial instruction that includes new material; computer-managed instruction (CMI), where the computer evaluates student test performance, then guides students to appropriate instructional resources, and keeps records of student progress; and computer-enriched instruction (CEI), where the computer (a) serves as a problem solving tool, (b) generates data at the student's request to illustrate relationships in social or physical reality, or (c) executes programs developed by the student. In all three categories, computer-based instruction (versus traditional instructional approaches such as lecture, discussion, and text) produced average advantages in tested understanding of course content that were statistically significant. The average effect-size advantages were: CAI, .27 SD; CMI, .43 SD; and CEI, .34 SD. Weighting the effect sizes by the number of studies in each category yielded an overall learning advantage for computer-based instruction of .31 SD.

Since the publication of Kulik and Kulik's (1991) meta-analysis, the impact of computer-based instruction on learning has continued to be the focus of substantial inquiry. I uncovered 24 additional studies published since 1991 that investigate the impact of computer-based instruction using experimental or quasi-experimental designs (e.g., Agarwal & Day, 1998; Huang & Aloi, 1991; Williamson & Abraham, 1995). Across all studies that provided requisite statistical information, computer-based classes had an advantage over traditional instructional approaches of .28 SD in tested knowledge acquisition. Though admittedly a rougher estimate, this is nonetheless quite consistent with the overall advantage of .31 SD derived from Kulik and Kulik's work. Moreover, there was also evidence, consistent with that reported by Kulik and Kulik, that students in computer-based classes required less instructional time than their counterparts in traditionally taught classes (e.g., Taraban & Rynearson, 1998; Tjaden & Martin, 1995).

It should be pointed out that the extensive body of research indicating consistent, though modest, impacts of computer-based instructional approaches on learning has given rise to some debate. On one side is the argument that the results of this research are questionable because the relative advantage for student learning of one instructional medium (e.g., computers) over another (e.g., lecture) will inevitably confound the instructional medium with the quality or type of instruction received (Clark, 1994). Consequently, the learning benefits attributed to computer-based instruction could just as easily be explained by the instructional methods they support or augment. Others (Kozma, 1994; Reiser, 1994), however, argue that the ways computers are employed is not irrelevant to instruction or student learning. Indeed, certain technological applications make certain kinds of instructional approaches possible or enhance their impact. What counts is how information technology integrated with instructional approaches can facilitate knowledge construction and learning for students.

Supplemental Instruction. Supplemental instruction (SI) is a structured intervention designed to increase mastery of content in "high risk" courses through the use of collaborative learning strategies. High-risk courses are those that typically have 30% D or F grades or withdrawals. The courses are frequently offered during the first year of college. SI provides regularly scheduled, out-of-class, peer-facilitated sessions offering students the chance to discuss and process course content. The leaders of these peer-facilitated sessions are other students who have previously taken the course and who are trained to help current students develop strategies for learning and understanding course content (Arendale, 1994; Congos, Langsam, & Schoeps, 1997).

In the last two decades, SI has been widely used throughout the country and has produced an extensive literature of comparative investigations of its impact. Arendale and Martin (1997) have synthesized the results of these studies, which are based on data from nearly 5,000 courses in 270 institutions. The studies were conducted in a broad range of disciplines, including biology, chemistry, history, economics, statistics, calculus, physics, and government. Course grades on a five-point scale, where 0 = "F" and 4 = "A," were the measure of content learning in all studies. Taking the statistical information provided on each study, I computed an effect size and concluded that SI leads to an estimated advantage in course content mastery over nonparticipation of about .39 SD. An additional finding reported by Arendale and Martin is that, across all studies, SI participants averaged a significantly lower percentage of D, F, and "incomplete" grades (23.1%) than did non-SI participants (37.1%). There appears to be little evidence in studies not covered by the Arendale and Martin synthesis that would change their conclusions (Kochenour et al., 1997; Warren, 1997–1998; Wittig & Thomerson, 1996).

A major threat to the internal validity of most studies of SI is that students self-select themselves into participation or nonparticipation in SI; and there is evidence that more motivated students choose SI participation (Visor, Johnson, & Cole, 1992). Recent SI studies, however, have controlled for self-selection either by random assignment of intact classes to SI or non-SI conditions (Peled & Kim, 1996) or by building a measure of academic motivation (i.e., cumulative grades) into the design of the study (Ramirez, 1997). In the presence of these controls for self-selection effects, SI participants still significantly outperformed their non-SI counterparts on measures of course achievement. A second rival hypothesis is that SI merely provides "double exposure" to the course content, once in a lecture and for a second time in the SI session. However, a quasi-experimental study conducted by Kenny (1989) reported that students who attended course lectures and SI sessions still had significantly higher levels of course achievement than similar students who attended lectures and special question-and-answer sessions led by graduate students. Thus, given equal exposure in terms of instructional time, SI participants still outperformed their non-SI peers.

Collaborative/Cooperative Learning. As defined by Smith and Mac-Gregor (1992):

> Collaborative learning is an umbrella term for a variety of educational approaches involving joint intellectual effort by students, or students and teachers together. In most collaborative learning situations students are working in groups of two or more, mutually searching for understanding, solutions or meanings, or creating a product. (p. 10)

The intellectual and philosophical justification for collaborative learning would appear to be that knowledge is more a socially held or socially based phenomenon than it is a body of information and concepts transmitted from expert to novice. Consequently, it is most effectively acquired through social or group interactions and activities in which peers actively engage in knowledge construction (Palinscar, Stevens, & Gavelek, 1989). Although the statistical information prevented estimation of an effect size, it would appear from the experimental or quasi-experimental evidence that learning in a collaborative context can significantly improve acquisition of course content over learning on one's own in statistics and research methods (Leppel, 1998), sociology (Son & Van Sickle, 1993), biology (Sokolove & Marbach-Ad, 2000), and college algebra (Thomas & Higbee, 1996).

Cooperative learning is typically considered the most operationally well-defined and procedurally structured form of collaborative learning. It is a systematic instructional strategy in which small groups of students work together to accomplish shared learning goals; and each student achieves his or her learning goals only if other members achieve theirs (Johnson, Johnson, & Smith, 1998). The common attributes of cooperative learning appear to be: (a) a common task or learning activity suitable for group work, (b) learning in small groups, (c) positive interdependence and cooperative behavior among group members, and (d) individual accountability and responsibility (Millis & Cottell, 1998). The research on the cognitive impacts of cooperative learning in postsecondary education is extensive. Fortunately, in the 1990s, several comprehensive meta-analyses have synthesized this literature. Syntheses of over 150 experimental and quasi-experimental studies with postsecondary samples by Johnson and Johnson (1993a) and Johnson et al. (1998) suggest that classes taught in a cooperative context provided respective advantages in course content mastery of between .49 and .54 SD over competitive classroom approaches, and between .51 and .53 SD over students learning on their own. These results held for verbal tasks (such as reading, writing, and oral presentation), quantitative tasks, and procedural tasks (such as swimming). Moreover, there is little to suggest that the preceding estimates of the positive learning effects of cooperative learning would be substantially altered by more recent research (e.g., Kim, Cohen, Booske, & Derry, 1998; Potthast, 1999).

There is an additional body of experimental and quasi-experimental evidence to suggest that cooperative learning may also facilitate the acquisition of more general problem-solving skills. Qin, Johnson, and Johnson (1995) conducted a meta-analysis of 43 experimental and quasi-experimental studies that considered the effects of cooperative versus individualistic or competitive approaches on general problem-solving skills. Problem solving was operationally defined as "a process that required participants to form a cognitive representation of a task, plan a procedure for solving it, and execute the procedure and check the results" (Qin et al., 1995, p. 181). Taking the raw statistical data provided by Qin et al. for the 20 studies conducted with postsecondary samples, I estimated that, compared to their counterparts not learning in a cooperative format, college students learning in cooperative groups had a statistically significant advantage in overall problem-solving skills of .47 SD. The advantage in problem solving accruing to students engaged in cooperative learning was essentially the same for both well-defined problems (.46 SD) and ill-defined problems (.49 SD). Well-defined problems are those with well-defined operational procedures and solutions (e.g., a chess problem), while ill-defined problems have uncertainty with regard to operational procedures and ultimate solutions (e.g., deciding which car to buy).

Active Learning. Active learning is a general instructional approach that attempts to exploit the learning that occurs when students are actively engaged in processing information in new and personally relevant ways and "constructing" their own knowledge (e.g., Baxter Magolda, 1998; Reynolds & Nunn, 1997). A modest body of experimental and quasi-experimental research suggests that such active student involvement in learning can facilitate the acquisition of course content. For example, Lang (1996), reported in Murray and Lang (1997), conducted an experiment in which course topics in an undergraduate psychology course were randomly assigned to be taught by either an "active participation" method or a control "lecture only" method. For the topics taught by the "active participation" method, at least 75% of class time was spent in activities requiring active student participation (e.g., small-group discussion, case study debates). At the end of the course, mean student performance on both multiple-choice and essay examination questions was significantly better for topics taught by active participation than by topics taught by lecture.

In addition to the experiment reported by Murray and Lang (1997), I uncovered 16 additional experimental or quasi-experimental studies that estimate the relative impact of active learning (e.g., Hake, 1998; Hall & McCurdy, 1990; McCarthy & Anderson, 2000). Though not totally consistent, the weight of evidence from this research suggests that students may demonstrate modestly better mastery of course content when actively engaged in learning. Using the data from those studies providing requisite statistical information, I estimate that active learning approaches provide a learning advantage over passive approaches of about .25 SD. It should be cautioned, however, that this is only a tentative estimate based on a relatively small body of studies.

Constructivist-Oriented Approaches.   There is an additional group of related instructional approaches that do not fit neatly into single categories such as collaborative learning, cooperative learning, or active learning. Instead, they typically combine elements of each of these approaches in various ways and are based on the premise that students learn best when they actively construct knowledge in socially interactive contexts that are often problem-based rather than passively receiving it from an "expert." For lack of a better term, I refer to these approaches as "constructivist-oriented." Research on the relative cognitive impacts of constructivist-oriented approaches appears to be in its nascent stages. Nevertheless, examples exist in a small number of experimental and quasi-experimental studies addressing variations on the constructivist theme such as constructivist teaching (Lord, 1997), "new-wave methods" (Hofer, 1994, 1998–99), problem-based learning (Schumow, 1999), and team problem-solving (Marra, Palmer, & Litzinger, 2000). In three of these studies, students learning under one of the various constructivist approaches had a statistically significant advantage over students learning in a traditional format (usually lecture) in course content mastery (Lord, 1997; Hofer, 1994, 1998–99) and problem-solving ability (Schumow, 1999). Furthermore, in the fourth study (Marra et al., 2000), students who completed a course in a constructivist team problem-solving format had significantly higher scores on a measure of intellectual development than did students waiting to take the course.

This difference persisted even in the presence of statistical controls for academic aptitude, sex, prior grades, class standing, and honors program participation.

Thus, the body of evidence on the impact of constructivist-oriented approaches is small and far from definitive. Yet, the early results of experimental and quasi-experimental investigations suggest the potential of these instructional formats to foster student learning and cognitive growth.

Service-Learning. A growing number of postsecondary institutions in the United States have become actively engaged in encouraging undergraduates to involve themselves in some form of volunteer service (Astin, Sax, & Avalos, 1999; Eyler & Giles, 1999). As argued by Astin et al. (1999), the importance that higher education leaders place on volunteer service as part of the undergraduate curriculum can be seen in the growth of a consortium of colleges known as the Campus Compact, which promotes service among students and faculty. Paralleling growth in postsecondary education's interest in service experiences has been an interest in assessing the educational impacts of service.

The body of evidence on the cognitive impacts of service-learning is small, and not always convincing. However, the weight of quasi-experimental studies, matched with extensive statistical controls, suggests that when service experiences are well integrated into a course, they may enhance the learning or cognitive growth that occurs (e.g., Astin & Sax, 1996; Batchelder & Root, 1994; Berson & Younkin, 1998; Eyler & Giles, 1997, 1999; Eyler, Giles, Lynch, & Gray, 1997; Marcus, Howard, & King, 1993; Strage, 2000). The operative part of this conclusion is the phrase "well integrated." Eyler and her colleagues argue that this condition is approached when: (a) service experiences are purposefully integrated with course content; (b) provision is made in course activities for reflection about the service experience; and (c) students apply subject matter learning to the service experience and vice versa. In short, to have an impact service experiences have to be highly integrated into course content, and provisions must be made for continuous reflection. Additional evidence suggests that the greater the extent to which service-learning courses meet the criteria for being integrative and reflective, the stronger the positive effects on learning (Ikeda, 2000), reflective judgment (Eyler, Giles, Lynch, & Gray, 1997), and the use of complex and multiple perspectives in formulating solutions to social problems (Eyler, Giles, Root, & Price, 1997). The simple addition of service experiences to a course had trivial impacts on these outcomes.

OUT-OF-CLASS INFLUENCES
ON FIRST-YEAR COGNITIVE OUTCOMES

If we know anything from the vast body of research on the impact of college, it is that not all of the important influences on learning or cognitive development occur in the classroom. There is ample evidence to indicate that students' interactions with their peers and the nature of their extracurricular experiences have important implications for cognitive growth. Moreover, much of this evidence is taken from the first year of college. For example, analyses of the National Study of Student Learning (Inman & Pascarella, 1998; Terenzini et al., 1994) found that first-year gains on a standardized measure of critical thinking were positively linked to a student's level of involvement in college clubs and organizations. This positive association persisted in the presence of controls for such confounding influences as precollege critical thinking level, academic motivation, student demographic characteristics, full- or part-time enrollment, work responsibilities, measures of academic effort/involvement, and institutional selectivity. Consistent findings are also reported by Baxter Magolda (1992) in a qualitative investigation of growth in students' epistemological sophistication and reasoning skills during college. What appears to underlie this link between extracurricular involvement and cognitive growth is the nature of the interactions one has with other students. The evidence suggests that peer interactions having the strongest net influence on various measures of first-year cognitive growth (e.g., critical thinking, reflective thinking) are those that: (a) extend and reinforce the ethos of the academic program, and/or (b) expose one to people, ideas, and perspectives that challenge his or her assumed views of the world (e.g., Kitchener, Wood, & Jensen, 1999, 2000; Whitt, Edison, Pascarella, Nora, & Terenzini, 1999).

The impact of exposure to diverse peers, ideas, and perspectives has been a particularly revealing line of inquiry. With statistical controls in place for important confounding influences (including precollege scores on the outcome), there is replicated evidence to indicate that students reporting the highest levels of exposure to multidimensional diversity (e.g., friendships or interactions with peers of a different race, attending multicultural/multisocial events, exposure to diversity themes or diverse views in the classroom, having discussions with peers whose values or political views are different from one's own) also report the greatest first-year gains in critical thinking (Pascarella, Palmer, Moye, & Pierson, 2001; Terenzini et al., 1994) and reflective thinking (Kitchener et al., 2000); as well as the largest four-year gains in thinking complexity (Gurin, 1999). Moreover, there is at least some evidence in this research to suggest the possibility that the largest cognitive benefits from first-year interactions with peers of a different race accrue to White students.

Not all student out-of-class involvements appear to facilitate cognitive growth in the first year of college. Analyses of multi-institutional samples using standardized measures of learning and cognitive development suggest that both fraternity membership and participation in intercollegiate revenue-producing sports (i.e., football and basketball) have significant negative effects on male first-year gains in reading comprehension, mathematics, and critical thinking (Pascarella, Edison, Whitt, et al., 1996; Pascarella, Bohr, Nora, & Terenzini, 1995b). These negative effects persisted even in the presence of statistical controls for such confounding influences as precollege scores on the dependent variables, academic motivation, student demographic characteristics, full- or part-time enrollment, work responsibilities, the academic selectivity of the institution attended, and, in the case of intercollegiate athletics, whether or not the institution attended fielded an NCAA Division I or non-Division I athletic program. There were no negative first-year cognitive impacts for men participating in non-revenue producing sports, but the magnitude of the negative effects for male football and basketball plays was similar at schools differing in selectivity and in whether or not they fielded a Division I or non-Division I athletic program. Greek affiliation and athletic participation did not have the same cognitive implications for women. Any first-year negative effects of sorority membership and intercollegiate athletic participation for women were substantially smaller in magnitude and less extensive than those for men.

In addition to Greek affiliation and intercollegiate athletic participation, multi-institutional studies using standardized outcome measures have also addressed the cognitive impacts of both on- and off-campus work during the first year of college (Pascarella, Bohr, Nora, Desler, & Zusman, 1994; Pascarella, Edison, Nora, Hagedorn, & Terenzini, 1998). These analyses suggest that work neither enhances nor inhibits first-year learning and cognitive gains. With statistical controls in place for such confounding influences as precollege scores on the dependent variables, academic motivation, demographic traits, full- or part-time enrollment, on- or off-campus residence, course work taken, and institutional selectivity, neither amount of on- or off-campus work had more than nonsignificant, trivial linear or curvilinear effects on first-year gains in reading comprehension, mathematics, and critical thinking. Moreover, the nonsignificant effects of work appeared to hold irrespective of differences in student characteristics

(e.g., ethnicity, gender, age, precollege test scores, full- or part-time enrollment) and whether or not the student attended a community college or
four-year institution.

CONDITIONAL EFFECTS ON FIRST-YEAR COGNITIVE OUTCOMES

One of the underlying assumptions of the evidence synthesized in this
chapter up to this point is that the average effects reported are general in
nature; that is, they are essentially the same for all students. However, it is
sometimes the case that these general effects can mask important differences in the magnitude of an effect for different kinds of students. When
the impact of a particular experience or intervention varies in magnitude
(or perhaps even direction) for students with different characteristics, it is
referred to as a conditional, or interaction, effect. Such conditional effects
assume that the individual differences students bring to college can shape
the impact of college on them.

Perhaps the most robust of all conditional effects in the literature on
college impact on learning and cognitive development are those involving the fit between learning style and instructional approach. Although
all the research on the topic was not conducted with first-year students,
the results would certainly seem to have applicability to the first year of
college. As suggested by Dunn and Stevenson (1997), learning style is the
"way each individual begins to concentrate on, process, internalize, and
remember new and difficult academic information and skills" (p. 353). It
can be measured by a number of existing instruments, examples of which
are the Productivity Environmental Preference Survey and the Learning
Style Inventory (Dunn & Dunn, 1993; Dunn, Dunn, & Price, 1990). Both
instruments elicit student self-diagnostic responses which yield a profile
of preferred learning style based on dimensions such as cognitive, environmental, emotional, sociological, and physiological (Dunn & Stevenson,
1997). Since students exhibit a rather broad range of these learning styles
(Dunn & Dunn, 1993), it seems reasonable to expect that any single instructional approach may yield different levels of learning for students with
different learning styles. Thus, learning can be enhanced when learning
styles are matched with appropriate instructional approaches.

The weight of evidence from a modest body of research does, in fact, suggest that college students demonstrate higher levels of learning or knowledge acquisition when they are exposed to instruction that matches their

preferred learning style than when they are exposed to instruction that does not. A meta-analysis of experimental and quasi-experimental studies testing the general model of matching instruction to diagnosed learning style was conducted by Dunn, Griggs, Olson, Beasley, and Gorman (1995). Their findings across all levels of education clearly suggest that students with different learning styles learn most efficiently from different instructional approaches. Taking only those studies from the meta-analysis conducted with postsecondary samples, I estimate that college students who receive instruction matched to their learning style demonstrate an average achievement advantage of .90 SD over similar students for whom no attempt was made to match instruction with their preferred learning style.

Beyond the replicated evidence on student learning styles, there are also a substantial number of conditional effects based on single-sample findings that are, as yet, unreplicated. Such unreplicated conditional effects need to be regarded as tentative. However, they are interesting if only because of what they suggest — that the cognitive impacts of college may be somewhat more complex and less straightforward than the evidence on general effects would indicate. Examples of these effects include the following:

1. Students with low tested academic ability may derive greater learning benefits from participation in supplemental instruction than those with high tested academic ability (Kochenour et al., 1997).

2. Students of color may benefit more from cooperative learning approaches than White students (Posner & Markstein, 1994).

3. The negative first-year impacts of fraternity membership on reading comprehension, mathematics, and critical thinking were larger for White men than for men of color (Pascarella, Edison, Whitt, et al., 1996). Similarly, Greek affiliation had a significantly stronger negative impact on first-year critical thinking gains for men than for women (Whitt, Pascarella, Pierson, Elkins, & Marth, in press).

4. Studying with peers had a positive impact on first-year critical thinking gains for African American students, but a negative effect for White students (Terenzini et al., 1994).

5. Working off-campus was negatively related to growth in reflective thinking for men, but working on-campus, or cumulative hours worked either on- or off-campus was positively related to growth in reflective thinking for women (Kitchener et al., 2000).

6. Full-time enrollment in college had a significantly stronger positive influence on first-year critical thinking gains for first-genera-

tion college students than for students whose parents had attended college (Terenzini, Springer, Yaeger, Pascarella, & Nora, 1996).

7. For four-year college students high in precollege tested academic ability, unstructured electronic-mail use had a significant, positive effect on gains in a composite measure of first-year learning (consisting of reading comprehension, mathematics, and critical thinking); but for students low in precollege academic ability, the corresponding effect was negative (Flowers, Pascarella, & Pierson, 1999).

8. The positive effects of cooperative learning may be significantly more pronounced for gains in complex cognitive functioning (e.g., analysis, synthesis, and/or evaluation) than for gains in less complex cognitive functioning (e.g., knowledge, comprehension) (Garside, 1996).

CONCLUSIONS AND IMPLICATIONS

What can we conclude from the extensive evidence on the cognitive effects of college? I believe a number of general conclusions are warranted. First, while it may not hold across all dimensions of cognitive or intellectual development, it would nevertheless appear that the first year of college is one in which students can make important gains in knowledge acquisition and reasoning skills. Indeed, the growth in some content areas (e.g., English, mathematics, social science) and in critical thinking that occurs during the first year of college represents a substantial part of the total growth in those areas attributable to the undergraduate experience.

Second, the extent of learning and cognitive growth that happens during the first year of college does not appear to be highly dependent on the characteristics of the institution one attends. Statistically reliable between-college effects on knowledge acquisition and cognitive growth tend to be inconsistent and, when they are uncovered, quite modest in magnitude. From the perspective of institutional leaders, this conclusion may be welcome. Many institutional characteristics (e.g., size, selectivity, private/public control, two- versus four-year, wealth) are extremely difficult, if not impossible, to change in any meaningful way. Thus, if institutional characteristics were in fact the major determinant of learning and cognitive growth in college, purposeful attempts to enhance or reshape the intellectual experience of undergraduates might prove largely impossible. Fortunately, however, this is not the case.

A third major conclusion is an extension of the second conclusion. The learning and cognitive growth that occurs during the first year of college is much more the result of within-college academic and nonacademic experiences than it is of between-institution characteristics. Irrespective of the characteristics of the institution one attends, there are a number of purposeful instructional behaviors and approaches one can implement that have been shown to have substantial impacts on knowledge acquisition and cognitive skills. The research of the last 20 years provides us with a diverse array of pedagogical tools to enrich and enliven the first-year academic experience. If one is concerned with improving the effectiveness of the dominant paradigm of instruction, an impressive body of evidence suggests that there are learnable teacher skills, such as clarity, expressiveness, and organization/preparation, that significantly facilitate student content acquisition. Conversely, there are pedagogical approaches such as collaborative/cooperative learning, active learning, and constructivist learning which fundamentally change the dominant teacher-student paradigm. These, too, appear to have a positive impact on student knowledge acquisition, as well as facilitating some dimensions of cognitive growth. Additionally, there are instructional approaches such as mastery learning, computer-based instruction, supplemental instruction and service learning, which may not fit neatly into any particular pedagogical paradigm, but which have been experimentally validated in terms of their impacts on learning and cognitive growth.

The "take-home message" from this vast body of research is that we are now equipped with a wide variety of vetted instructional behaviors and pedagogical approaches (e.g., teachers teaching students; students teaching, and learning from, other students; using information technology and service experiences to enhance learning; students "constructing" rather than receiving knowledge; and the like). As a result, we have the potential to make the first-year academic experience in American postsecondary education the most dynamic in its history. This may have important instructional implications for institution-wide courses designed to help students adjust to, and make the most of college. What better arena to apply our new understanding of effective teaching behaviors and instructional approaches than in a common course experience that involves large numbers of first-year students? The use of instructional approaches such as cooperative learning, constructivist learning, mastery learning, and computer-based learning might not only facilitate student acquisition of the content of such courses; it could conceivably produce several additional benefits. First, a variety of instructional approaches may provide something of a novelty effect that

helps maintain student interest in the course content. Second, such pedagogical approaches may increase generalizable learning and social skills
that assist students, not only in their other course work, but also in the
quality of their interactions with other students. Third, if some degree of
choice is feasible, students might select different instructional approaches
covering the same content, and thereby gain a better understanding of
their own preferred learning style. Finally, faculty who participate in these
common first-year courses might use them as something of a laboratory to:
(a) sharpen important instructional skills such as clarity and organization,
and/or (b) become more adept at implementing and understanding the
impacts of important new pedagogical approaches.

A fourth major conclusion is that the nature of a student's non-classroom interactions with peers can have a significant influence on first-year
intellectual growth. Interactions that extend and reinforce what happens
in class and expose one to different people, ideas, and perspectives are the
most influential. From this perspective, an institution's attempt to increase
student-body racial, ethnic, or cultural diversity is not simply the projection
of a political or ideological agenda, it also makes good sense educationally.
Indeed, the ways in which an institution develops programmatic initiatives
to exploit the education potential of student peer groups may have important implications for its impact on learning and cognitive growth. The first
step in this direction is to acknowledge that much of what students learn in
college comes from other students.

A fifth and final conclusion is that the cognitive impact of any first-year
academic or non-academic experience may vary in magnitude for different
kinds of students. As the national undergraduate student population becomes more diverse in terms of such characteristics as race, socioeconomic
background, academic preparation, native language, and the cultural capi-
tal they bring to college, we should anticipate that fewer educational experiences will have similar effects for all students engaged in them. Perhaps
the important question to ask in future research about the cognitive outcomes of the first year of college is not which academic and non-academic
experiences are most influential, but rather which experiences are most
influential for which particular type of student?

REFERENCES

Agarwal, R., & Day, E. (1998). The impact of the Internet on economic education. *Journal of Economic Education, 29*, 99–110.

Aleamoni, L. (1999). Student rating myths versus research facts from 1924 to 1998. *Journal of Personnel Evaluation in Education, 13,* 153–166.

Anaya, G. (1996). College experiences and student learning: The influence of active learning, college environments and cocurricular activities. *Journal of College Student Development, 37,* 611–622.

Anaya, G. (1999, April). *Within-college, curricular and co-curricular correlates of performance on the MCAT.* Paper presented at the annual meeting of the American Educational Research Association, Montreal, Canada.

Arendale, D. (1994). Understanding the supplemental instruction model. In D. Martin & D. Arendale (Eds.), *Supplemental instruction: Increasing achievement and retention* (pp. 11–21). San Francisco: Jossey-Bass.

Arendale, D., & Martin, D. (1997). *Review of research concerning the effectiveness of supplemental instruction from the University of Missouri-Kansas City and other institutions from the across the United States.* Kansas City: The University of Missouri. (ERIC Document Reproduction Service ED 370 502)

Astin, A. (1968). Undergraduate achievement and institutional excellence. *Science, 161,* 661–668.

Astin, A. (1993). *What matters in college? Four critical years revisited.* San Francisco: Jossey-Bass.

Astin, A. (1999). How the liberal arts college affects students. *Daedalus, 128,* 77–100.

Astin, A., & Astin, H. (1993). *Undergraduate science education: The impact of different college environments on the educational pipeline in the sciences.* Los Angeles: University of California, Higher Education Research Institute, Graduate School of Education.

Astin, A., & Sax, L. (1996). *How undergraduates are affected by service participation.* Unpublished manuscript, University of California, Los Angeles.

Astin, A., Sax, L., & Avalos, J. (1999). Long-term effects of volunteerism during the undergraduate years. *Review of Higher Education, 22,* 187–202.

Baird, L. (1988). The college environment revisited. In J. Smart (Ed.), *Higher education: Handbook of theory and research* (Vol. 4, pp. 1–52). New York: Agathon Press.

Baird, L. (1991, May). *What can studies of college environments contribute to institutional research?* Paper presented at the annual meeting of the Association for Institutional Research, San Francisco.

Batchelder, T., & Root, S. (1994). Effects of an undergraduate program to integrate academic learning and service: Cognitive, prosocial cognitive, and identity outcomes. *Journal of Adolescence, 17,* 341–355.

Baxter Magolda, M. (1990). Gender differences in epistemological development. *Journal of College Student Development, 31,* 555–561.

Baxter Magolda, M. (1992). Cocurricular influences on college students' intellectual development. *Journal of College Student Development, 33,* 203–213.

Baxter Magolda, M. (1998). Developing self-authorship in young adult life. *Journal of College Student Development, 39,* 143–156.

Becker, W., & Powers, J. (2001). Student performance, attrition, and class size given missing student data. *Economics of Education Review, 20,* 377–388.

Berson, J., & Younkin, W. (1998, November). *Doing well by doing good: A study of the effects of a service-learning experience on student success.* Paper presented at the annual meeting of the Association for the Study of Higher Education, Miami, FL.

Biner, P., Welsh, K., Barone, N., Summers, M., & Dean, R. (1997). The impact of remote-site group size on student satisfaction and relative performance in interactive telecourses. *American Journal of Distance Education, 11,* 23–33.

Bloom, B. (1968). Learning for mastery. *Evaluation Comment, 1*(2), 1–12.

Bohr, L., Pascarella, E., Nora, A., & Terenzini, P. (1995). Do Black students learn more at historically black or predominantly White colleges? *Journal of College Student Development, 36,* 75–85.

Bohr, L., Pascarella, E., Nora, A., Zusman, B., Jacobs, M., & Desler, M. (1994). Cognitive effects of 2-year and 4-year colleges: A preliminary study. *Community College Review, 22,* 4–11.

Bowen, H. (1977). *Investment in learning.* San Francisco: Jossey-Bass.

Cashin, W. (1999). *Student ratings of teaching: Their uses and misuses.* Unpublished manuscript, Kansas State University, Manhattan, KS.

Clark, R. (1994). Media will never influence learning. *Educational Technology, Research, and Development, 42,* 21–29.

Congos, D., Langsam, D., & Schoeps, N. (1997). Supplemental instruction: A successful approach to learning how to learn college introductory biology. *Journal of Teaching and Learning, 2*(1), 2–17.

d'Apollonia, S., & Abrami, P. (1997). Navigating student ratings of instruction. *American Psychologist, 52,* 1198–1208.

Doyle, S., Edison, M., & Pascarella, E. (1998, November). The *"seven principles of good practice in undergraduate education" as process indicators of cognitive development in college: A longitudinal study.* Paper presented at the annual meeting of the Association for the Study of Higher Education, Miami, FL.

Dunn, R., & Dunn, K. (1993). *Teaching secondary students through their individual learning styles.* Boston: Allyn and Bacon.

Dunn, R., Dunn, K., & Price, G. (1990). *Learning style inventory.* Lawrence, KS: Price Systems.

Dunn, R., Griggs, S., Olson, J., Beasley, M., & Gorman, B. (1995). A meta analytic validation of the Dunn and Dunn learning styles model. *Journal of Educational Research, 88,* 353–362.

Dunn, R., & Stevenson, J. (1997). Teaching diverse college students to study with a learning-styles prescription. *College Student Journal, 31,* 333–339.

Ehrenberg, R. G., Brewer, D. J., Gamoran, A., & Willms, J. D. (2001). Class size and student achievement. *Psychological Science in he Public Interest, 2*(May), 1–30.

Eyler, J., & Giles, D. (1997). The importance of program quality in service-learning. In A. Waterman (Ed.), *Service-learning: Applications from the research* (pp. 57–76). Hillsdale, NJ: Lawrence Erlbaum Associates.

Eyler, J., & Giles, D. (1999). *Where's the learning in service learning?* San Francisco: Jossey-Bass.

Eyler, J., Giles, D., Lynch, C., & Gray, C. (1997, April). *Service-learning and the development of reflective judgment.* Paper presented at the annual meeting of the American Educational Research Association, Chicago.

Eyler, J., Giles, D., Root, S., & Price, J. (1997, April). *Service-learning and the development of expert citizens.* Paper presented at the annual meeting of the American Educational Research Association, Chicago.

Facione, N. (1997). *Critical thinking assessment in nursing education programs: An aggregate data analysis.* Millbrae, CA: The California Academic Press.

Feldman, K. (1997). Identifying exemplary teachers and teaching: Evidence from student ratings. In R. Perry & J. Smart (Eds.), *Effective teaching in higher education: Research and practice* (pp. 368–395). Edison, NJ: Agathon Press.

Feldman, K., & Newcomb, T. (1969). *The impact of college on students*. San Francisco: Jossey-Bass.

Flowers, L., Pascarella, E., & Pierson, C. (1999). *Information technology use and cognitive outcomes in the first year of college*. Unpublished manuscript, University of Iowa, Iowa City.

Flowers, L., Osterlind, S., Pascarella, E., & Pierson, C. (2001). How much do students learn in college: Cross-sectional estimates using the College Basic Academic Subjects Examination. *Journal of Higher Education, 72*, 565–583.

Gardiner, L. (1994). *Redesigning higher education: Producing dramatic gains in student learning*. Washington, DC: Clearinghouse on Higher Education, The George Washington University.

Garside, C. (1996). Look who's talking: A comparison of lecture and group discussion teaching strategies in developing critical thinking skills. *Communication Education, 45*, 212–227.

Goldfinch, J. (1996). The effectiveness of school-type classes compared to the traditional lecture/tutorial method for teaching quantitative methods to business students. *Studies in Higher Education, 21*, 207–220.

Green, K. (1996). The coming ubiquity of information technology. *Change, 28*(2), 24–28.

Gurin, P. (1999). Expert report of Patricia Gurin. Retrieved 2000 from http://www.umich.edu/~newsinfo/admission/expert/gurinapb.html

Guskey, T. (1985). *Implementing mastery learning*. Belmont, CA: Wadsworth.

Guskey, T., & Pigott, T. (1988). Research on group-based mastery learning programs: A meta-analysis. *Journal of Educational Research, 81*, 197–216.

Hagedorn, L., Pascarella, E., Edison, M., Braxton, J., Nora, A., & Terenzini, P. (1999). Does institutional context influence the development of critical thinking? A research note. *Review of Higher Education, 22*, 247–263.

Hake, R. (1998). Interactive-engagement vs. traditional methods: A six-thousand-student survey of mechanics test data for introductory physics courses. *American Journal of Physics, 66*, 64–74.

Hall, D., & McCurdy, D. (1990). A comparative study of a BSCS-style and a traditional laboratory approach on student achievement at two private liberal arts colleges. *Journal of Research in Science Teaching, 27*, 628–636.

Heath, D. (1968). *Growing up in college*. San Francisco: Jossey-Bass.

Hines, C., Cruickshank, D., & Kennedy, J. (1985). Teacher clarity and its relationship to student achievement and satisfaction. *American Educational Research Journal, 22*, 87–99.

Hofer, B. (1994, August). *Epistemological beliefs and first-year college students: Motivation and cognition in different instructional contexts*. Paper presented at the annual meeting of the American Psychological Association, Los Angeles.

Hofer, B. (1998–99). Instructional context in the college mathematics classroom: Epistemological beliefs and student motivation. *Journal of Staff, Program, & Organization Development, 16*, 73–82.

Huang, S., & Aloi, J. (1991). The impact of using interactive video in teaching general biology. *American Biology Teacher, 53*, 281–284.

Ikeda, E. (2000, April). *How reflection enhances learning in service-learning courses*. Paper presented at the annual meeting of the American Educational Research Association, New Orleans.

Inman, P., & Pascarella, E. (1998). The impact of college residence on the development of critical thinking skills in college freshmen. *Journal of College Student Development, 39,* 557–568.

Johnson, D., & Johnson, R. (1993a). *Cooperation among adults: Impact on individual learning versus team productivity.* Unpublished manuscript, University of Minnesota, Minneapolis.

Johnson, D., & Johnson, R. (1993b). Creative and critical thinking through academic controversy. *American Behavioral Scientist, 37,* 40–53.

Johnson, D., Johnson, R., & Smith, K. (1998). *Active learning: Cooperation in the college classroom* (2nd ed.). Edina, MN: Interaction Book Company.

Keil, J., & Partell, P. (1998, May). *The effect of class size on student performance and retention at Binghampton University.* Paper presented at the annual meeting of the Association for Institutional Research, Minneapolis, MN.

Kennedy, P., & Siegfried, J. (1997). Class size and achievement in introductory economics: Evidence from the TUCE III data. *Economics of Education Review, 16,* 385–394.

Kenny, P. (1989, April). *Effects of supplemental instruction on student performance in a college level mathematics course.* Paper presented at the annual meeting of the American Educational Research Association, San Francisco.

Kim, J.-B., Cohen, A., Booske, J., & Derry, S. (1998, April). *Application of cooperative learning in an introductory engineering course.* Paper presented at the annual meeting of the American Educational Research Association.

Kitchener, K., Wood, P., & Jensen, L. (1999, August). *Curricular, co-curricular, and institutional influence on real-world problem-solving.* Paper presented at the annual meeting of the American Psychological Association, Boston.

Kitchener, K., Wood, P., & Jensen, L. (2000, August). *Promoting epistemic cognition and complex judgment in college students.* Paper presented at the annual meeting of the American Psychological Association, Washington, DC.

Knox, W., Lindsay, P., & Kolb, M. (1992). Higher education, college characteristics, and student experiences: Long-term effects on educational satisfactions and perceptions. *Journal of Higher Education, 63,* 303–328.

Kochenour, E., Jolley, D., Kaup, J., Patrick, D., Roach, K., & Wenzler, L. (1997). Supplemental instruction: An effective component of student affairs programming. *Journal of College Student Development, 38,* 577–586.

Kozma, R. (1994). Will media influence learning? Reframing the debate. *Educational Technology Research and Development, 42,* 1–19.

Kuh, G., & Vesper, N. (1999, April). *Do computers enhance or detract from student learning?* Paper presented at the annual meeting of the American Educational Research Association, Montreal, Canada.

Kulik, C., & Kulik, J. (1991). Effectiveness of computer-based instruction: An updated analysis. *Computers in Human Behavior, 7,* 75–94.

Kulik, C., Kulik, J., & Bangert-Drowns, R. (1990). Effectiveness of mastery learning programs: A meta-analysis. *Review of Educational Research, 60,* 265–299.

Lang, M. (1996). *Effects of class participation on student achievement and motivation.* Unpublished honors thesis, University of Western Ontario, London, Canada.

Leppel, K. (1998). The use of class-specific group exercises in undergraduate statistics, or

"How many body piercings do you have?" *Journal on Excellence in College Teaching, 9,* 3–11.

Liao, Y.-K., & Bright, G. (1991). Effects of computer-assisted instruction and computer programming on cognitive outcomes: A meta-analysis. *Journal of Educational Computing Research, 7,* 251–268.

Lopus, J., & Maxwell, N. (1995). A cost effectiveness analysis of large and small classes in the university. *Educational Evaluation and Policy Analysis, 17,* 167–178.

Lord, T. (1997). A comparison between traditional and constructivist teaching in college biology. *Innovative Higher Education, 21,* 197–216.

Marcus, G., Howard, J., & King, D. (1993). Integrating community service and classroom instruction enhances learning: Results from an experiment. *Educational Evaluation and Policy Analysis, 15,* 410–419.

Marra, R., Palmer, B., & Litzinger, T. (2000). The effects of a first-year engineering design course on student intellectual development as measured by the Perry scheme. *Journal of Engineering Education, 89,* 39–45.

Marsh, H., & Dunkin, M. (1997). Students' evaluations of university teaching: A multidimensional perspective. In R. Perry & J. Smart (Eds.), *Effective teaching in higher education: Research and practice* (pp. 241–320). New York: Agathon.

McCarthy, J., & Anderson, L. (2000). Active learning techniques versus traditional teaching styles: Two experiments from history and political science. *Innovative Higher Education, 24,* 279–294.

McComb, M. (1994). Benefits of computer-mediated communication in college courses. *Communication Education, 43,* 159–170.

Millis, B., & Cottell, P. (1998). *Cooperative learning for higher education faculty.* Phoenix, AZ: Oryx Press.

Murray, H., & Lang, M. (1997). Does classroom participation improve student learning? *Teaching and Learning in Higher Education, 20,* 7–9.

Opp, R. (1991). *The impact of college on NTE performance.* Unpublished doctoral dissertation, University of California, Los Angeles.

Osterlind, S. (1997). *Collegians' achievement in general education: A national look.* Washington, DC: George Washington University.

Pace, C. (1997, November). *Connecting institutional types to student outcomes.* Paper presented at the annual meeting of the Association for the Study of Higher Education, Albuquerque, NM.

Palinscar, A., Stevens, D., & Gavelek, J. (1989). Collaborating with teachers in the interest of student collaboration. *International Journal of Educational Research, 13,* 41–53.

Pascarella, E. (1989). The development of critical thinking: Does college make a difference. *Journal of College Student Development, 30,* 19–26.

Pascarella, E., Bohr, L., Nora, A., Desler, M., & Zusman, B. (1994). Impacts of on-campus and off-campus work on first year cognitive outcomes. *Journal of College Student Development, 35,* 364–370.

Pascarella, E., Bohr, L., Nora, A., & Terenzini, P. (1995a). Cognitive effects of 2-year and 4-year colleges: New evidence. *Educational Evaluation and Policy Analysis, 17,* 83–96.

Pascarella, E., Bohr, L., Nora, A., & Terenzini, P. (1995b). Intercollegiate athletic participation and freshman-year cognitive outcomes. *Journal of Higher Education, 66,* 369–387.

Pascarella, E., Bohr, L., Nora, A., & Terenzini, P. (1996). Is differential exposure to college linked to the development of critical thinking? *Research in Higher Education, 37,* 159–174.

Pascarella, E., Edison, M., Nora, A., Hagedorn, L., & Braxton, J. (1996). Effects of teacher organization/preparation and teacher skill/clarity on general cognitive skills in college. *Journal of College Student Development, 37*, 7–19.

Pascarella, E., Edison, M., Nora, A., Hagedorn, L., & Terenzini, P. (1998). Does work inhibit cognitive development during college? *Education Evaluation and Policy Analysis, 20*, 75–93.

Pascarella, E., Edison, M., Whitt, E., Nora, A., Hagedorn, L., & Terenzini, P. (1996). Cognitive effects of Greek affiliation during the first year of college. *NASPA Journal, 33*, 242–259.

Pascarella, E., Palmer, B., Moye, M., & Pierson, C. (2001). Do diversity experiences influence the development of critical thinking? *Journal of College Student Development, 42*, 257–271.

Pascarella, E., & Terenzini, P. (1991). *How college affects students: Findings and insights from twenty years of research.* San Francisco: Jossey-Bass.

Peled, O., & Kim, A. (1996). Evaluation of supplemental instruction at the college level. *The Learning Assistance Review, 1*(2), 23–31.

Perry, R. (1991). Perceived control in college students: Implications for instruction in higher education. In J. Smart (Ed.), *Higher education: Handbook of theory and research* (Vol. 7, pp. 1–56). New York: Agathon Press.

Posner, H., & Markstein, J. (1994). Cooperative learning in introductory cell and molecular biology. *Journal of College Science Teaching, 23*, 231–233.

Potthast, M. (1999). Outcomes of using small-group cooperative learning experiences in introductory statistics courses. *College Student Journal, 33*, 34–42.

Qin, Z., Johnson, D., & Johnson, R. (1995). Cooperative versus competitive efforts and problem solving. *Review of Educational Research, 65*, 129–143.

Raimondo, H., Esposito, L., & Gershenberg, I. (1990). Introductory class size and student performance in intermediate theory courses. *Journal of Economic Education, 21*, 369–381.

Ramirez, G. (1997). Supplemental instruction: The long-term impact. *Journal of Developmental Education, 21*, 2–4, 6, 8, 10, 28.

Reynolds, K., & Nunn, C. (1997, November). *Engaging classrooms: Student participation and the instructional factors that shape it.* Paper presented at the annual meeting of the Association for the Study of Higher Education, Albuquerque, NM.

Reiser, R. (1994). Clark's invitation to the dance: An instructional designer's response. *Educational Technology, Research, and Development, 42*, 45–48.

Scheck, C., Kinicki, A., & Webster, J. (1994). The effect of class size on student performance: Development and assessment of a process model. *Journal of Education for Business, 70*, 104–111.

Schonwetter, D., Menec, V., & Perry, R. (1995, April). *An empirical comparison of two effective college teaching behaviors: Expressiveness and organization.* Paper presented at the annual meeting of the American Educational Research Association, San Francisco.

Schonwetter, D., Perry, R., & Struthers, C. (1994). Students' perceptions of control and success in the college classroom: Affects and achievement in different instructional conditions. *Journal of Experimental Education, 61*, 227–246.

Schumow, L. (1999, April). *Problem-based learning in undergraduate educational psychology: Contributor to student learning and motivation?* Paper presented at the annual meeting of the American Educational Research Association, Montreal, Canada.

Smart, J. (1997). Academic subenvironments and differential patterns of self-perceived growth during college: A test of Holland's theory. *Journal of College Student Development, 38,* 68–77.

Smart, J., & Feldman, K. (1998). "Accentuation effects" of dissimilar departments: An application and explanation of Holland's theory. *Research in Higher Education, 39,* 385–418.

Smith, B., & MacGregor, J. (1992). What is collaborative learning? In A. Goodsell, M. Maher, V. Tinto, B. Smith, & J. MacGregor (Eds.), *Collaborative learning: A sourcebook for higher education* (pp. 9–22). University Park, PA: National Center on Postsecondary Teaching, Learning, and Assessment.

Smith, D. (1977). College classroom interactions and critical thinking. *Journal of Educational Psychology, 69,* 180–190.

Sokolove, P., & Marbach-Ad, G. (2000, April). *Out-of-class group study improves student performance on exams: Comparison of outcomes in active learning and traditional college biology classes.* Paper presented at the annual meeting of the American Educational Research Association, New Orleans.

Son, B., & Van Sickle, R. (1993, April). *Problem-solving instruction and students' acquisition, retention and structuring of economics knowledge.* Paper presented at the annual meeting of the American Educational Research Association, Atlanta, GA.

Strage, A. (2000, April). *Service-learning as a tool for enhancing student outcomes in a college-level lecture course.* Paper presented at the annual meeting of the American Educational Research Association, New Orleans.

Strauss, L., & Volkwein, J. (2001, May). *Comparing student performance and growth in two and four year institutions.* Paper presented at the annual forum of the Association for Institutional Research, Long Beach, CA.

Taraban, R., & Rynearson, K. (1998). Computer-based comprehension research in a content area. *Journal of Development Education, 21*(Spring), 10 ff.

Terenzini, P., Springer, L., Yaeger, P., Pascarella, E., & Nora, A. (1994, November). *The multiple influences on students' critical thinking skills.* Paper presented at the annual meeting of the Association for the Study of Higher Education, Orlando, FL.

Terenzini, P., Springer, L., Yaeger, P., Pascarella, E., & Nora, A. (1996). First-generation college students: Characteristics, experiences, and cognitive development. *Research in Higher Education, 37,* 1–22.

Thomas, P., & Higbee, J. (1996). Enhancing mathematics achievement through collaborative problem solving. *The Learning Assistance Review, 1*(1), 38–46.

Thompson, P. (1991). The effect of section size on student performance in a statistics course. *College Student Journal, 25,* 388–395.

Tjaden, B., & Martin, C. (1995). Learning effects of CAI on college students. *Computers and Education, 24,* 271–277.

Toutkoushian, R., & Smart, J. (2001). Do institutional characteristics affect student gains from college? *Review of Higher Education, 25,* 39–61.

Upcraft, L., Gardner, J., & Associates (1989). *The freshman year experience.* San Francisco: Jossey-Bass.

Visor, J., Johnson, J., & Cole, L. (1992). Supplemental instruction and self-esteem. *Supplemental Instruction News* (Fall), 1, 7.

Warren, B. (1997–1998). Supporting large classes with supplemental instruction (SI). *Journal of Staff, Program, & Organizational Development, 15,* 47–54.

Weimer, M., & Lenze, L. (1997). Instructional interventions: Review of the literature on efforts to improve instruction. In R. Perry & J. Smart (Eds.), *Effective teaching in higher education: Research and practice* (pp. 154–168). New York: Agathon Press.

Whitmire, E., & Lawrence, J. (1996, November). *Undergraduate students' development of critical thinking skills: An institutional and disciplinary analysis and comparison with academic library use and other measures.* Paper presented at the annual meeting of the Association for the Study of Higher Education, Memphis, TN.

Whitt, E., Edison, M., Pascarella, E., Nora, A., & Terenzini, P. (1999). Interaction with peers and objective and self-reported cognitive outcomes across three years of college. *Journal of College Student Development, 40,* 61–78.

Whitt, E., Pascarella, E., Pierson, C., Elkins, B., & Marth, B. (in press). *Sex and gender in college: Evidence of differences in experiences and outcomes.* Nashville, TN: Vanderbilt University Press.

Williamson, V., & Abraham, M. (1995). The effects of computer animation on the particular mental models of college chemistry students. *Journal of Research in Science Teaching, 32,* 521–534.

Wittig, G., & Thomerson, J. (1996, October). *Supplemental instruction improves student retention and performance in biology.* Paper presented at the 89th meeting of the Illinois State Academy of Science, Bloomington, IL.

Wood, A., & Murray, H. (1999, April). *Effects of teacher enthusiasm on student attention, motivation, and memory encoding.* Paper presented at the annual meeting of the American Educational Research Association, Montreal, Canada.

Zietz, J., & Cochran, H. (1997). Containing cost without sacrificing achievement: Some evidence from college-level economics classes. *Journal of Education Finance, 23,* 177–192.

6

Assessing Programs and Other Student Experiences Designed to Enrich the First-Year Experience

JOHN H. SCHUH

Iowa State University

To claim that higher education is experiencing a variety of stresses is to understate the obvious. Many institutions are beset by chronic problems that are manifested by concerns about college price escalation (The National Commission on the Cost of Higher Education, 1998), decreasing affordability for most American families (The National Center for Public Policy and Higher Education, 2002), changes in public policy relative to college choice (Davis, 2003; The Institute for Higher Education Policy, 2002), and more limited access to institutions of higher education for students from modest economic backgrounds (Terenzini, Cabrera, & Bernal, 2001; Wolanin, 2003). In addition to these financial challenges, others have raised concerns about poor graduation rates (Wingspread Group, 1993) and what students have learned (Hamrick, Evans, & Schuh, 2002).

As senior leaders, policy makers, and others struggle with these challenges, institutions of higher education have begun to realize that they must provide data that clearly and convincingly demonstrate that they are acting as good stewards of the public's trust. One of the ways that institutions can demonstrate that they are serving as good stewards of the public trust is to conduct regular, rigorous assessment studies. No aspect of higher education is immune from having to provide evidence that it is accomplishing their stated objectives. In fact, accreditation bodies increasingly are asking institutions as part of their self-studies to include data that demonstrate that they are accomplishing their stated objectives (see, for example, WASC 2001 Handbook of Accreditation).

This chapter is designed to provide an overview of how to assess programs, services, and experiences of first-year students. First, I start with a very brief discussion of how theory can be used to inform assessment projects. Then I provide a framework for assessment, including providing specific reasons for conducting assessment, questions that can be used to guide assessment projects, a discussion of various kinds of assessment that are appropriate for first-year student programs, services, and experiences, and a few thoughts on how to get started. This chapter concludes with two case studies that are examples of assessing programs at fictitious institutions of higher education.

Assessment is a complex subject, and any number of books has been written in the past decade that address this topic in detail. Consequently, for the person who has undertaken numerous assessment projects, the chapter may appear to lack details, and in many respects that is correct. However, a number of resources are identified as references in the chapter, and they can provide additional depth if such is desired by the reader. I also need to point out that many of the ideas in this chapter are products of the discussions and work that I have done on assessment with Lee Upcraft (e.g., Schuh & Upcraft, 2001; Upcraft & Schuh, 1996). We decided long ago that our thinking on assessment was so intertwined that it is impossible to separate Lee's ideas from mine and vice versa. Consequently, we have given each other permission to write about assessment freely using each other's ideas without attribution.

USING THEORY TO GUIDE ASSESSMENT

Theories are available to help explain how students grow and develop (e.g., Chickering & Reisser, 1993; Perry, 1968). Similarly, theories have been developed that help in understanding why it is that some students persist in their college experiences and ultimately graduate while others are less successful and drop out. Perhaps the most useful of these theories is one developed by Tinto (1987), who asserted that students who are involved in an academic and social sense are more likely to persist than those who are not. Tinto (1998) also concluded that "to the degree that involvement matters, we also know that involvement matters most during the first year of college. Attrition is, for most institutions, most frequent during the first year of college" (p. 169).

Tinto's observations provide a useful framework for the development and assessment of first-year programs. If programs are developed to facilitate or expedite the kinds of integration to which he refers, then the assessment of these programs should be undertaken to measure the extent to which integration occurs. Orientation programs often are developed to help first-year students succeed academically and to facilitate the adjustment of these students to college (Perigo & Upcraft, 1989). In this context, then, assessment projects should be undertaken to measure the degrees to which these actually happen. Does the orientation program facilitate academic success? Does it help students with their adjustment to college? These questions, which flow directly from Tinto's theory, can be used to frame specific assessment projects. Other pertinent questions include the following: Do students feel more confident about their ability to handle the academic challenges of college after completing the orientation program? Does an extended orientation program help students with time management and study skills? Do students who participate in a learning community feel like they have a social group with which to do other things in addition to attending class?

Programs that are developed without a theoretical basis run the risk of simply chasing the latest educational fad. Using theory to inform program development and the assessment of it will help insure that the desired outcomes from the first-year experience actually will occur. Once the theory is in place for assessment, the next step is to develop a framework for assessment, the topic of the next section of this chapter.

A FRAMEWORK FOR ASSESSMENT

This section of this chapter provides a framework for assessment activities, looking at such issues as the reasons for assessment, questions that guide the assessment process, types of assessment, and how to get assessment projects started. Because this is a substantial amount of material to cover, the reader should note that only a brief discussion of each of these topics is provided. For a more lengthy discussion of these topics, the reader is referred to Upcraft and Schuh (1996), Rossi, Freeman, and Lipsey (1999), Palomba and Banta (1999), and Schuh and Upcraft (2001).

Assessment Defined

A variety of definitions of assessment have been developed over the years. One that seems to fit a variety of situations was developed by Marchese (cited by Palomba & Banta, 1999). It is as follows:

> Assessment is the systematic collection, review and use of information about educational programs undertaken for the purpose of improving student learning and development. (p. 4)

Upcraft and Schuh (1996) emphasize that assessment is undertaken to determine unit effectiveness, and they stress that assessment data are then used to make improvements in the delivery of programs and the experiences of students. To simply conduct assessment projects for their own sake is to miss the point. Assessment is part of a process of improvement, and in the case of first-year students, learning opportunities are designed to assist in the crucial transition that students make from their high school years to college. Determining how the transition process can be improved is a crucial reason for conducting assessments. Assessment projects typically employ specific research methods, but should not be confused with conducting research. Research projects typically are undertaken to test theories that can be applied widely. Assessment projects are more focused, and their findings usually are not applied beyond the site where they are conducted (Upcraft & Schuh, 2002).

Reasons for Assessment

Typically, three reasons are offered for why assessment activities should be undertaken. These include measuring effectiveness, accountability, and improvement. In measuring effectiveness, determining the extent to which programs accomplish their objectives is a key purpose. For example, do orientation programs for first-year students achieve their stated goals of providing information to students while at the same time introducing them to their classmates? Do orientation programs influence first-year student persistence rates positively? Do extended orientation programs, such as first-year student tutorials, meet their goals? These and other questions can be used to determine the effectiveness of first-year student programs.

Accountability is the second reason to engage in assessment projects. If resources are shifted from one program to another, are the goals of the new programs achieved through measurable results? For example, if funds are devoted to an extended orientation program such as a first-year student tutorial, do the persistence rates of the participants in the tutorials exceed those of students who do not participate? If an extended program for parents is put in place, can the time the parents take away from their employment be justified? In times of increasing accountability for higher education, assessment projects can help provide evidence that the accountability dimension of initiatives is satisfied.

The third reason for conducting assessment projects is to provide data that can be used to improve programs and services. A qualitative assessment, for example, of the advising program can be used to generate ideas for refining the approach an institution takes to advising for first-year students. Such information can be collected through the use of focus groups, for example, to learn how useful students found their academic advising process in academic program planning for their first year.

Guiding Questions for Assessment

In developing various approaches for conducting assessment project, Lee Upcraft and I assembled a list of questions that we believe are quite useful to those who are planning assessment. These questions are listed hereafter, with just a bit of explanation. For additional details, we refer the reader to Upcraft and Schuh (1996).

1. What is the problem? More time should be taken in developing an answer to this question than the others. It provides the framework for the assessment project. Let's say that an extended orientation program, consisting of a series of meetings for first-year students after the semester has begun has just been implemented. The meetings are voluntary and are conducted by academic advisers. In this case we may determine that the reason to conduct the assessment is that we want to find out if the assessment project has achieved its stated objective, which is to improve the persistence rate of first-year students from the fall to the spring term.

2. What is the specific purpose of the assessment? The purpose of the assessment results directly from the larger problem. In the case of our example, the purpose is to determine if the persistence rate of first-year

students has been affected by participating in the extended orientation program.

3. What data are needed? Data form the heart of the assessment project and provide the basis upon which decisions are made. For our example we need information about persistence rates of students who participated in the extended orientation program, and those with whom they will be compared.

4. What is the best assessment method? While we recommend that multiple methods be used in assessment projects (meaning both quantitative and qualitative methodological approaches), such will not always be possible. It is important to note that the assessment method is chosen after the project's purposes have been determined, rather than selecting one method over another because of familiarity or comfort with a specific research method. In this case a quantitative approach makes the most sense.

5. Whom should we study? While this question can be quite problematic in some cases, such as evaluating a campus-wide food service, in the case of this program, the students we will study are those who participated in the program and perhaps a matched sample of non-participants.

6. How should the data be collected? Again, this can be a complex question. Do we develop a questionnaire, mail it to potential participants, use a telephone or web-based data collection approach, or something else? In the case of our project, the data should be available in the institution's records, since we will be looking at the persistence rate of students who were enrolled in the fall term and whether they returned in the spring.

7. What instrument should be used? This question suggests that a quantitative approach has been chosen and an instrument needs to be selected from a commercial publisher of instruments or one needs to be developed specifically for the assessment. A variety of questions need to be considered in the choice of an instrument. If a commercial instrument is selected, are the costs acceptable? Does the instrument assess constructs of interest? Can additional locally developed questions be added to the core instrument? If a locally developed instrument is used, are its psychometric properties acceptable? Is a person available locally to develop the instrument? Can a pilot test be arranged? These questions and others (see Upcraft & Schuh, 1996, for additional questions) need to be considered carefully before selecting an instrument. In a qualitative assessment, if focus groups were to be conducted, then an interview protocol would need to be prepared. In the case of the example, an instrument is not needed since our data are available, presumably, through the Registrar's Office. In other cases, we

might need to take time to determine the most appropriate instrument for our project and perhaps develop our own.

8. Who should collect the data? If a unit collects data about its own programs, critics might claim that there is a conflict of interest, and they may be correct. To avoid this problem, blending people from the unit with other members of the campus community can be done. Practically speaking, the "outsiders" might conduct some telephone interviews or focus groups. In the case of our example, the data are provided by the Registrar's Office, so there is no potential conflict-of-interest problem.

9. How should the data be analyzed? This question suggests selecting the most appropriate statistical technique or employing an approach to analyze qualitative data, such as the constant comparative method (Glaser & Strauss, 1967). In our example we can use a matched sample t-test that is designed to compare the persistence rate of the participants with a matched sample of non-participants. The students are matched on the basis of their high school rank, their SAT score, whether or not they are first-generation college students, and the extent to which they are eligible for Pell grants and Stafford loans, a proxy for SES.

10. How should the results be reported? Sometimes there is a temptation to prepare a lengthy report of the results, with a focus on the inquiry methods that were used. We urge that the resulting reports be short, focus on the problem, the results, and the recommendations for practice (Schuh & Upcraft, 2001). Reports need to be targeted at their audience and may be of varying length, from quite short for senior institutional officers to a bit more lengthy for program planners. In the case of this assessment, senior officers can receive a report of not more than two pages including graphics that illustrate the results. Those who have delivered the program should receive more detail, also with graphics and illustrations. Regardless of the length of the report, we urge that recommendations for improving the program be included as appropriate.

11. How should the data be used in the evaluation process? Assessment, from our point of view, leads to evaluation. Evaluation in this case means that programs, initiatives, or other interventions are adjusted or modified so that they can be even more potent. If our program worked, what can we do to increase its effect? If it did not have the desired result, should a major overhaul be conducted or should the program be discontinued? These questions and others are part of the evaluation process. It is the final step in conducting an assessment, until the cycle is repeated if the program is offered in the future.

Types of Assessment

In our work on assessment, Lee Upcraft and I identified a number of types of assessments that potentially are conducted in student affairs. For the purpose of this chapter each is identified with a short explanation. More information is available in Upcraft and Schuh (1996) or Schuh and Upcraft (2001).

Keeping Track of Participants.   This is the most basic form of assessment and it has to do with identifying who uses the service or participates in activities. For first-year experiences, the universe of participants consists of all first-year students and can be defined easily by the Registrar's Office. First-year experience program participants would include, for example, students participating in orientation programs, their parents and other family members, students who enroll in seminars for first-year students, and so on.

Identifying the Needs of First-Year Students.   After understanding who participates in first-year student programs, the next step is to measure their needs. Various commercial needs-assessment questionnaires are available (for example, ACT publishes such an instrument). Focus groups also can be conducted to learn more about student needs. Student development theory (for example, Chickering & Reisser, 1993) also can be used to shape programs for first-year students. Programs and other experiences based on a needs assessment, then, can be developed to meet the needs of entering students.

Measuring User Satisfaction.   After needs are measured and programs and other experiences are developed, the next step is to measure satisfaction with them. Were expectations met? If not, why not? What can be done to improve them? These questions and others form the heart of a satisfaction assessment.

Assessing Outcomes.   Probably the most important, and perhaps the most difficult, form of assessment is outcomes assessment. In this form of assessment we are trying to determine the effect of the experience on the participants, often measured in terms of learning or student growth and development. Outcomes assessment usually requires sophisticated research skills, and we urge those conducting the assessment to develop partnerships with those on campus who possess such research skills if the assessors are not confident with outcomes assessment methodology.

Comparing With Peer Institutions. Most institutions have identified peers, are members of a system of campuses, participate in an athletic conference, or in some way have identified a set of institutions with which they compare themselves. In these situations, institutions identify benchmarks for comparison purposes. Examples of common benchmarks are persistence rates, graduation rates, and percentages of income from tuition and fees and so on. At times, it might make sense to use this form of assessment to compare the portfolio of first-year programs of one institution with those of its peer group, or the rate of first-year students who persist to their sophomore year might be compared. It is important to note, however, that even if institutions are similar, they may not be alike and as a consequence comparisons always have to be made in context.

Using Professional Standards. The Council for Advancement of Standards (CAS; see Miller, 1997) has developed standards for a wide number of programs and services for students. Included among these are standards for student orientation programs, one of the key programs for first-year students. The CAS standards are particularly useful for doing self-studies or determining if programs meet the minimum standards published by CAS.

Assessing for Accreditation. Increasingly, the regional accrediting associations are asking institutions, as part of their self-studies, to include evidence demonstrating that students are learning from their various experiences on campus. Those responsible for first-year student programs, then, will have to provide such evidence, as is the case for other units, academic and non-academic, on campus. The Middle States Commission on Higher Education has developed particularly useful document to assist in conducting such assessments; it is available on line at <www.msche.org>.

Getting Started

At times unit leaders find that one of the most challenging aspects of the assessment process is getting started. Staff are resistant to conducting assessment, supervisors may be reluctant to devote the resources to this process, and in the end, no one can be quite sure what story the results will tell. So the problem, then, is to how to get started.

One of the best concepts for getting started in dealing with difficult problems has been provided by Karl Weick. Weick (1984) suggests that instead of trying to solve large, complex problems with equally complex strategies, one should start simply, try to solve modest problems, and then work toward the more complex problems. He has characterized this process as "small wins" and it applies to the assessment of first-year programs very nicely.

Instead of trying to assess all of the first-year programs included in a campus's portfolio, a more appropriate approach would be to assess programs one at a time, starting with the least complex and moving to the most complicated. This might mean looking at a simple, one-day orientation program offered for students who are unable to attend a regular, two-day orientation program in the summer, and then moving on to more complex programs, perhaps culminating with assessing a semester-long seminar for first-year students.

Weick's view is that success begets success, has a way of disarming critics, and provides a basis for additional, more complex activities in the future. His approach makes particularly good sense in the context of assessment, which is an activity that can be frightening and at times intimidating. Starting with simple projects and building on success toward the more complex seems to be a very good approach, and it is recommended especially for those who are developing assessment projects for the first time.

CASE STUDIES

The next section of this chapter provides two case studies as examples of assessment projects. They are provided to illustrate how the ideas and principles introduced earlier in this chapter can be used to solve practical assessment problems faced by those responsible for programs for first-year students.

Midwest College Tutorials

Midwest College (MC) has been concerned about the persistence rates of first-year students to the sophomore year for the past three years. During this time period, resources have become increasingly tight, and it has become clear to the senior leaders of the college that recruiting transfer students to "replace" dropouts after the first year is an expensive proposition. Moreover, the obligation of the college to assist students in the transition process from high school to college strikes many at the college, including a number of faculty, as a moral responsibility.

MC is a private college located in Midwest City, a city of 100,000 in the middle of the state. The college boasts an enrollment of 4,000, all undergraduates. The range of the academic background of MC students is quite broad. Many excellent students attend MC, but there are some marginal students who are admitted each year under a number of special programs. These appear to be the students most at risk, if retention data are accurate. A maximum of 100 new students are admitted under special programs each year with a stipulation that they never comprise more than 10% of the entering class, but about half of them never make it to the sophomore year.

To deal with this problem, a faculty committee has proposed to the senior academic officer that the college develop special tutorial programs for the students at risk called "first-year tutorials." At-risk students are defined as those students with an ACT score of 22 or lower, or who ranked in the third quartile of their high school graduating class. For next fall's entering class of first-year students, 90 students were identified by these criteria. The tutorial programs would involve sessions directed by faculty who teach the English courses and mathematics courses that these students will take as part of their distribution requirements in both the fall and the spring semester. Senior students will serve as tutors for these special sessions, which would be offered once per week. While students would not be required to participate in these sessions, they would be encouraged to do so. If they agreed to participate, they would have to attend all the sessions.

The senior academic officer agreed to all of this, including providing stipends for the senior tutors and additional compensation for the faculty. The cost of the program was such that the senior academic officer insisted on an assessment of its impact on students. She asserted that if the college was serious about trying to improve retention, it ought to have measures in place that would evaluate the effect of the program. The faculty agreed with that approach and brought in a faculty member from the psychology department to develop an assessment plan.

The Assessment Plan. The assessment plan that was developed used the following questions as a guide:

- *What is the problem?* The problem that this project is trying to address has to do with trying to determine if an intervention related to retention works.
- *What is the purpose of the assessment?* The purpose of the assessment is to determine if the "first-year tutorials" have the desired effect of improving the retention rate of first-year students.

- *What data are needed?* The grade point averages for all first-year students will be needed at the end of the first year, and after their sophomore year begins, data will be needed to determine which students returned for their sophomore year.
- *What is the best assessment method?* The best assessment method is quantitative for this study.
- *Who should be studied?* All first-year students who were admitted under special programs. These were students who had an ACT score of 22 or lower and/or who were in the third quartile of the high school graduating class. Whether they participated in the special tutorials or not, these students would be of interest.
- *What instruments should be used?* In this study a special instrument is not needed. All of the data will be in institutional databases that can be accessed through the Office of Institutional Research.
- *How should the data be collected?* Data collection is not a problem because they are located in the institutional database.
- *How should the data be recorded?* Again, recording data is not a problem since the data are in the institutional database.
- *How should the data be analyzed?* Data will be analyzed by conducting a comparative study of those students who participated in the special tutorial program with those who did not. Two comparisons will be drawn: one will be the grade point averages that the students earned in these courses and the other will be whether they returned for the sophomore year. For the grade point averages, a one-way analysis of variance will be conducted and for the persistence data, chi-squares will be calculated.
- *How should the data be reported?* A short report should be produced for the senior academic officer and others interested in this study.
- *How should the data be used in the evaluation process?* The data will be central in the evaluation process. If there is a significant difference in the grade point averages and persistence information, then it is likely that the programs should be continued. If the results are less clear, it is possible that additional data will have to be collected.

Learning Community Alpha

The vice president for student affairs (VPSA) and the vice president for academic affairs (VPAA) at Mideast University (ME) jointly attended a conference on the first-year experience and learned that many colleges and universities had developed learning communities with great results. Those who presented papers at the conference reported that the grade point averages of learning community participants had been influenced positively by their participation and that those who participated in such experiences were more likely to return for their sophomore year than those who had not.

Mideast University is a very traditional public institution that has high academic standards and is slow to change. It enrolls 8,000 students, 7,000 of whom are undergraduates. Students come from all over the country to attend ME and they are prepared very well in an academic sense for their college-level work. They are not as strong in terms of their interpersonal skills, and although they work well with faculty, they work less well with each other.

Faculty, in particular, have been used to doing things their way and were disinterested in change. The VPAA had discussed the possibility of implementing learning communities at ME with members of the steering committee of the Faculty Council with little success. These leaders were dubious of starting this kind of program and certainly did not want precious resources drained from academic programs to support a program that had unclear objectives and effects on students. On the other hand, they were quite oriented toward students and generally supported initiatives that had clear benefits for students.

The VPSA did not have much better luck in talking about learning communities with her senior staff. The development of learning communities looked like more work for them and, as the dean of students pointed out, the Division of Student Affairs had lost three positions in the past two years and to ask staff to take on new projects just did not make sense. However, the literature they read was full of good reports about the effects of learning communities on students, and several senior staff grudgingly admitted that such initiatives had promise.

Finally, the VPAA and VPSA were able to convince their constituent groups that a pilot project (Project Alpha) was worth considering. Agreement was reached to implement one learning community in the next academic year. This would be for history majors, one of the strongest programs in the University. The elements of the program were that students would live together in the same residence hall, that they would take an English course, a math course, and a history course together, and that a senior peer advisor would live on the same floor of the residence hall to which they were assigned. In all, 18 students were recruited for the program.

Everyone agreed that an evaluation of Learning Community Alpha was necessary to determine what effects, if any, the program had on students.

Since no one was quite sure what the effects of the learning community would be on students, a qualitative study was planned with the help of the sociology department.

The Assessment Plan. The assessment plan that was developed used the following questions as a guide:

- *What is the problem?* The problem to be addressed in this assessment was to determine the effects, if any, participating in a learning community had on students.
- *What is the purpose of the assessment?* The purpose of the assessment is to identify the effects of participating in a learning community on students.
- *What data are needed?* Data are needed that identify the effects of participating in Learning Community Alpha on students. Since no data are available upon which to build, descriptions of the effects will be quite powerful.
- *What is the best assessment method?* No one at ME is quite sure what the effects of participating in a learning community will be, so a qualitative study is proposed. This will generate foundational data upon which to make decisions about the efficacy of the program.
- *Whom should we study?* Those who are identified as participants in the study include the 18 students, their peer advisor, and the faculty who teach the three courses in which they are jointly enrolled.
- *How should the data be collected?* Focus groups and individual interviews are the likely ways that the data should be collected. The 18 students can be divided into three groups, and focus groups can be held for each of the three groups. The peer adviser can be interviewed separately, and the three faculty members could be interviewed as a group or individually, depending on their schedules.
- *What instruments should be used?* Interview protocols will need to be developed for the student groups, the interview with the peer advisor, and the interview(s) with faculty members. Since the study is interested in outcomes, such questions for the students as "What did you learn from participating in the Learning Community Alpha?" "How did participating in Learning Community Alpha affect your plans?" should be asked. The peer advisor could be asked questions along the lines of "How did the students appear to be affected by participating in Learning Community Alpha?" The faculty could be asked similar questions.

- *How should the data be collected?* Data should be a collected through focus groups and individual interviews. The students also could be observed in class and in their activities out of class.
- *How should the data be recorded?* The interviews should be tape recorded. Notes might be taken as well, in the interviews and focus groups. Field notes should be taken during the observation phase of the data collection.
- *How should the data be analyzed?* Those conducting the analysis should look for themes, patterns, and trends in the raw data. Ultimately these will form the basis for the report, but negative cases also should be identified and reported.
- *How should the data be reported?* The data should be shared with the faculty in the form of a report. The report is likely to be a bit longer than a typical assessment report since the data are in the form of words, and providing richness to the report will add to its value.
- *How should the data be used in the evaluation process?* The data should form the basis for determining whether or not to continue Learning Community Alpha, developing other learning communities, or canceling it. The outcomes of the program identified in the assessment project will form the basis for this discussion.

EXAMPLES OF ASSESSMENTS

Given the ever-increasing level of accountability expected on our college campuses of program planners, student services professionals, and others (Upcraft & Schuh, 1996), it should come as no surprise that examples of assessment projects are abundant in recently published literature. Several examples are available of projects or programs directed at first-year students. Among these are assessment of residential learning communities (Pike, 1999; Pike, Schroeder, & Berry, 1997); a social support discussion intervention program (Pratt et al., 2000); and a series of structured experiences for first-year students (Ting, Grant, & Plenert, 2000). These reports are strong examples of how assessments are conducted to provide evidence that sustains the value of the experiences for first-year students. Another excellent example of a program assessment was published by Hensen and Shelley (2003), although the study was not focused exclusively on first-year students.

CONCLUSION

In the contemporary environment of higher education, assessing the effect of programs, services, and experiences is a crucial activity. Determining the efficacy of programs designed for first-year students through assessment activities is no exception. Assessment data can be used for the purposes of accountability, improvement, and demonstration of effectiveness. This chapter has provided a brief overview of various approaches to assessment and has recommended that those contemplating assessment projects begin their work by developing simple, basic projects and then moving on to more complex studies. Finally, assessment data need to be used to increase the potency of programs designed for first-year students.

REFERENCES

Chickering, A. W., & Reisser, L. (1993). *Education and identity* (2nd ed.). San Francisco: Jossey-Bass.

Davis, J. S. (2003). *Unintended consequences of tuition discounting.* Indianapolis, IN: Lumina Foundation.

Glaser, B. G., & Strauss, A. L. (1967). *The discovery of grounded theory.* Chicago: Aldine.

Hamrick, F. A., Evans, N. J., & Schuh, J. H. (2002). *Foundations of student affairs practice: How philosophy, theory and research strengthen educational outcomes.* San Francisco: Jossey-Bass.

Hensen, K. A., & Shelley, M. C., II. (2003). The impact of a supplemental instruction: Results from a large, public, Midwestern university. *Journal of College Student Development, 44,* 250–259.

The Institute for Higher Education Policy. (2002). *The policy of choice: Expanding student options in higher education.* Washington, DC: Author.

Middle States Commission on Higher Education. (2002). *Student learning assessment: Options and resources.* Philadelphia, PA: Author. Retrieved December 30, 2002, from http://www/msche.org

Miller, T. K. (Ed.). (1997). *CAS. The book of professional standards.* Washington, DC: Council for the Advancement of Standards.

The National Center for Public Policy and Higher Education. (2002). *Losing ground: A national status report on the affordability of American higher education.* San Jose, CA: Author.

The National Commission on the Cost of Higher Education. (1998). *Straight talk about college costs and prices.* NP: Author.

Palomba, C. A., & Banta, T. W. (1999). *Assessment essentials: Planning, implementing and improving assessment in higher education.* San Francisco: Jossey-Bass.

Perigo, D. L., & Upcraft, M. L. (1989). Orientation programs. In M. L. Upcraft, J. N. Gardner, and Associates, *The freshman year experience* (pp. 82–94). San Francisco: Jossey-Bass.

Perry, W. G., Jr. (1968). *Forms of intellectual and ethical development in the college years: A scheme.* New York: Holt, Rinehart & Wonton.

Pike, G. R. (1999). The effects of residential learning communities and traditional residential living arrangements on education gains during the first year of college. *Journal of College Student Development, 40,* 269–284.

Pike, G. R., Schroeder, C. C., & Berry, T. R. (1997). Enhancing the educational impact of residence halls: The relationship between residential learning communities and first-year college experiences and persistence. *Journal of College Student Development, 38,* 609–621.

Pratt, M. W., Bowers, C., Terzian, B., Hunsberger, B., Mackey, K., Thomas, N., et al. (2000). Facilitating the transition to university: Evaluation of a social support discussion intervention program. *Journal of College Student Development, 41,* 427–441.

Rossi, P. H. Freeman. H. E., & Lipsey, M. W. (1999). *Evaluation: A systematic approach* (6th ed.). Thousand Oaks, CA: Sage.

Schuh, J. H., & Upcraft, M. L. (2001). *Assessment practice in student affairs: An applications manual.* San Francisco: Jossey-Bass.

Terenzini, P. T., Cabrera, A. F., & Bernal, E. M. (2001). *Swimming against the tide: The poor in American higher education.* New York: College Entrance Examination Board.

Ting, S-M., Grant, S., & Plenert, S. L. (2000). The Excellence-Commitment-and-Effective-Learning (ExCEL) Group: An integrated approach for first-year college students' success. *Journal of College Student Development, 41,* 355–362.

Tinto, V. (1987). *Leaving college: Rethinking the causes and cures of student attrition.* Chicago: University of Chicago Press.

Tinto, V. (1998). Colleges as communities: Taking research on student persistence seriously. *The Review of Higher Education, 21*(2), 167–177.

Upcraft, M. L., & Schuh, J. H. (1996). *Assessment in student affairs: A guide for practitioners.* San Francisco: Jossey-Bass.

Upcraft, M. L., & Schuh, J. H. (2002). Assessment vs. research: Why we should care about the difference. *About Campus, 7*(1), 16–20.

Western Association of Schools and Colleges. (2001). *Handbook of accreditation.* Alameda, CA: Author.

Weick, K. E. (1984). Small wins: Redefining the scale of social problems. *American Psychologist, 39*(1), 40–44.

Wingspread Group of Higher Education. (1993). *An American imperative: Higher expectations for higher education.* Racine, WI: The Johnson Foundation.

Wolanin, T. R. (Ed.). (2003). *Reauthorizing the higher education act.* Washington, DC: Institute for Higher Education Policy.

IV

Cutting-Edge Approaches
to Engendering
First-Year College Success

7

Going Online:
Promoting Student Success
Via Distance Learning

CHRISTOPHER R. POIRIER
ROBERT S. FELDMAN
University of Massachusetts, Amherst

Distance learning is beginning to play a significant role in the education of first-year college students. For some—particularly non-traditional students—it represents the sole means by which their college education proceeds. Other first-year students use distance learning as an adjunct to their more traditional, on-campus courses. In any case, it is clear that distance learning is playing an increasingly important part in the education of 21st-century first-year college students.

Despite the growing use of distance education, there is a relative paucity of careful research that demonstrates its efficacy and effectiveness. In this chapter, we examine distance learning, considering its advantages and disadvantages, and describing the variety of ways in which it is used. We focus on objective research on distance learning and speculate on how it can best be used to promote student success. We also discuss our own efforts in conducting a student success course using distance learning.

THE PREVALENCE
OF DISTANCE LEARNING

Although it is often thought of as a recent innovation, in fact distance learning has been an integral part of higher education for over a century. The earliest evidence of distance learning consisted of correspondence study. Beginning in the middle of the 19th century, several universities offered correspondence courses by allowing instructors and students to send printed documents back and forth. In the 1900s, different technologies including radio, telephone, television, pre-recorded video, and two-way interactive video conferencing were developed. Although some of these technologies are still used today, the adoption of computer technology is significantly changing the way instructors teach and students learn in the 21st century. The affordability of the personal computer, the greater accessibility to the Internet, and the interactive capabilities afforded by the computer have allowed institutions around the world to offer online distance learning courses. According to the National Center for Education Statistics (2002), in 1999–2000, 60% of distance learning students took their courses online.

Over the past decade, there has been a significant increase in the number of institutions offering online courses; therefore, the number and variety of online course offerings has skyrocketed. There are many reasons for the rapid increase. For one, more people have computers connected to the Internet. In the United States, 26% of homes had Internet access in 1998. In 2000, the percentage increased to 41.5 (U.S. Bureau of the Census, 2001). Results from the Pew Internet and American Life Project (2002) found that 85% of college students own their own computer, and 86% of college students have gone online.

A second reason for the increase is that online courses can serve both traditional and non-traditional students. For instance, people who live far from a college campus or work full-time now have the opportunity to take college courses via a personal computer. In 2002, approximately 78% of non-traditional adult students took a distance learning course (Parker, 2003).

Third, recent studies have shown that online courses are effective (Graham, 2001; Lawson, 2000; Poirier & Feldman, 2004; Waschull, 2001; Wegner, Holloway, & Garton, 1999). Studies conducted on courses across many different disciplines have reached the conclusion that online students can be at least as successful as traditional students. The studies have included instructors and students with diverse backgrounds and have controlled for a multitude of variables that may be involved in bringing about student success.

DIFFERENCES BETWEEN ONLINE AND TRADITIONAL COURSES

There are several distinct differences between online and traditional courses. For one, the physical environment is different: the virtual classroom replaces the traditional campus classroom. A personal computer equipped with a mouse, speakers, and a connection to the Internet replaces the traditional blackboard and chalk. Online courses are most often delivered over the Internet by a course delivery platform. A platform provides a course template that instructors modify to display course content. WebCT, eCollege, and Blackboard offer three of the most popular ones. For instance, thousands of institutions from around the world use the WebCT platform (WebCT, 2003). Most platforms are user friendly, and although there are some differences between platforms, the most common platforms offer similar tools.

There are three general clusters of tools: course content, communication, and assessment tools. Course content tools allow instructors to add course content by uploading text, audio, and video files. The course syllabus, lecture slides or notes, introductory greetings, learning objectives, and other supplementary materials may be added.

There are two broad types of communication tools: synchronous and asynchronous. Synchronous communication tools require all parties to be online at the same time. Video-conferencing, chat rooms, and whiteboards are examples of synchronous communication. On the other hand, asynchronous tools such as e-mail, threaded discussions, and message boards, allow people to be online at different times. These tools, arguably the most important tools for a successful online course, allow students and instructors to interact with each other at any time of the day or night.

Finally, assessment tools include quizzes, exams, and gradebooks. Instructors can design objective and subjective tests and have them graded automatically. Online gradebooks allow students to view their grades, and in some cases, to view feedback.

Another difference between traditional and online courses is how instructors spend their time. Foremost, instructors do not deliver a series of weekly lectures. However, they are responsible for posting assignments, moderating discussions, preparing feedback, and editing course content.

Although instructors of traditional courses share these same responsibilities, the online environment may be challenging for first-time instructors. Some reports estimate that instructors spend more hours per week teaching their online courses than their traditional courses (Bremner, 1998; Graham, 2001). Because overcoming the limited face-to-face contact is a serious challenge for instructors, they may spend more time interacting with their students. In addition, most online courses are writing intensive, so instructors spend more time grading students' assignments.

A third difference relates to the assessment of student learning. Assessing student performance in an online environment can be a major challenge. Students enrolled in traditional courses sit in a confined classroom and take proctored exams; students in many online courses sit at home and take unproctored exams. Because of this difference, many instructors decrease the significance of traditional testing. Instead, threaded discussions, chats, writing assignments, and group activities are used to assess learning. Therefore, online instructors generally create a greater number and variety of assignments (Dereshiwsky, 2001).

Advantages of Online Courses

There are several advantages of online course delivery. First, online courses are accessible to almost anyone with Internet access. Students from different states or countries can take the same course. Also, students who cannot reach a college campus for any reason can enroll in online courses. With a computer and Internet access, students can log in from their home or any other environment that is comfortable.

Another advantage is that online courses may be flexible and self-paced. Students are not required to attend lecture two or three times per week. Instead, students in many courses are allowed to set aside specific times to log-in and complete work. For instance, because many online students are employed, completing course work during the evening hours allows students with full-time jobs to take courses. Other students may prefer waking up early to complete work. For most online courses, students have more control over the course schedule.

A third advantage is that online courses may allow more interaction between students and instructors. Although face-to-face contact may be limited or nonexistent, which may be considered a disadvantage, e-mail, chat, and threaded discussions allow students and instructors to interact more often. Online students may interact with their instructors multiple times each week, which may lead to more discussions and active participation by all students. Furthermore, students with a fear of public speaking may be more likely to flourish in this environment. Taking away the public speaking aspect of the course may allow these students to share their ideas more easily. Nearly half of college students report that e-mail allows them to express ideas that they would not have expressed in front of a class (Pew Internet and American Life Project, 2002).

Another potential advantage is that online courses incorporate more writing assignments, which may improve students' writing skills. Typically, online courses are writing intensive because of the nature of the online assignments. Therefore, students spend more time writing, and they receive more feedback from their instructors. In addition, because many online discussions and assignments are asynchronous, the students have more time to plan and write ideas.

Finally, students enjoy using computers, surfing the Web, and chatting online. In addition, students use the Web because it provides easy access to information. Approximately 80% of college students have reported that the Internet has had a positive impact on their college academic career, and more than half of college students e-mail their instructors to receive and discuss grades or to report absences (Pew Internet and American Life Project, 2002). Most instructors incorporate websites and chatrooms into their online courses to make their courses more appealing. These assignments may increase enthusiasm for the material, make learning more interesting, and subsequently improve student learning.

Disadvantages of Online Courses

Although the advantages of online courses are significant, there are some disadvantages of the online delivery method. However, it should be noted that a well-trained instructor teaching a well-designed course can overcome most disadvantages.

One potential disadvantage is that online courses eliminate face-to-face contact between instructors and students. Many instructors and students report that they miss the social aspect of the traditional classroom, and some students have reported feeling socially isolated (Graham, 2001). Consequently, the attrition rate is higher for online courses. Rates at some institutions exceed 40% (Carr & Ledwith, 2000). However, with a high level of interactivity between students and instructors, and among students, feelings of social isolation and attrition rates may be minimized.

Related to this issue, many students have expressed that it is difficult to express emotions online and easy to misinterpret one's written communication (Dereshiwsky, Moan, & Gahungu, 2002). Without face-to-face contact, the visual cues are lost, which makes interpreting an e-mail or any other text message challenging. Students and instructors may become frustrated by repeated misinterpretations and communication breakdowns.

Another potential disadvantage of online courses is that they rely primarily on computer technology. If technology fails, even an exceptionally designed course will fail. When students experience computer problems, they may become frustrated and drop the course (Graham, 2001). Some of the common problems include slow processors, outdated software, and slow Internet connections. Also, course delivery platforms can crash, which is frustrating for both students and instructors. In some cases, students are not as computer savvy as they should be. For instance, poor typing skills and limited knowledge of how computers work may impede student success.

Fourth, because many online courses are self-paced, some students may struggle because self-paced courses demand significant time management skills, motivation, and self-responsibility. Students without these skills may procrastinate and struggle in the online learning environment. Not unlike traditional students, online students who procrastinate will struggle to succeed.

Finally, the assessment of student learning is more difficult. For instance, administering traditional exams may not be feasible. Many instructors do not have the resources available to set up a proctoring system for their online students. Instead, instructors use multiple types of assessments. One drawback is that using a variety of assessments may take more planning.

IS DISTANCE LEARNING EFFECTIVE?

Are distance learning students as successful as traditional students? Results from around the world suggest that the answer is affirmative (Institute for Higher Education Policy, 1999; Russell, 1999). Studies employing a variety of research methods, courses of study, course delivery modalities, and instructor and student profiles have shown that distance learning students perform at least as well as traditional students. Russell (1999) reviewed over 300 studies comparing distance learning and traditional courses and found that the majority of the studies found no difference in the effectiveness of the two methods of teaching.

A review of studies published in the 1990s reached a similar conclusion (Institute for Higher Education Policy, 1999). Distance learning students have similar grades and attitudes about courses when compared with traditional students. In addition, both students and instructors have positive attitudes toward distance learning. However, these reviews (i.e., Institute for Higher Education Policy, 1999; Russell, 1999) include courses delivered by a variety of distance learning technologies. Recently, researchers have focused on comparing online and traditional courses (Graham, 2001; Poirier & Feldman, 2004; Waschull, 2001; Wegner, Holloway, & Garton, 1999). The conclusion from these studies represents typical research in this area: Online students are at least as successful as traditional students, and they report positive feelings about their online course experiences.

However, there are limitations of the research. First, in most studies, students selected the course delivery method instead of being randomly assigned to one of the courses (Graham, 2001; Wegner et al., 1999; see Institute for Higher Education Policy, 1999). Because of this lack of control, it is difficult to interpret the results of these studies. For instance, students who self-select an online course may be more computer savvy, intelligent, or motivated.

Another limitation is the method of assessment used in many online courses. Students in online courses typically take unproctored exams (e.g., Waschull, 2001). Students may have an advantage because they can use their books, notes, and other resources (e.g., people). Comparing online and traditional students' grades under these circumstances is impossible.

To address these issues, and to evaluate whether or not our own undergraduate students could be successful in an online learning environment, we conducted a study comparing online and traditional students taking introductory psychology (Poirier & Feldman, 2004). Twenty-three traditional, undergraduate students, mostly first-year students, participated. Students were enrolled at the University of Massachusetts at Amherst, the flagship campus of the state system. It has approximately 24,000 students, 18,000 of whom are undergraduates. During the first week of classes, we constructed a waiting list for students who were interested in taking the course online or in a traditional classroom. By creating a waiting list, we were able to randomly assign students to the courses. From the list of students, we randomly assigned 11 students to the traditional course and 12 students to the online course.

The students enrolled in the traditional course met for 75 min twice per week for 15 weeks. Class meetings consisted of a combination of lecture, discussion, writing activities, videos, and exams. Out-of-class requirements included readings from the textbook, three online discussions, and three 2-page papers.

The students in the online course accessed an online classroom via eCollege at least twice per week for 15 weeks. In addition, these students were required to take their exams in a regular classroom with the students from the traditional course. This allowed us to create a controlled environment so that we could compare the online and traditional student's test grades. Except for exam days, the online students did not meet face-to-face with the instructor.

The online course consisted of text and audio introductions, learning objectives, reading assignments, Web activities, and discussion topics posted on the course delivery platform. Students and the instructor used e-mail and threaded discussions to communicate and interact. Students were required to participate in two online discussions per week. Online students read the same chapters and completed the same 2-page papers as the traditional students. In addition, they took nearly identical multiple-choice exams.

To compare the two courses, we analyzed the students' exam and paper grades and their course evaluations. For the exams, 23 of the 28 multiple-choice questions were identical between courses and used in the comparison. The paper grades ranged from 1 (*poor*) to 7 (*excellent*). The course evaluation consisted of four scales: instructor evaluation, overall course rating, interaction/feedback rating, and amount of time spent on the course. For most of the 30 items, students used a rating scale ranging from 1 (*negative*) to 7 (*positive*).

The results of the study showed that students could be successful online learners. On exams, the online students outperformed the traditional students: the online students correctly answered approximately 80% of the exam questions, while the traditional students correctly answered 72%. These results demonstrate that students can be successful even when there's nearly no face-to-face contact between the instructor and students.

Unlike the exam grade analysis, the analysis of the paper grades revealed no significant difference between the two groups of students. The traditional and online students had nearly identical mean paper grades, and the majority of the grades were in the "A" range. Taking the course online had no impact on the students' ability to write papers.

In addition to the grade analyses, we compared the students' course evaluations. The course evaluations were positive for both courses. However, the online students gave more positive ratings on a few of the items. For instance, the online students gave higher ratings of the instructor and the amount and quality of interaction and feedback. Conversely, there was no significant difference between the online and traditional students on items related to the overall experience with the course. However, the online students reported that they enjoyed the course and stated that they would like to take another online course in the future.

The results of the study are significant for at least two reasons. For one, the students were randomly assigned to one of the courses. Our study employed a waiting-list procedure to help ensure that the online and traditional students were similar at the beginning of the semester. Hence, the differences detected between the groups were most likely caused by the different course modality and not by the online students being more computer savvy, intelligent, or motivated.

Second, the findings are significant because they show that first-year students can be successful online students. For the majority of the online students, this was one of their first college courses and their first online course experience. Although at the start of the course the online students may have been proficient at sending e-mail and instant messages and browsing Web sites, they had never experienced taking an online college course. So we were pleased that the students, although novices, managed to perform at a high level.

We posit that the students' success was the result of the variety of assignments and activities and the asynchronous nature of the course. Although the online students did not attend lecture, they were provided with text and audio chapter introductions, learning objectives, Web activities, writing assignments, and threaded discussions. The Web activities and discussions required the students to be active learners. Moreover, these assignments and activities were asynchronous, so the students could log on at different times of the day to complete work. This may have provided the online students with an advantage: they could log in when they were ready to learn. For instance, if they worked better in the morning, they could complete their work early. With a traditional course, students have a set class schedule and do not have the luxury of showing up when they are ready to think critically, participate in discussions, and master course content.

Requiring students to participate in at least two threaded discussions per week was the key component of the course. Many studies have documented that interaction among students and instructors is the key to online success (Chen, 1997; Hiltz, 1993; Kerka, 1996; Picciano, 2002; Schrum, 1995; Simich-Dudgeon, 1998). The students in the online course expressed that interaction between students and the instructor was important. Moreover, the majority of the students noted that feedback from other students enhanced learning.

TEACHING STUDENT SUCCESS
COURSES ONLINE

Collectively, the results of our own research and that of other researchers clearly shows that students can succeed at least as effectively in online
courses as they can in traditional, classroom-based courses. Yet, to the
best of our knowledge, all the research conducted to date has focused on
courses with traditional, discipline-based content.

But what about student success in freshmen seminar courses designed to
help incoming students adjust to college life and achieve academic success?
The beginning of college is arguably the most difficult transition in life. During the first term of college, students often report high levels of stress and
social concerns. Consequently, many students leave college during or immediately following their first year. However, if there is a smooth transition
from high school to college, students are more likely to be successful (Nelson,
Scott, & Bryan, 1984). Research suggests that students who take student
success courses gain academic skills and social integration, achieve higher
grade point averages, and ultimately are more likely to complete their college
education (Barefoot, Warnock, Dickinson, Richardson, & Roberts, 1998;
Davis-Underwood & Lee, 1994; Schwitzer, McGovern, & Robbins, 1991).

To date, virtually all student success courses have been taught in traditional classrooms. However, we reasoned that, given the data supporting the efficacy of distance learning, conducting a student success course
online would be feasible. Certainly, students who are enrolled in all-online
college programs would find it useful. But even traditional students in
residence on a college campus might find the online nature of the course
advantageous. Because they could take the course in the summer, prior
to coming to campus, they could jump-start their educational experience.
And even students who are already on campus, currently taking courses,
might benefit from an online student success course that supplements their
traditional courses.

In order to investigate the efficacy and benefits of delivering student
success courses via distance learning, we designed an exploratory investigation in which we taught an online student success course. We designed
the course to meet two goals. First, we wanted to provide students with a
systematic, balanced presentation of the skills required to achieve success
in college. Second, we wanted to help students to build a network of friends.
Therefore, they would arrive on campus already knowing a small group of
people. Knowing other students may reduce stress and make the transition
to college easier. Consequently, the students would have a greater chance

of achieving academic success and they would be more likely to have a positive experience adjusting to life on campus.

Students' participation in the one-credit online course, dubbed "POWER-UP for Student Success," was solicited through a brochure that was mailed to all entering students in June, prior to their September enrollment at the University of Massachusetts at Amherst. The entering first-year class typically contains around 4,000 students. Eighteen students enrolled in the course, which was offered online using the university-supported eCollege course management system.

The course, offered approximately one month before the beginning of the Fall semester, required students to log in each day for three weeks. During the first two days, students participated in a series of introductory discussions and activities to build a sense of community. For instance, in the open introductions, the students were asked to share where they were from, why they selected the University of Massachusetts, what their hobbies were, and anything else of interest. In addition, they were prompted to post follow-up questions to their peers. Within a few hours, an online community formed as students "met" their classmates.

During the remainder of the course, students completed seven units, each covering a different topic. The topics included time management; learning styles; note taking; test taking; reading, writing, and speaking skills; and memory. For each unit, students completed a variety of assignments and read a chapter from *P.O.W.E.R. Learning: Strategies for Success in College and Life* (Feldman, 2003). Because the text was available both in traditional form and in a completely online version (available over the Web), it was particularly easy to use in the distance learning venue. Each reading assignment required students to complete interactive exercises, which allowed them to gain hands-on experience with the material covered in the book.

Students also participated in one online discussion per unit. They were required to reply to the instructors' initial question and to respond to at least one classmate's answer. The discussions served two purposes. First, they allowed the students to share and discuss their thoughts and feelings regarding the material and exercises in the text. Second, the students got to know each other and had an opportunity to learn from their classmates' experiences. Also, because we monitored and participated in the discussions, the students learned from our feedback.

In addition to the reading and discussion assignments, the students completed a brief writing assignment and at least one Web-related activity per unit. Each writing assignment consisted of a series of questions related to the topic covered in the textbook. The Web assignments allowed the students to extend their learning beyond the text.

All assignments (i.e., discussion, writing assignment, and Web activity) were graded on a 4-point scale ranging from 0 (*poor*) to 3 (*excellent*). Students received a Pass or Fail grade at the end of the course.

The course proceeded smoothly, and all 18 students completed the course with a passing grade. The course evaluations suggest that we achieved the goals of the course. For one, the students reported that knowing other students would be beneficial. Many of the students stated that this was the most important reason for taking the course. Second, the students believed that the course prepared them for a successful academic career at the University of Massachusetts. Overall, the students gave high ratings for the course. Nearly 75% of the students rated the course as better than average. Seventy-five percent of the students stated that they learned more in this course than in other courses.

Although the course was deemed a success, there were a few drawbacks. For one, the online environment made some things difficult. For instance, because the course was only three weeks long, getting the books to the students on time was a significant problem. During the first few days of the course, some students had not yet received their books. For future courses, we will be certain that the students receive their books on time or that they have access to an online version of the text for the entire course.

Second, we do not know yet if the students ultimately will be successful college students since follow-up evaluations have not yet been conducted. Furthermore, although the students reported that knowing other students prior to arriving on campus was beneficial, we do not yet know the extent of their actual interaction after arriving on campus.

Third, the students (or perhaps their parents) self-selected the course, and we did not have a comparable control group of students who did not take the course. Because our students selected the course delivery method instead of being randomly assigned to one of the courses, it is difficult to interpret unequivocally the effectiveness of the course. For instance, it is conceivable that our students may have enjoyed the online course because they already were more social, intelligent, or motivated than other first-year students and not because of the benefits of the course.

CONCLUSION

The results of our pilot project suggest that teaching student success online can be effective. This conclusion is congruent with research that has clearly demonstrated that online distance learning courses are at least as effective as traditional courses (Graham, 2001; Poirier & Feldman, 2004; Waschull, 2001; Wegner, Holloway, & Garton, 1999).

However, additional research is necessary because the results of our pilot project are limited and certainly not definitive. For example, random assignment should be used to ensure that the differences observed between groups are caused by the assignment to a specific type of course. In addition, the students' academic achievement and overall adjustment to college life should be measured.

The increase in the number of online course offerings will continue to rise as more people gain access to the Internet. Students who do not have the time or resources needed to reach a college campus are likely to take advantage of online courses. In addition, because online courses do not require physical space, institutions may turn to online course delivery to decrease costs associated with maintaining campus facilities. Therefore, the future of higher education will most likely be influenced by the development of new online course offerings, which will potentially allow more students to reach their academic goals.

Ultimately, student success in college courses is likely the result of *what* students and instructors do, not *how* they do it. According to Ragan (1998), "good teaching is good teaching" (p. 1), and the method of delivering a course is less important than the nature of the activities in which students are engaged. Student success is the result of well-designed course activities that stimulate students to think, gain knowledge, and master course content.

REFERENCES

Barefoot, B., Warnock, C., Dickinson, M., Richardson, S., & Roberts, M. (Eds.) (1998). *Exploring the evidence: Reporting outcomes of first-year seminars, Vol. II.* Monograph #25. Columbia, SC: National Resource Center for the First-Year Experience and Students in Transition

Bremner, F. (1998, November 16). On-line college classes get high marks among students. Cyber courses handy but more work for teacher. *USA Today,* p. 16E.

Carr, R., & Ledwith, F. (2000). Helping disadvantaged students. *Teaching at a Distance, 18,* 77–85.

Chen, L. (1997). Distance delivery systems in terms of pedagogical considerations: A reevaluation. *Educational Technology, 37*(4), 34–38.

Davis-Underwood, M., & Lee, J. A. (1994). An evaluation of The University of North Carolina at Charlotte Freshmen Seminar. *Journal of College Student Development, 35,* 491–492.

Dereshiwsky, M. I. (2001). "A" is for assessment: Identifying online assessment practices and perceptions. *USDLA Journal, 15*(1). Retrieved May 7, 2004, from http://www.usdla.org/html/journal/JAN01_Issue/article02.html

Dereshiwsky, M. I., Moan, E. R., & Gahungu, A. (2002). Faculty perceptions regarding issues of civility in online instructional communication. *USDLA Journal, 16*(6). Retrieved May 7, 2004, from http://www.usdla.org/html/journal/JUN02_Issue/article01.html

Feldman, R. S. (2003). *P.O.W.E.R. Learning: Strategies for success in college and life* (2nd ed.). New York: McGraw-Hill.

Graham, T. A. (2001). Teaching child development via the Internet: Opportunities and pitfalls. *Teaching of Psychology, 28*, 67–71.

Hiltz, S. R. (1993). Correlates of Learning in a Virtual Classroom. *International Journal of Man-Machine Studies, 39*, 71–98.

Institute for Higher Education Policy. (1999, April). *What's the difference? A review of contemporary research on the effectiveness of distance learning in higher education.* Washington, DC: Author. Retrieved May 7, 2004, from: http://www.ihep.com/Pubs/PDF/Difference.pdf

Kerka, S. (1996). *Distance learning, the Internet, and the World Wide Web.* Washington, DC: Office of Educational Research and Improvement. (ERIC Document Reproduction Service No. ED 395 214)

Lawson, T. J. (2000). Teaching a social psychology course on the Web. *Teaching of Psychology, 27*, 285–291.

National Center for Education Statistics. (2002). *Findings from the condition of education 2002: Nontraditional undergraduates.* Retrieved May 7, 2004, from http://nces.ed.gov//programs/coe/2002/analyses/nontraditional/sa05.asp

Nelson, R. B., Scott, T. B., & Bryan, W. A. (1984). Precollege characteristics and early college experiences as predictors of freshman year persistence. *Journal of College Student Personnel, 25*, 50–54.

Parker, A. (2003). Identifying predictors of academic persistence in distance education. *USDLA Journal, 17*(1). Retrieved May 7, 2004, from http://www.usdla.org/html/journal/JAN03_Issue/article06.html

Pew Internet and American Life Project. (2002). *The Internet goes to college: How students are living in the future with today's technology.* Retrieved May 7, 2004, from http://www.pewtrusts.com/pdf/vf_pew_internet_college.pdf

Picciano, A. G. (2002). Beyond student perceptions: Issues of interaction, presence, and performance in an online course. *Journal of Asynchronous Learning Networks, 6*(1). Retrieved May 7, 2004, from http://www.aln.org/publications/jaln/v6n1/v6n1_picciano.asp

Poirier, C. R., & Feldman, R. S. (2004). Teaching in cyberspace: Online versus traditional instruction using a waiting-list experimental design. *Teaching of Psychology, 31*, 59–62.

Ragan, L. C. (1998). Good teaching is good teaching: An emerging set of guiding principles and practices for the design and development of distance education. *DEOSNEWS, 8*(12). Retrieved May 7, 2004, from: http://www.ed.psu.edu/acsde/deos/deosnews/deosnews8_12.asp

Russell, T. (1999). *The no significant phenomenon.* Chapel Hill: Office of Instructional Telecommunications, North Carolina State University.

Schrum, L. (1995). *Online courses: What have we learned?* Paper presented at the World Conference of Computers in Education, England. (ERIC Document Reproduction Service No. ED 385 245)

Schwitzer, A. M., McGovern, T. V., & Robbins, S. B. (1991). Adjustment outcomes of a freshmen seminar: A utilization-focused approach. *Journal of College Student Development, 32,* 484–489.

Simich-Dudgeon, C. (1998). Developing a college Web-based course: Lessons learned. *Distance Education, 19*(2), 337–357.

U.S. Bureau of the Census. (2001). *Home computers and internet use in the United States: August 2000.* Washington, DC: Author.

Waschull, S. B. (2001). The online delivery of psychology courses: Attrition, performance, and evaluation. *Teaching of Psychology, 28,* 143–147.

WebCT. (2003). *WebCT customers.* Retrieved May 7, 2004, from http://www.webct.com/company/viewpage?name=company_webct_customers

Wegner, S. B., Holloway, K. C., & Garton, E. M. (1999). The effects of Internet-based instruction on student learning. *Journal of Asynchronous Learning, 3,* 98–106. Retrieved May 7, 2004, from http://www.aln.org/publications/jaln/v3n2/v3n2_wegner.asp

8

Engaging the First-Year Student

JONI WEBB PETSCHAUER
CINDY WALLACE
Appalachian State University

SETTING HIGH EXPECTATIONS FOR ENGAGEMENT

Appalachian State University is recognized as an exemplary institution for the attention it gives to its freshmen in the context of learning communities. This is the reason the institution has been selected as one of *TIME* magazine's four exemplary national models for freshman learning (Rutherford, 2001), one of the Policy Center on the First Year of College's thirteen Institutions of Excellence (2002–2003), and a national recipient of the Noel Levitz Retention Excellence Award (Noel & Levitz, 2002). These accolades resulted from integrating new ideas into a rich legacy of placing first-year students at the center of its mission. During the last thirty years, senior administrators have strongly supported freshman initiatives and have committed personnel and financial resources to their development and institutionalization. Assessment has guided the gradual and consistent modification of policies and programs, results of which are included in this chapter. The goals of this work have remained consistent—to become a "premier comprehensive university and model learning community" (Appalachian State University, 1998, *Campus Strategic Plan*) while supporting first-year students in developing connections and relationships with faculty, staff, and other students; providing each student with an intentionally integrative academic experience; and insuring that the university's reputation as a student-friendly institution remains intact.

PRE-ENROLLMENT AND ENROLLMENT MESSAGES

Appalachian's approach to engaging freshmen is comprehensive and seamless and ultimately focuses the entire campus community on the learning enterprise. It begins with significant pre-enrollment activities that connect prospective students to the educational decision-making process and resources as early as the middle school years. Critical early intervention ensures that students are academically prepared, informed about financial options and welcomed to the campus through participation in specially designed, pre-college programs. These efforts, supported in part by the non-profit partnership of College Foundation of North Carolina (www .cfnc.org), assist in preparing every student in the state for a college education. Students establish a web-based account as early as the seventh grade that allows them to plan, pay, and apply for college as well as introduces them directly to Appalachian State University and other North Carolina campuses. By the time they apply for admission, they have developed a basic awareness of the language, processes, and tools necessary for social and academic success in college.

The official admissions process introduces students to expectations, experiences and opportunities through a common academic message carried throughout recruiting materials, visitations and personal contact. "Academic excellence, a living laboratory, a community of educators, of scholars, an academic atmosphere that is serious, but supportive...." These words and phrases are pulled from the pages and sites of recruiting materials that teach prospective students about who we are and what will be expected of them. Indeed that is the fundamental reason for a campus-wide communication plan (Appalachian State University, 2003a).

Consistent messages and specific activities serve to remind and reinforce the idea that each student is about to embark on an academic journey. Among the most important activities are the fall and spring semester open houses that provide an opportunity for *prospective* students, parents, faculty and administrators to meet and personally address questions and concerns. Additionally, special topic workshops that focus on the various freshman programs and services are available during these weekend visits. All of these efforts provide opportunities for institutional representatives to connect with students and families and establish the basis for four years of trust. Through these interactions, the institution's academic image becomes a promise for an education and a better life. It is crucial for us to deliver on this promise and honor that commitment.

The Admissions Office coordinates communication throughout the application process, connecting students with services such as Residence Life, Financial Aid, Orientation and the Registrar's Office as well as appropriate academic programs and faculty. From the start, admissions officers and student ambassadors personalize the institution for prospective students. Upon the student's decision to attend Appalachian, each student is assigned an electronic account and instructed to go online and register for orientation, complete online placement testing, and communicate with the Academic Advising Center. Each admitted student completes a Preliminary Course Registration Form, which provides a comprehensive academic profile of an individual's academic preparedness and educational intentions. This profile informs an advisor about a student's intellectual curiosity, aptitudes, skills, and interest in a variety of academic majors and engages a student in the process of thinking about and articulating an academic plan. A tentative schedule of classes is designed and based on this profile for 95% of the freshman class *prior to* their attendance at a summer orientation session (Appalachian State University, 2003e).

Reflecting student responses to such questions as "What do you hope to learn while in college?" and "What are you curious about?" in a set of courses is both a provocative and practical process (Appalachian State University, 2003f). Through this activity, institutional representatives are able to lobby for and provide appropriate resources to meet the academic needs of the incoming class. Anyone who has worked with a course scheduling process understands how frustrating and unsettling it is to have first-year students struggle to put a schedule together when most, if not all, of the seats are filled. Such experiences create unnecessary anxiety and wasted energy during the first critical, face-to-face academic conversation. Issues and concerns regarding course and seat availability or faculty assignments should be negotiated with departments and colleges as a part of an institution's daily work and not as a reaction to the presence of first-year students and their parents during summer orientation. What message do we send when we wait until the last minute to make decisions and solve resource problems? Would we tolerate such behavior from our students? It is far more productive for the academic advisor and student to modify a schedule during the summer orientation session based on a continuing conversation that began with the Admissions application and well-designed Preliminary Course Registration Form. An example of how this effort can be further enhanced is illustrated by the work of Dr. Tom Rhyne, chair of Appalachian's Chemistry Department, who individually contacted every student who expressed interest in the Forensic Science learning community prior to their attendance at Orientation. This is the kind of personal, academically focused connection that sets the stage for students to sense the level of commitment and invitation for engagement.

A sequence of orientation events provides students and their parents with an introduction to critical individuals and policies. All students must attend the academically focused, two-day, campus-based Phase 1 Orientation program held in the summer to establish key relationships regarding the life of the campus (Appalachian State University, 2003f). During summer orientation, academic policies and responsibilities, core curriculum, course planning and adjustment are discussed in a small group setting. Orientation and academic advising must be associated in this work; when students meet and feel secure with a significant academic resource (advisor), they are more committed to their courses and reassured about course choices. A custom-designed academic planning booklet is given to each student that provides a supplemental resource for a student's first year at Appalachian (Appalachian State University, 2003b). This academic manual is also used as a required text in most of Appalachian's Freshman Seminar classes (Appalachian State University, 2003c).

Parent Orientation, held concurrently with Phase 1 Orientation in the summer, provides parents with an opportunity to learn about the academic and social expectations of their sons or daughters. This event is part of the comprehensive and coherent plan to both encourage and balance the level of engagement that parents bring to their students' college experience. Legislative initiatives, public policy and educational invitation during the K–12 experience have shaped both a student's and parent's expectations for oversight and involvement prior to college. Defining appropriate points of contact and communication once a student enrolls in college is a sensitive issue that should be addressed openly by administrators, faculty, staff, and students. Trust is earned through clear policies and procedures that both support open communication between parents and students and encourage independence.

It is during Phase 1 Orientation that students learn about the Summer Reading program and receive their first college assignment to read a specially chosen book prior to their return in the fall. The selection of a common book broadens the notion of academic community and provides a platform to introduce students and the local community to lifelong learning experiences (Appalachian State University, 2003b). Scheduling speakers, forums, discussions, and service projects that explore themes from a shared reading and opening them up to students and local community members alike creates a supportive environment in which to build a broader appreciation for diverse opinions.

Setting the stage for a college experience through an academic filter is a must, but attention must be given to the social development of students. Complementing the intellectual development of students is an array of personal development experiences such as First Ascent, an outdoor adventure program, and the Plemmons Fellows, a scholarship for students with proven leadership qualities. Upon their return in the fall, students participate in Phase 2 Orientation, which introduces them to clubs, organizations, and additional leadership opportunities. Phase 2 Orientation continues the message of academic and social connection through its coordination of small groups of students who participate in two faculty-led conversations. The first session provides an opportunity for informal sharing of academic expectations and general tips for success in the first year. The second discussion focuses on the summer reading assignment. Participation by faculty, staff, student development professionals, and academic administrators is broad-based and serves as an example of how campus-wide partnerships assist first-year students in making a successful transition to their new environment. These are the kinds of experiences that provide voice and energy to the out-of-classroom activities and truly enhance the campus's academic climate.

In addition to activities, external and internal assessment tools such as the Noel-Levitz College Student Inventory, Educational Benchmarking Inventories, Myers-Briggs Type Indicator, and system-wide freshman surveys allow the campus to teach and gather data regarding expectations for academic and social engagement (Policy Center on the First Year of College, 2002–2003). Furthermore, the results suggest ways for a campus to prioritize and organize its resources and discussions about services.

THE FRESHMAN YEAR

Student success in the first year has been deeply ingrained in the fabric of Appalachian from the early days of its founding, insuring that academic rigor and excellence are obtained and that the personal developmental needs of students are addressed. Attention to academic success is paramount, particularly in the first year. In addition to all freshmen being assigned an academic advisor (most frequently based on a learning community assignment) to assist them with negotiating the academic environment, they have access to a gamut of coordinated resources developed specifically to ensure academic success (Appalachian State University, 2003b). All students, but particularly freshmen, receive academic assistance through the university's tutoring program, Supplemental Instruction, and learning skills courses and workshops. Students considered most at-risk on campus — economically disadvantaged, first-generation, disabled, and/or athletes — are involved in special services geared to their individual academic needs. Early warning processes for all first-year students are in place to assure that academic progress and engagement is monitored, and problems are identified and dealt with in a timely manner. The development of social and leadership skills in students is important at Appalachian, particularly as these activities maximize the academic experience. Over 250 clubs and organizations with faculty advisors exist to support this growth (Appalachian State University, 2001–2003, p. 17).

At the heart of Appalachian's success is a broad continuum of learning community offerings, specifically designed for the first-year student. Approximately 85% of Appalachian freshmen participate in a learning community program during the first semester. Learning communities provide a programmatic structure for bringing together students, faculty, and academic support team members to learn specific skills, explore similar interests, and solve common problems. By registering interested freshmen in groups of selected courses, students have an opportunity to integrate class material more fully while meeting individuals and learning about resources and services that will support their academic efforts. This is particularly true when one of the courses is a well-developed Freshman Seminar or other anchor course that intentionally connects campus resources to the curriculum. Through the learning community faculty, students make connections to academic departments that support their educational and possibly their professional goals. Through their academic support team (advisors, librarians, peer leaders and tutors), they make connections to services that support their academic success (Wallace & Petschauer, 2003).

Importantly, learning communities are not limited to students who are certain of their educational direction. One significant potential outcome associated with co-enrollment options such as learning communities is the ability to engage students who do not yet have an academic direction with a group of learners who can be directly supported by a facilitated academic discourse from the start. Students who are undecided do not have to feel isolated in their quest for an educational purpose. End-of-the semester evaluation comments suggest that cognitive and social development is addressed by learning communities:

> "I knew many of the students that were in my classes. This made me feel comfortable and it helped me learn what was out there."

> "Yes, by joining this group I got a chance to get closer to the faculty associated with this major and access to the classes."

> "It (the learning community) is a great way to meet friends and work together to get through freshman year." (Appalachian State University, 2000 and 2001b)

Faculty members have an opportunity to present their discipline through a common theme or within the context of possible careers to an interested group of students. Furthermore, faculty have regular access to an academic support team that can address specific student concerns that detract from the academic focus of the classroom. Finally, faculty have an opportunity to explore their discipline in a cross-disciplinary context and with colleagues outside of their department. Faculty response to working with freshman learning communities has been positive and informative. The following end-of-semester evaluation comments by learning community instructors reflect programmatic goals:

> "Student familiarity and support with one another was established early, which led to positive results: studying together, improved grades, good discussions."

> "Dialogue with other teachers gave me insights and other perspectives regarding individual students."

> "Wonderful community building. The class really bonded and took care of each other. Students seemed more motivated; attendance was better." (Appalachian State University, 2000 and 2001a)

Academic support services represented by librarians, academic advisors, orientation leaders, tutors, and peer leaders have defined groups and an academic context with which to direct resources and assistance. Student development professionals such as residence life assistants and professionals, career planning and financial aid specialists, personal development counselors, health professionals, and facilitators of clubs, organizations, and other student groups need to filter co-curricular activities and programs through the academic mission—thus reinforcing the primary reason for attending college. Safety officers, campus police, secretaries, records keepers, housekeepers, physical plant employees, construction and design planners, and food service workers involve themselves in the lives of students through the creation of safe, healthy, accurate, and adequate learning environments. In fact, in Appalachian's most recent residential learning community efforts, many from this collective group were involved in the conversation from the start rather than as an afterthought.

Academic advisors play a pivotal role in coordinating academic success resources based on faculty and student feedback. All learning community coursework receives core curriculum or general elective credit and does not limit a student's ultimate choice of majors. The following is a brief description of the academically focused learning communities available for first-year students. Some of these programs have existed since the late 1960s or early 1970s; others are newly implemented. All, however, work in concert to provide an intentionally integrative and academically focused first-year experience for freshmen.

Freshman Learning Communities in General Studies (FLC) enrolls over half of the freshman class. This program provides a way for small groups of students (15–25) who share similar academic interests or career aspirations to take two or three classes together during the first semester of their freshman year; virtually every FLC in General Studies includes the Freshman Seminar course (U S 1150) — a three-hour, graded graduation credit class — as one of the classes. The co-enrollment aspect allows students to more easily form study groups and integrate class material while making friends, exploring majors, and discovering potential career choices (Appalachian State University, 2001–2003, p. 76; 2003d).

Freshman Seminar offers first-semester students a carefully structured orientation to college, an introduction to academic and personal success strategies, and an opportunity for self-discovery and self-realization. It draws on national models and extensive research for much of its conceptual framework, but is tailored to fit the unique needs and challenges faced by freshmen at Appalachian. The course acquaints students with the opportunities and demands of higher education through a mix of activities, lectures, discussions, and participation in community events. In small classes (15–25), students build learning skills, practice time management and other life skills; examine the purpose of higher education and learn to set goals for their first semester and beyond; and take time to volunteer in the community, eat meals together, and attend cultural events. It is important that the goals of this course complement your institution's culture and be committed to your campus mission statement (Appalachian State University, 2001–2003, p. 76; 2003d).

On the Appalachian campus, the Freshman Seminar course supports the goal of maintaining a strong sense of community. Additionally, it complements planning priorities that emphasize the importance of enhancing the undergraduate experience and addresses recommendations urging careful consideration of freshman needs. Beyond these ideas, Appalachian's Freshman Seminar supports broader educational goals by providing learning experiences that permit personal growth and development, encouraging interaction among faculty and students, and demonstrating the interrelatedness of knowledge and the importance of lifelong learning. It assists students in making a successful transition to college while discovering the resources and opportunities offered by Appalachian. It promises to strengthen learning skills, broaden individual horizons, and facilitate students in their move toward intellectual and individual independence. As a fundamental element in Appalachian's Freshman Learning Community program, students are co-enrolled with their Freshman Seminar classmates in at least one other freshman-level course. This allows students, faculty and academic support team members to engage in a planned cross-disciplinary experience in the first semester, support each other's learning goals, and enhance the academic climate of the campus (Appalachian State University, 2003d; Brantz, Friedman, & Glass, 2003, pp. 1–4).

Faculty members are encouraged to tailor Freshman Seminar in ways that reflect their own expertise, but there is a core set of course requirements that each section of the course is expected to deliver. Additionally, faculty and academic support teams participate in a number of ongoing faculty development activities to ensure their ability in carrying out this work. What every campus must do is develop course content or services in light of a broadly understood and accepted first-year mission. Appalachian's Freshman Seminar course requirements set the stage for engaging the first year student and faculty in learning and are based on best practices in undergraduate education. They include:

- Regular writing
- Library use
- Learning styles
- Learning skills
- Convocation
- Computing
- Supplemental reading
- Campus Resource Tour

- Service Learning
- Group Interaction Course (GIC)
- Career and Major Planning
- Cultural events
- Time management
- Campus involvement
- International Programs

(Wallace & Petschauer, 2003, pp. 19–24; Appalachian State University, 2003c, pp. 1–8)

Watauga College, founded in 1972, is an interdisciplinary residential living-learning community that offers specially designed general education courses for first- and second-year students. Students live together in the same residence hall to encourage the integration of the academic program with students' personal and social development. The Watauga program is challenging, with small classes (12 to 18 students) that are discussion oriented to encourage students to develop and articulate their own views. Approximately 120 freshmen participate in this program, which promotes student-faculty contact inside and outside of the classroom (Appalachian State University, 2001–2003, p. 77; 2003d). In fall 2003, the Watauga College moved to a new living-learning facility on the campus. Built to support the delivery of a newly restructured curriculum, this facility reflects true campus collaboration. The Great Hall provides an open gathering space for meals, speakers, and other elements of "commons time." Faculty offices and student rooms connect to make the living and learning seamless. The curriculum guides the out-of-class activities, and the agreed-upon rules for living together are intentional. Even the residence hall staff are called "guides" and not "resident assistants."

Honors education at Appalachian delivers intellectual excitement and scholarly engagement for the 400 or so students who take honors classes each year. Approximately the top 10% of the entering class is invited to participate in this program. Freshmen join upper class Honors students in small classes that promote critical thinking and analysis through a scholarly and rigorous approach. Beyond the classroom, Honors seeks to maintain a stimulating and supportive community for serious students through co-curricular activities and programs. All freshmen are invited to participate in the Honors Connection seminar for co-curricular credit, and a quarter of entering freshmen live in Coffey Hall, a residence for honors students (Appalachian State University, 2001–2003, p. 78; 2003d).

Appalachian's Teaching Fellows program is one of the oldest in the state and has always been one of the largest with 60 students enrolling each year. Funded by North Carolina's legislature as a way to attract good students into the teaching profession, the program provides a scholarship to promising high school seniors from across the state. The students pay the state back by teaching for at least four years after graduation in one of the state's public schools. Students must apply for the scholarship during October of their senior year in high school and are selected through a screening process. A wide range of special seminars, field trips, and service activities are provided for Fellows to help improve their readiness for work with a very diverse population of students in the public schools of the state.

Starting in 2003, all freshman Teaching Fellows are housed in the new living-learning center on campus (Appalachian State University, 2001–2003,
p. 77; 2003d).

The Army ROTC program supports Appalachian's learning community
goals and has been on the campus for over three decades. The Military
Science 1000 class offers an introduction to the military, providing students
with knowledge of the Army organization, mission, branches, leadership,
and problem solving processes during classroom instruction. Additionally,
students participate in outdoor adventure activities during labs. Student
can take military science classes for up to two years without making an
obligation to the Army (Appalachian State University, 2001–2003, p. 76;
2003d).

The Student Support Services (SSS) program provides academic support services to moderate income and/or first-generation college students. ↙
Long-term academic advising, early academic programming assessment,
one-on-one and small group tutoring, freshman study hall, financial aid
planning and career decision-making are among the efforts designed to assist these students become college graduates (Appalachian State University,
2001–2003, p. 77; 2003d).

The W.H. Plemmons Scholars program is a selective four-year leadership experience that identifies students who have been actively involved in
their high school or community in service and leadership roles and wish
to continue that commitment in college. Freshmen are selected through
an application process and are enrolled in a leadership course designed
specifically to assist them in adapting to college and developing their leadership potential (Appalachian State University, 2003d).

This variety of programs and services at Appalachian exist to insure a
smooth transition for freshmen. The breadth and depth of learning communities indicates that no one learning community model can meet the
needs of an entering class at a comprehensive institution. Some are residential; some last one semester — others last longer; some are major specific — others work well for deciding students; and all support faculty and
staff in their work with small groups of students both inside and outside
of the classroom. Importantly, these efforts include both a revitalization
of existing services and the development of new ones that have a tremen-
dous impact on first-year students. Some of the programs were created
by student development, and others grew out of the academic house.
Important to this work is the constant communication and collaboration
among diverse campus members. During the past decade, academic affairs
and student development partnerships have been fostered by formal and

informal councils, committees, task forces, and work teams. The Learning Communities Council, Student Orientation Committee, Student Services Committee, Retention Task Force, Hubbard Center for Faculty and Staff Development, Academic Advising Council, and Core Curriculum Council serve to illustrate this idea. Such broad-based cooperation and involvement is vital for a campus in developing genuinely meaningful first year programs. And once such conversations occur, it becomes difficult to consider new initiatives without calling on like-minded colleagues.

ASSESSMENT

Assessment is driven by the need to respond to external and internal policy makers. When developing a philosophy and framework for regular and informative assessment, it is useful to remember not to test (it's a four-letter word). Always take time to give voice to those who experience the effort through personalized and low-threat activities such as focus groups, interviews, response papers, journals, and letters. Our students are wisened to and cynical about the surveys and testing results that simply serve to measure levels of achievement (or not) rather than reflect the cognitive and social development that is shaped by the first-year experience over the course of an undergraduate education.

Integrated into all programs and services for freshmen is a campus-wide assessment model designed to assist educators and administrators in proving the value of attending to freshmen and improving the programs provided for them. Indeed, assessment and evaluation are so important to the institutional decision-making and planning process that they are part of Appalachian's academic calendar. Prior to the implementation of an easily monitored and accessed online assessment process, student participation was ensured through University Focus and Assessment Days. Classes were cancelled and early registration permission was granted in order to gather qualitative and quantitative data from students—particularly freshmen. Today, data continues to be collected in the form of student satisfaction surveys, competency tests, focus group participation; locally developed program surveys; enrollment, retention and performance data; UNC Office of the President surveys; and nationally-developed assessment tools such as CIRP, CSEQ, CSXQ, NSSE, NCTLA, EBI First-Year Initiative Benchmarking Survey and Study, Student Environment Benchmarking Survey (EBI), and Noel-Levitz College Student Inventory (CSI). The Office of Institutional Research, Assessment and Planning (IRAP), in conjunction with the Student

Development and Academic Affairs, coordinates freshman assessment and assists various academic departments and divisions as well as co-curricular program units in gathering data about freshmen for evaluation purposes. The results guide administrators in monitoring success and modifying programs and policies. All units are expected to communicate evaluation efforts in the Annual Report to the Chancellor. This information is collected and used by appropriate units and groups as part of the institution's ongoing strategic planning process. Despite current budget concerns in North Carolina and because of assessment efforts, freshmen still come first at Appalachian (Policy Center on the First Year of College, 2001–2003).

Evidence of assessment efforts that influence freshman programming can be seen in the following examples:

1. Several studies regarding freshman learning community involvement led to a decision to increase the number of intentionally connective academic experiences for freshmen. Since 1998, learning community enrollment has grown from approximately 500 freshmen (21%) to over 2,000 freshmen (83.6%).

2. Retention studies have been used to monitor Appalachian's first- to second-year retention rates, particularly as this information reveals historical trends and compares with other institutions. Appalachian traditionally enjoys high retention rates for a public comprehensive institution (81%–86%) and is most frequently the third highest in the UNC system. Students enrolled in a freshman learning community are statistically and significantly higher (3%–5%) than those not enrolled.

3. Graduation rates are extremely important comparisons. Freshman Seminar's longitudinal data (the program was implemented in 1987) has shown that students who were enrolled in that course persist in college and graduate at higher rates (5%–7%) than students who did not take the course.

4. 2001 NSSE results found that Appalachian's first-year students' responses exceeded other Master's comparisons by statistically significant differences in the following areas: quality of advising, and the institutional emphases of (a) providing the support needed to succeed academically, and (b) encouraging contact among students from different economic, social and racial or ethnic backgrounds. These results inform practices and planning for advisor caseloads as well as provide support for recruiting ethnically different and international students.

5. The Noel Levitz College Student Inventory and Retention Management System has been used to generate a "dropout proneness" scale for

individuals. Students who enter Appalachian with high drop-out proneness and are in learning communities persist at significantly higher rates than similar students who are not in learning communities. Due to this information, the College Student Inventory is now administered the first day of Phase 1 Orientation, allowing advisors access to reports in time to suggest learning communities or other forms of intervention.

6. In order to study the General Education curriculum, in which students are enrolled primarily during the first year, various assessments have been done. Cohort testing in the areas of writing, math/science reasoning, critical thinking, social science, and speaking skills have taken place, with a sophomore- or junior-year follow-up. The results stimulated discussion among members of the University Assessment Committee and the Core Curriculum Council as to how and why students may improve in some areas and not in others.

7. The Student Development Task and Lifestyle Assessment (SDTLA) has been used to examine the impact of involvement in out-of-classroom experiences and first-year student services on psychosocial development and has been used to modify university policies. Specifically, the Office of Student Development studies the impact of Greek, club, and/or organizational affiliation, particularly as it influenced alcohol and drug use, smoking, sleep, and sexual activity of first-year students. The university's commitment to a successful academic transition was affirmed by the recent decision to delay freshman participation in fraternity and sorority rush until the spring semester because of these studies. Additionally, these results informed discussions that led to the "freshman-only" housing option. Information gathered from a campus climate survey added to knowledge collected from focus groups of minority students about their experiences at Appalachian.

8. Focus groups made up of students representing Freshman Learning Communities, Summer Preview, Watauga College, and departmental experiences have been conducted to learn more about how to improve specific programs and campus-wide offerings. The Office of Institutional Research, Assessment and Planning assists by coordinating and recording these efforts.

9. Assessment will always be part of Appalachian's future work with freshmen. Some of the studies to be used in the future include: EBI First-Year Initiative Study to compare results of students among various learning communities; NSSE to assess growth or change in student engagement; internal measures regarding core curriculum designators; and focus groups and surveys with students in the new living-learning center.

(Wallace, Petschauer, Williams, Hogan, & Langdon, 2003)

FINAL THOUGHTS

Much of Appalachian's success can be attributed to its long standing commitment to students and the surrounding mountain community. Furthermore, a relatively stable faculty and administration—from 1899 until 2003, only five presidents/chancellors served the campus—has provided a continued conversation about student success. But even if your campus does not enjoy these particular elements of Appalachian's environment, many student-focused activities already exist on your campus. And, if they are the result of intentional collaboration, then it is all the better. If not, then take the ideas that work and place them in a more connective conversation or use any combination of ideas to forward a new agenda in developing a first-year mission that is campus wide and accountable. Just remember that much of what you want to do must be done in the context of a specific campus or department. No matter how good the "new idea" is, there is a chance it will not work well the first time you test it. When campus culture and best practice collide, there are always unintended results—some good and some not so good. We recommend that you find a group of people you trust and do it, assess it, laugh about it, modify it and give it another try.

Appalachian's national recognition is the result of trying out many different ideas, assessing them, and learning from each of them. Some of the most important lessons came from efforts that no longer exist on the campus. An example of this would be Project EXCEL, a computer-based learning community taught during the 1999–2000 academic year. Designed as a technology enhanced educational experience, freshmen were enrolled in a two-semester sequence of specific general education courses. The faculty members participated in training and committed to integrating technology into their sections of English, history, biology, math, and Freshman Seminar. Specific goals included "improve the learning of students and the teaching of faculty." The results of the effort were fantastic—students reported high satisfaction and passed their classes, faculty employed computing in disciplines that were not traditionally technology-rich environments and the freshman-to-sophomore retention rate was 98% (and the one student who did not return actually transferred to another institution) (Appalachian State University, 1999–2000, "Project EXCEL—Reasons to End"). But the level of micro-management and human energy needed to administer this experience for a relatively miniscule percentage of the freshman population (59 students) proved overwhelming. An important feature for any new program is its ability to be institutionalized and/or replicated for greater numbers. Project EXCEL could be managed for a small group but the resource, curricular and systemic changes required to implement this option for greater numbers of students and faculty were unrealistic, particularly in light of competing values.

The fear of failure often interrupts the enthusiasm for action or publicly engaged learning or institutional change. Faculty and students are guilty of not speaking because they might look foolish, get it wrong or appear less than competent. Yet, it is in that very environment that learning can occur. And in order for true engagement to occur, trust must be built. Every classroom and campus must become a *community*. Implicit in that word is a commitment to watch over, guide, facilitate, listen, understand and support one another. Taking time to develop trust is critical to developing a community that will sustain intellectual risk taking.

There are always campus-specific processes for implementing new initiatives: financial and human resources, organizational/administrative structures, existing alliances for getting things done. Ask yourself: Who are the policy makers? Who are your campus worker bees? Who are your idea people? Where are they—both up and down the line? Almost any university is willing to support one good idea, particularly when success can be shown. Start small, identify what works, and be honest about what didn't. Post it, publish it, put it out for scrutiny. Invite your greatest critics to assist you in solving the problems that they believe exist. Partner with people and offices that are like-minded. You don't have to be responsible for it all but you must accept the responsibility for facilitating discussions and being open to ideas that you didn't have. Suggest ways to re-approach an idea. Develop meaningful accountability at every stage that creates opportunities for everyone on campus to learn about the enterprise. Often this entails creating a new institutional memory which is particularly important now that so many institutions are turning over its faculty and staff through retirement and attrition. Be certain that your assessment is both formative and summative in nature. Stories and numbers are needed. Remember the old chestnut—chancellors like stories, deans need numbers, faculty feed minds, student development touches hearts—the whole university community is bigger than any one part.

In summary, it is about the potential of the freshman experience. It is about how we bring individuals to our campuses and how we set the stage for every possibility that subsequently occurs. We must attend to developmental and sequential experiences that indicate high expectations from the start. We must be willing to experiment with new ideas but always in a realistic environment. Financial constraints will continue to exist. Our campus demographics will change—students, faculty, and staff will be challenged to understand each other and the unique pressures each group faces. Higher education has moved from the luxury of random, individually led experimentation for the benefit of an elite population to an expectation for efficient, effective educational models that meet the needs of a diverse, mobile, increasingly demanding nation.

Focusing on first-year students is one way to embark on this conversation. It transcends discipline, departments, and divisions. It is the whole of the academic experience and it is found in the first steps of a student's journey.

REFERENCES

Appalachian State University. (1998). *Campus strategic plan.* Boone, NC: Author. Retrieved January 25, 2003, from http://www.appstate.edu/www_docs/depart/irp/planning/SPV.pdf

Appalachian State University. (2000 and 2001b). *Freshman Learning Communities (FLC) student evaluation summary* (internal program survey). Boone, NC: Office of Freshman Learning Communities in General Studies.

Appalachian State University. (2001–2003) *General bulletin.* Boone, NC: Office of Academic Affairs.

Appalachian State University. (2003a). *2003–2004 Prospectus.* Boone, NC: Office of Admissions.

Appalachian State University. (2003b). *Academic planning manual.* Boone, NC: Office of General Studies.

Appalachian State University. (2003c). *Faculty resource manual.* Boone, NC: Office of Freshman Seminar. http://www.freshmanseminar.appstate.edu/fs_faculty.htm

Appalachian State University. (2003d). *Freshman learning communities brochure.* Boone, NC: Office of Freshman Learning Communities in General Studies.

Appalachian State University. (2003e, July 2). *Internal report for freshman schedules built* (Ref. No. RJA451_A). Boone, NC: Office of General Studies.

Appalachian State University. (2003f). Preliminary course registration form. *First Connection: Freshman Orientation Phase I and Course Registration.* Boone, NC: Office of General Studies.

Brantz, R., Friedman, D., & Glass, E. (2003). (3rd ed.) *New connections: A handbook for freshman seminar.* Dubuque, IA: Kendall/Hunt Publishing Company.

Noel, L., & Levitz, R. (2002). *Lee Noel and Randi Levitz retention excellence awards.* Retrieved January 25, 2003, from http://www.noellevitz.com/library/awards/retention/index

Policy Center on the First Year of College (2002–2003). Appalachian State University. In *Institutions of excellence in the first year.* Retrieved December 19, 2003, from http://www.brevard.edu/fyc/instofexcellence/data.htm

Rutherford, M. (2001, September 10). Appalachian State. *TIME,* pp. 68–71.

Wallace, C., & Petschauer, J. (2003). *Instructor's resource manual and test bank to accompany P.O.W.E.R. learning strategies for success in college and life* (2nd ed.). New York: McGraw-Hill.

Wallace, C., Petschauer, J., Williams, L., Hogan, T., & Langdon, H. (2003). *Hallmarks of Excellence Proposal for Appalachian State University for the Policy Center on the First Year of College.* Boone, NC: Office of Enrollment Services.

9

Building Learning Communities for First-Year Students

JODI LEVINE LAUFGRABEN
Temple University

Campus experiments with learning communities are flourishing because many faculty sense that this structure promises an effective way to address some of the most pressing concerns of the academy —disengaged, passive, and unevenly prepared students, a fragmented curriculum with little connection between and among students, and a high freshman to sophomore year attrition rate.

—Strommer (1999, p. 41)

Consider the ideal environment we hope to create for our first-year students and what they say when they experience this type of setting. A welcoming and supportive learning environment: "I wasn't afraid to ask questions in class or to approach professors or students in my learning communities classes. Everything was so open and friendly." Opportunities for students to form supportive relationships with peers and teachers: "There were many advantages of the program. I was able to meet a lot of new people, which allowed me to make new friends and form a 'network' of students I could call when I had a question about the day's class." Good teaching and deeper learning: "The learning community really helped me to draw parallels between my classes. I've learned about racism, economics, class structure and society as a whole. I will use what I've been taught in the future."

Learning communities — clusters of courses organized around a curricular theme which students take as a group — strengthen and enrich students' connections to each other, their teachers, and the subject matter they are studying (Levine Laufgraben, 2004). Learning communities aim to improve the first year of college by (a) enhancing the curriculum; (b) supporting the transition to college by creating connections between and among students and their peers, teachers, and disciplines; (c) extending learning beyond the classroom; and (d) empowering students to be more active participants in their learning and in their academic decision making.

A national survey of first-year academic practices conducted by the Policy Center on the First Year of College (Barefoot, 2002), confirmed the pervasiveness of learning communities in the undergraduate program. According to the survey, 62% of the respondents reported enrolling student cohorts in two or more linked courses. Learning communities were most likely to be found at research universities and least likely to be found at small, bachelor's degree-granting campuses. Larger universities, particularly public institutions with larger percentages of working and commuting students, recognize the value of learning communities in creating the small-college atmosphere already in place at liberal arts or small, private institutions. While there is no "one size fits all" approach to learning communities, successful curricular learning communities share common elements: curricular restructuring, active and collaborative pedagogies, student cohorts, and opportunities to create community among and between students and teachers.

LEARNING COMMUNITIES
AS GOOD PRACTICE

The literature on student success and development (Astin, 1993; Ewell, 1997; Pascarella & Terenzini, 1991; Tinto, 1994) provides the theoretical foundation on which to build learning communities. According to Astin (1993), frequent student-faculty interaction, frequent student-student interaction, amount of time devoted to studying, tutoring, cooperative learning, and giving class presentations all positively impact student development (pp.

423–424). Greater intellectual interactions between students and their peers and teachers, and more active, collaborative types of learning characterize learning community classrooms. Learning communities create the type of environment Astin describes, particularly for first-year students.

Chickering and Gamson's (1987) "Seven Principles for Good Practice in Undergraduate Education" summarized years of research on the undergraduate experience. Good practice:

1. Encourages student-faculty contact.
2. Encourages cooperation among students.
3. Encourages active learning.
4. Gives prompt feedback.
5. Emphasizes time on task.
6. Communicates high expectations.
7. Respects diverse talents and ways of learning.

Learning communities offer a structure within which these principles can be implemented, particularly in classrooms with large numbers of first-year students, classrooms not traditionally characterized by this type of cooperative, active learning.

Learning communities, according to Ewell (1997), represent one effective structure that promotes learning. Learners create their learning actively and uniquely; they are not empty vessels into which knowledge can be poured. Learning is about making meaning, and students learn constantly, both with us and without us. Direct experience also impacts students' understanding; students learn most effectively in the context of a compelling problem. Learning also requires reflection and is most likely to occur in a supportive environment characterized by personal support and interaction with others (p. 4). Learning community curriculum is characterized by the application of concepts to real situations and opportunities for experiential and cross-disciplinary learning. The learning community classroom includes interpersonal collaboration and frequent faculty feedback on student performance.

LEARNING COMMUNITIES MODELS

With the rapid increase in the number of learning community programs in higher education today, the term *learning communities* has taken on different meanings. This chapter describes curricular learning communities:

> A variety of approaches that link or cluster classes during a given term, often around an interdisciplinary theme, that enroll a common cohort of students. This represents an intentional restructuring of students' time, credit, and learning experiences to build community among students, among students and their teachers, and among disciplines. (MacGregor, Smith, Mathews, & Gabelnick, 2001)

In the broadest sense of the term, any classroom in which students and faculty are engaged in intellectual matters is a learning community. But what are learning communities in practice? Bystrom (1997) operationalized this definition and stated what those involved in learning communities work mean by the term:

> First, we mean, in addition to active and collaborative classroom methods, a curricular structure which includes collaboration among teachers. . . . Second, we mean a structure that addresses the issue of curricular coherence by purposeful links among courses in disciplines. For us, then, a learning community is a course of study designed by two or more faculty which includes work in different disciplines integrated around a particular issue or theme. (p. 247)

Learning Community initiatives share several basic characteristics. According to Shapiro and Levine (1999), successful learning communities:

1. Organize students and faculty into smaller groups.
2. Encourage integration of the curriculum.
3. Help students establish academic and social support networks.
4. Provide a setting for students to be socialized to the expectations of college.
5. Bring faculty together in more meaningful ways.
6. Focus faculty and students on learning outcomes.
7. Provide a setting for community-based delivery of academic support programs.
8. Offer a critical lens for examining the first-year experience. (p. 3)

The approach to learning communities will vary across institutions. There are, however, four commonly described models: (a) paired or clustered courses; (b) cohorts in large courses or FIGs (freshmen interest groups); (c) team-taught or coordinated studies programs; and (d) residence-based learning communities, models that intentionally link the classroom-based learning community with a residential life component. These models also vary in terms of levels of faculty collaboration and curricular integration; with the FIG (freshman interest group) model being the least intensive and the team-taught/coordinated studies approach representing the most radical restructuring of student and faculty time and courses.

Paired or Clustered Courses

Paired- or clustered-course learning communities link individually taught courses through cohort and often block scheduling (scheduling of courses in back-to-back time slots). A paired-course learning community typically enrolls a group of 20–30 students in two courses. Offerings tend to be existing courses that traditionally enroll significant numbers of first-year students. One of the two courses in the pairing is usually a basic composition or communications course. These courses tend to be more interdisciplinary in nature and promote a classroom environment in which students and faculty get to know each other (Levine Laufgraben, 2004; MacGregor et al., 2001; Shapiro & Levine, 1999). In learning communities designed to support students' transition to college, pairings might also include sections of a one- to three-credit student success or first-year experience course.

In paired-course learning communities, classes are often linked based on logical curricular connections and skill areas. The linked-course learning communities at Temple University pair two general education courses or a general education requirement with an introductory course in the major. Courses are individually taught, but faculty work together to create a curricular theme for their communities and to integrate content across their courses. A recent learning community for first-year theater students paired college composition with a collaborative arts course. The theme for this community was "Creating Meaning." As described by the teaching team:

> This community will explore the ways that perception and meaning are influenced. Students will approach this theme from two perspectives, as members of an academic community and as artists. The artist asks two questions: What do I want to say? How can I say it? The cultural historian, recognizing that artists are not separate from their society and culture, asks which forces affect an artist's answers. What influences the audiences who view the work? This Learning Community will ask its students to tackle both sets of questions—to be artists and academics. Students will create their own meaning using unfamiliar forms of theatrical expression and they will investigate other artist's meanings using the discourse of academia. (D. Ingram, personal communication, October 2003)

Clusters.   Clusters expand the paired-course model by linking three or four individually taught courses around a theme. Clusters are often small and usually enroll cohorts of 20–30 students. One course tends to be a writing course and the community usually includes a weekly seminar. These seminars are the setting for synthesis and community-building activities. Some cluster models include larger lecture-type courses in which the community cohort enrolls as a subset, as well as smaller, cluster-only seminars or small writing classes.

At LaGuardia Community College, liberal arts and science majors can choose from a list of six to eight cluster offerings each semester. Each cluster is organized around a curricular theme and includes two liberal arts and science courses, college composition, a research paper course, and an integrated hour. Some frequently offered clusters include:

- Harlem on My Mind: American Music, The Art of Theatre, English Composition, The Research Paper, Integrated Hour.
- Names, Labels and Stereotypes: Oral Communication, Critical Thinking, English Composition, The Research Paper, Integrated Hour.
- Women's Lives; Women's Struggles: Introduction to Sociology, Women and Society, English Composition, The Research Paper, Integrated Hour.
- Sociology and Culture of the Family: English Composition, The Research Paper, Introduction to Sociology, Sociology of the Family, Integrated Hour. (Learning Communities at LaGuardia Community College, City University of New York, retrieved from http://www.lagcc.cuny.edu/STUINFO/firstyear/learningcomm.asp)

Cohorts in Large Courses or FIGs

Freshman interest groups (FIGs), learning communities organized around a curricular theme, represent the simplest learning community model in terms of organization and cost (Gabelnick, MacGregor, Matthews, & Smith, 1990). This model is more commonly used at large universities or at institutions where first-year students typically register for at least one or two large lecture courses. In FIGs, learning community students represent a subset of the total enrollment. If the lecture course involves a smaller recitation or discussion section, FIG students are typically enrolled in a designated "learning community-only" section. In addition to one or two large courses, FIGs commonly include a smaller writing course and a weekly seminar limited to FIG students. An undergraduate peer teacher may lead the weekly seminar (Levine Laufgraben, 2004; Shapiro & Levine, 1999).

A less common approach is the Federated Learning Community in which student cohorts enroll in larger courses along with a teacher who serves as master learner. Like the FIG, the Federated Learning Community integrates courses around a theme. The master learner, who typically does not have any teaching responsibilities beyond the community, facilitates a weekly seminar to help students synthesize what they are learning.

The University of Washington annually enrolls nearly 75% of its entering freshman in FIGs each autumn quarter (Smith, 2003). FIGs are organized around curricular interests and themes. Students interested in "the natural world" can select from a list of FIGs that include courses from a variety of natural science, humanities, and/or social science disciplines: biology, chemistry, geology, math, classics, drama, and anthropology. The FIG website (http://depts.washington.edu/figs/index.php) promotes the benefits of enrolling in a FIG:

- It makes the registration process very easy; you can register for most or all of your classes at once.
- Take classes with the same 20–25 students, so even a lecture class will seem small.
- Take courses that fulfill general education requirements.
- Meet students with similar interests (after all, you chose to register for the same classes!).
- Form your own UW community.

Team-Taught Learning Communities or Coordinated Studies Programs

Team-taught learning communities or coordinated studies programs enroll a cohort of students in two or more courses organized around an interdisciplinary theme. Total community enrollment varies, but it can range from 40–75 students. On campuses facing fiscal pressures, enrollment in the learning community might be closer to 75 students (Macgregor et al., 2001). In larger team-taught programs, the cohort is often subdivided into smaller seminar groups to achieve a faculty:student ratio of one faculty member to 20 or 25 students (Gabelnick et al., 1990).

Team-taught programs represent the most extensive approach in terms of curricular integration and faculty involvement. Faculty and student involvement can be part- or full-time, involving two to five courses. On many campuses, the learning community constitutes the students' and faculty members' entire schedules for at least a semester and sometimes an entire academic year.

Themes are faculty-generated and interdisciplinary. Themes can be broad and liberal-arts based, emphasize skill development in related disciplines, or prepare students for study or practice in professions. Small-group discussion sections are an important part of the community. Students and a faculty member break off into smaller groups to build upon what is being learned in the other courses in the community and/or to discuss assigned texts.

Freshmen in George Mason University's New Century College enroll in a 32-credit, freshman learning community experience that consists of four 8-credit integrated learning communities:

- Community of Learners
- The Natural World
- The Social World
- Self as Citizen (New Century College website, http://www.ncc.gmu .edu/divisionI.html)

The communities are taken sequentially and fulfill most of the university's general education requirements (Oates, 2003, p. 48). The communities are team-taught by two or more faculty representing different disciplinary perspectives. Students can benefit in many ways from this level of faculty and student teamwork and collaboration. A faculty member in New Century College describes the benefits for students:

> The benefits are numerous, but having just read my students' portfolios for the end of the first unit I can say three specific things. First, students generally report that this is their first real opportunity to engage in critical reading, dialogue, and writing. Many report that the [standardized] exams put the focus in the high school classroom on memorization. Secondly, students appreciate the voice and authority (and responsibility!) that a [learning community] brings. They appreciate the opportunity to create knowledge, learn from their peers, and have conversations [and] make meaning with faculty who don't have all the answers. Finally, I see a shift in students from "What is my grade?" or "What is the basic requirement for this course?" to "What am I learning?" and "How can I learn more about this topic in other ways?" There was a real shift from interest in grades to interest in learning for my students this past unit. (K. Eby, personal communication, October 2003)

Residence-Based Programs

Residence-based learning communities adapt a particular curricular model to include a residential component. The curricular component of residence-based programs typically resembles one of the three learning communities approaches described previously: clusters, FIGs, or team-taught programs. Residence-based learning communities involve more than assigning students with similar majors to the same floor of a residence hall. In residence-based learning communities, student cohorts enroll in specified curricular offerings and reside together in dedicated living space.

Residence-based learning communities are designed to integrate curricular and co-curricular experiences and therefore may be the most radical of the four learning communities approaches described in this chapter. Residence-based learning communities require change within multiple university systems: curriculum, teaching, and housing (Shapiro & Levine, 1999). Academic and co-curricular community activities are scheduled in residence halls, and in many instances classes actually meet in classrooms located in residential spaces (Levine Laufgraben, 2004; Shapiro & Levine, 1999).

The Michigan Community Scholars Program (MCSP) is one of several living-learning programs at the University of Michigan. MCSP "integrates community service-learning and intercultural understanding and dialogue in a residential learning community" (Schoem, 2003, p. 45). Students enroll in a three-credit "The Student in the University" course, a freshman seminar or community-service course, and are encouraged to enroll in sections of English or math designed and designated for community scholar's students. The program experience also includes leadership opportunities and co-curricular activities. Academic support services, including tutoring and study groups, are offered in the residence hall (Michigan Community Scholars Website, http://www.lsa.umich.edu/mcs/).

Selecting an Approach

In making decisions about learning communities, the institutions often must choose between the benefits of one model and the feasibility of another given the campus' organization and faculty culture (Shapiro & Levine, 1999). No one model or approach is "better" than another. All four structures reflect the characteristics of learning communities, but with varying degrees of student and faculty engagement and curricular integration. For a learning communities program to be successful, the model or approach to learning communities must fit the student, faculty, and institutional culture.

Implementation, regardless of the model, requires an understanding of the campus' capacity for change. By definition, learning communities represent a radical "restructuring of students' time, credit, and learning experiences" and this type of change represents a major transformation in thinking and operating for many institutions. Those involved in implementing learning communities need to identify opportunities for change: general education reform, accreditation review or a new chief academic officer are some examples of change levers. Implementing learning communities also involves creating a leadership and support structure to accommodate learning communities. What are the goals for the program, and who needs to be involved in the planning? Do not assume that everyone on campus will embrace the idea of learning communities. Be prepared to address sources of resistance, and avoid the program being overly associated with one individual. Identifying resources is another important step in creating a campus culture for learning communities. What are the fiscal and human resources need to achieve the program's goals (Shapiro & Levine, 1999)?

While campuses should be wary of simply replicating another campus' program by installing another's model for their own institution, learning from the experiences of others can be very helpful. A Learning Communities Directory is maintained by the National Learning Communities Project in partnership with the Washington Center for Improving the Quality of Undergraduate Education (http://learningcommons.evergreen.edu/) at The Evergreen State College. This database is a useful, online resource for locating examples of learning communities programs by model, institution type, or student populations served.

Placing Learning Communities in the First Year

Learning communities take root in different places in the undergraduate program:

- First-year experience.
- General education.
- Developmental studies.
- Writing programs.
- Study in major or minor.
- Professional or vocational preparation programs.

Learning communities located in first-year experience, general education, and developmental studies programs represent the more common learning communities approaches for improving the first year of college.

First-Year Experience Learning Communities. Learning communities embedded in a first-year experience program aim to support students' academic and social transitions to college. Designed primarily for first-semester college freshmen, learning communities is typically one component in a comprehensive first-year experience program that might also include orientation, a common/summer reading experience, and a student success course. Learning community programs for first-year students often include academic advising services, tutoring and other support services and co-curricular activities.

Learning communities for first-year students at IUPUI aim to improve student retention. A unique component of their program is the freshman seminar course. The seminar is taught by an instructional team that consists of a faculty member working with a librarian, a technologist, a counselor, and a student mentor. Each team member has a clearly articulated role in supporting student learning and success. The faculty member takes the lead in organizing and teaching the seminar and helps students understand the expectations for academic learning. The advisor provides information about academic policies and resources and assists students with academic goal setting. The librarian (information technologist) orients students to the university library and offers basic information literacy instruction. The student mentor, a role model for new students, leads discussions on resources and activities and provides feedback to the other members of the team on what the students are thinking and feeling (*Template for First-Year Seminars at IUPUI*, 2002).

General Education Learning Communities. Learning communities provide one strategy for creating coherence in a general education program. Satisfying general education requirements through learning communities helps students see the relationship between courses and the purpose of the general education curriculum. "Requirements" — lists of approved courses that students must take — become programs.

Portland State's University Studies program is a four-year, interdisciplinary general education program modeled on learning communities principles. The program is founded on four goals: communication, inquiry and critical thinking, the diversity of human experience, and social responsibility and ethical issues. Entering students enroll in "Freshman

Inquiry (FRINQ);" a year-long, theme-based and team-designed curriculum to support the transition to college. Each FRINQ program has a theme. Recent themes include: Chaos and Community; Columbia Basin; Cyborg Millenium; Sex, Mind and the Mask: The Constructed Self; Forbidden Knowledge; The Power of Place; Meaning and Madness at the Margins; and Sustainability and Justice. The learning community approach then extends vertically through the senior year. Sophomores enroll in a Sophomore Inquiry course that is the gateway to an upper-division cluster. In Sophomore Inquiry, students are introduced to the ideas, research, theory, and perspectives central to the cluster (see the University Studies Website, http://www.ous.pdx.edu/). At the senior level, students enroll in Senior Inquiry, an interdisciplinary, community-based learning experience.

Developmental Studies. The use of learning communities is one effective approach to better support the academic needs of students who enter college with deficiencies in one or more basic skill areas. Some campuses form communities by linking a remedial or developmental course with a general education or discipline-based course; other institutions create clusters or team-taught learning communities in which at least one or as many as all of the courses are developmental (Tinto, 1998). If the community includes academic courses, students receive the additional academic support they need while also making progress toward a degree.

New Student House at LaGuardia Community College is a program for students with basic skill needs in at least three areas: reading, writing, and speech. The cluster then includes a fourth, content-area course. Past New Student House programs have included college-level courses in Communication, Critical Thinking, Introduction to Business, and Computer Science. The curriculum is highly integrated and includes shared assignments and large-group meetings. Field trips provide a co-curricular component. A counselor who teaches the seminar that is part of the cluster meets regularly with other faculty teaching in the program to discuss student needs (Learning Communities Website, LaGuardia Community College, http://www.lagcc.cuny.edu/STUINFO/firstyear/learningcomm.asp).

A ten-year longitudinal study of New Student House shows a significantly higher pass rate in basic skills reading and English for those in the learning community compared to students enrolled in non-learning-community sections. A significantly higher pass rate among students in the cluster's college-level course was also noted when compared to the pass rates of first-year students who took the same course in a stand-alone version (Learning Communities website, LaGuardia Community College, http://www.lagcc.cuny.edu/STUINFO/firstyear/learningcomm.asp).

CREATING LEARNING COMMUNITIES

What conditions need to be present to successfully build and sustain learning communities? Successful learning community initiatives share a commitment to the following elements:

1. Clearly defined and articulated program goals.
2. Dedicated resources.
3. Committed program leadership and a broadening pool of participants and stakeholders.
4. Credible evidence of program impact and achievement.
5. Mechanisms for ongoing improvement and change.

Goals

Clearly articulated goal statements express what learning communities are intended to do, whom they will serve, and how the broader objectives can be accomplished. They address the environment for learning and the expectations for those responsible for that learning: students, teachers, and staff. The purposes of learning communities will vary by campus. Many institutions implement learning communities to improve student performance, persistence, or satisfaction with the college experience. Learning communities can also optimize the academic and social experience for students. Goals for students might include:

- Improve retention.
- Increase student learning and achievement.
- Increase time on task both in and out of class.
- Promote active learning and teamwork skills.
- Develop student leadership.
- Increase the success rate for under-represented students.
- Increase entry and completion in certain majors. (Smith, MacGregor, Matthews, & Gabelnick, 2004)

Who teaches in learning communities can also vary from campus to campus. At Temple University, the term *learning communities faculty* refers to any individual who teaches courses as part of a community. This includes professors, part-time instructors, graduate assistants, student affairs staff, academic advisers, and undergraduate peer teachers (Levine Laufgraben, 2004). Goals for faculty include:

- Increase experimentation within curriculum.
- Broaden pedagogical repertoire of faculty.
- Increase faculty engagement with one another.
- Promote deeper interaction among faculty and students.
- Promote interaction between junior and senior faculty.
- Promote stronger relationships among faculty and student affairs staff. (Smith et al., 2004)

For academic and student affairs staff who participate in learning communities, goals include more meaningful partnerships with faculty, greater opportunities to recruit students to organizations and to cultivate student leadership development, increased participation in student activities and campus events, and enhanced interactions with students.

Related to goals for students, faculty, and staff are goals for the curriculum. Learning communities can:

- Increase the coherence of general education.
- Create a more interdisciplinary curriculum.
- Allow for skills (e.g., writing, speaking, and technology) to be delivered across the curriculum.
- Create greater alignment between courses in the major or minor.
- Enhance preparation for advanced study by improving student learning in foundation or preparatory courses.
- Allow for more engagement with the curriculum outside of the formal classroom. (Smith et al., 2004)

Learning communities can also benefit the campus as a whole. Institutional goals for learning communities include:

- Enhance the quality of undergraduate education.
- Foster a climate of innovation.
- Increase the sense of community within the institution.
- Promote meaningful collaboration between faculty and staff, faculty and administration.

- Promote a culture of assessment, of learning about student learning. (Smith et al., 2004)

If a learning community program includes a service or experiential learning component, an additional goal includes increasing connections between the institution and the neighboring community.

Resources

Particularly during the start-up phase, planning support for faculty and staff is critical (MacGregor et al., 2001). This is a difficult fiscal time for colleges and universities, particularly public institutions. Many function in the universe of "do more with less." Human and fiscal resource issues to consider when creating a learning communities program:

- Align resource expenditures with goals.
- Secure dedicated leadership positions (Coordinator, Director, Faculty Fellow).
- Gain departmental support (dedicated faculty; courses).
- Secure a permanent budget — this might involve moving beyond grant funds to institutional operating funds.
- Provide resources for faculty development and assessment.
- Demonstrate fiscal accountability — regular evidence of program impact to justify ongoing support.

Leadership and Support Base

The long-term success of a learning community program requires that the effort not become overly associated with one person and that it move beyond early adopters. Often learning communities initiatives begin when a president, provost, or other senior officer asks an individual or group of individuals to "look into learning communities" or "get a few communities started." The early stakeholders are almost always people already recognized on campus as good teachers, dedicated committee members, creative teachers, and risk-takers. Expanding the circle from this point is the challenge. Growing a support base involves:

- Reaching out to departments and educating colleagues about the benefits of learning communities.

- Finding ways to include all interested faculty and staff who want to be involved with learning communities.
- Conducting good assessment and sharing results.
- Partnering with like programs for faculty development or recruitment events.
- Spreading the word and getting the program recognized around campus and with prospective students and their families.
- Extending public "thank-yous" to all who support the program.

Credible Evidence of Program Achievement

"Assessing and evaluating learning communities requires a research approach that takes into account the multiple perspectives and academic and social interactions at work in these environments" (Shapiro & Levine, 1999, p. 151). This involves assessment for both "proving and improving" the effectiveness of learning communities. Good assessment is ongoing, is linked to program goals, and begins before the first community is even offered.

Institutions assess their learning communities in different ways. A report based on the responses of learning community programs registered with the Learning Communities Directory, a database compiled and updated by the National Learning Communities project, revealed that the majority of institutions (86%, 134 out of 155 respondents) assess the effectiveness of their learning communities by student satisfaction; 65% assess faculty/student affairs satisfaction with the program; 72% analyze year-to-year retention at the university/college; and 69% assess retention within the program. Annual program enrollment is another measure of effectiveness (http://learningcommons.evergreen.edu/03_start_entry.asp#8).

Mechanisms for Ongoing Improvement

It is essential that learning communities programs create regular opportunities to review assessment results, revisit program goals, and implement improvements. Information should be shared regularly with the stakeholders most invested in the success of the program: faculty, students, and staff. Present assessment results to faculty at annual faculty development activities.

Use information to direct planning. The information gathered is not only evidence of the impact of the program, but also a catalyst for future planning and decision making. Data can be used to make informed decisions about expanding the program, adding new learning communities approaches to existing ones, or providing additional support services for first-year students.

THE IMPACT OF LEARNING COMMUNITIES

The literature on the impact of learning communities on students, faculty, and the institution is growing. Studies vary from nationally recognized research, like that of Vincent Tinto, to good examples of local assessment. What counts as "evidence" of program impact and success varies from campus to campus. A variety of evidence should be collected to present a snapshot of what happens to students and teachers when they participate in learning communities. This description should also capture the nature and level of organizational change that has occurred in the process of designing and implementing learning communities (Shapiro & Levine, 1999, p. 168). Most importantly, the data a campus decides to collect and the methods they use to gather this information should be closely related to stated goals.

Students

Participation in learning communities has a positive impact on student success, student achievement, and retention (Tinto, Love, & Russo, 1993). Examples of quantitative evidence of program impact on student achievement include:

- Grade point average comparisons of learning communities and non-learning communities participants.
- Credit hours attempted and completed; progress toward degree for learning communities and non-learning-communities participants.
- Comparison of student performance in courses taught in both learning communities and non-learning-communities settings.
- Comparison of student scores on placement tests or departmental exams pre- and post-learning communities or for learning-communities and non-learning-communities participants

A Temple University study revealed that learning community participants were retained to the second fall semester at rates 5% to 9% higher than comparison groups of non-participants (Levine & Degnan, 2000). Researchers at the University of Missouri-Columbia found first-year students in the FIG cohort earned a higher mean grade point average than non-participants. A longitudinal retention study for the same group demonstrated a 12% higher retention rate for FIG members after three years (Student Life Studies Abstracts, 1996).

Qualitative measures of student achievement might include transcript studies that document students' paths towards degree, interviews with learning communities participants and non-participants on what they learned in courses taught in both learning-community and non-learning-community settings, and portfolio reviews of student work. Studies reveal that learning communities help first-year students adapt more quickly to the college classroom environment. First-year students in learning communities are more likely to participate in class discussions, raise questions, and seek an instructor's assistance than non-participants (Reumann-Moore, El-Haj, & Gold, 1997; Tinto et al., 1993).

Participation in learning communities also positively influences students' intellectual development (MacGregor, 1987). Researchers working with the QUANTA Interdisciplinary Learning Communities Program at Daytona Beach Community College measured students' cognitive development using the Measure of Intellectual Development (MID), an instrument that applies Perry's Scheme of Intellectual Development. Student essays were compared over the course of the academic year to determine if learning community participants showed greater movement along the Perry Scale. The majority of these first-year students showed at least a change of one-third position, and when the QUANTA results were compared to findings from a study of national norms, learning community participants showed greater growth and development than students in non-learning communities classes (Avens & Zelley, 1992).

Other research shows that learning community students report greater intellectual and social engagement in college. They report greater satisfaction with their classes and teachers, and are also more likely to participate in a range of academic and social activities (Tinto et al., 1993; Reumann-Moore et al., 1997). At the University of Wisconsin, first-year students in the Bradley Learning Community reported greater satisfaction with the first year and greater participation in the University's opening-of-the-school-year activities than non-participants. Learning community participants were also more likely to become orientation leaders (Brower, 1997).

Who participates in learning communities can also be an assessment issue. A key research question to ask is, "Are the students enrolled in learning communities the ones we want to attract given the goals for our program?" (J. MacGregor, personal communication, November 2003). Some programs, such as the College Park Scholars (CPS) at the University of Maryland, aim to attract motivated and high-achieving students. CPS is a community-based program for academically talented first- and second-year students (http://www.scholars.umd.edu/). Applicants to the university are invited to apply based on their academic achievement and high school performance. Other programs might aim to attract developmental students or other special populations with the goals of improving student performance.

There are studies designed to take into account the volunteer, self-selection issues. Iowa State University found that students participating in learning communities had higher ACT scores and average high school rankings than non-participating students. To determine if the higher first-time GPA by learning communities students was because the program attracted better-prepared students, they used ACT and high school rank as covariates to control for their effects (Huba, Ellerston, Cook, & Epperson, 2003). When they controlled for these factors, they found that the adjusted average first-semester GPA of learning communities students was significantly higher than that of the non-participant group.

To determine the effectiveness of the Integrated Mathematics, Physics, Engineering and Chemistry (IMPEC) Program at North Carolina State University, researchers studied the performance of three groups: fall 1995 participants in the program, students who volunteered for the program and were not selected, and freshmen who did not volunteer. IMPEC was designed to provide: "(1) motivation and context for the fundamental material taught in the first-year mathematics and science courses; (2) a realistic and positive orientation to the engineering profession, and (3) training in the problem-solving, study, and communication skills that correlate with success in engineering school and equip individuals to be lifelong learners" (Felder, Bernold, Burniston, Dail, & Gastineau, 1996). IMPEC students participated in courses team-taught by faculty from mathematics, chemistry, physics, and engineering. The hands-on curriculum presented scientific and mathematical content in the context of real-world engineering problems.

Researchers found that during the 1995–1996 academic year, IMPEC participants had higher pass rates in the engineering core courses than students in both control groups. IMPEC students also did equal or better than non-participants on common final examination questions for calculus, chemistry, and physics courses. The IMPEC students were more likely to credit their engineering courses with improving their problem solving, studying, teamwork, time management, reading, writing, speaking, and computing skills than students in the comparison groups and also reported increased confidence in their chemistry, engineering, computing, speaking, and writing abilities (Felder et al., 1997).

Faculty

For faculty, participation in learning communities typically leads to greater attention to pedagogy and enhanced collegiality across disciplines. Faculty teaching in learning communities are more likely to say that they changed their teaching practices or philosophy toward teaching and learning in some manner (Reumann-Moore et al., 1997). Learning community faculty also report greater use of group work or collaborative learning strategies in their classrooms. They experience more out-of-class contact with students and an increased awareness of students' academic and personal needs.

Faculty commitment is essential to the long-term success of learning communities. Planning and teaching in a learning community is time intensive. Kim Eby, Assistant Professor of Integrative Studies at George Mason's New Century College, described the preparation faculty need to teach in learning communities: "There are two necessary and complimentary steps for interdisciplinary teaching and learning. First, faculty must develop what I call self-disciplinary awareness and, second, faculty must become learners" (Eby, 2001, p. 29). From this kind of teaching and learning, faculty stand to gain a clearer vision of their beliefs, deeper understanding of student needs, and new knowledge beyond their individual and disciplinary perspectives (p. 30).

There must be structures for faculty development and recognition of faculty work. Faculty development for learning communities typically focuses on three areas: (a) understanding learning communities; (b) curriculum and pedagogy; and (c) assessment and reflection (Levine Laufgraben & Shapiro, 2004). Faculty development activities range from brown bag lunches to on-campus workshops to multi-day planning retreats.

Many of the faculty members involved in learning communities are full-time, tenured professors. One reason for a lesser involvement of junior, tenure-track faculty is that the type of collaborative and interdisciplinary work associated with learning communities is not consistent with tenure and promotion systems (Oates, 2001). This is a challenge in securing faculty buy-in. Faculty involvement can be encouraged by promoting the benefits and personal rewards of teaching in communities: collegiality, opportunities to try and master new forms of pedagogy, intellectual engagement with students and peers, and a supportive teaching and learning environment.

The Campus

The impact of learning communities reaches beyond first-year students and faculty and leads to institutional transformation as well. For a campus, the implementation of learning communities leads to increased opportunities for cross-department collaboration and for partnerships between units, such as academic affairs and student affairs. In addition, the process of implementing and sustaining learning communities typically leads to increased attention to — and resources for — teaching, learning, assessment, and student support.

At the institution level, campuses stand to learn a great deal through the increased attention to students' academic and social experiences that naturally occurs while planning and implementing learning communities, particularly for first-year students. The campus can learn a great deal about what students experience in terms of orientation, residence life, academic advising, registration, financial aid, and support services. Focus group sessions to gather information on students perceptions' of learning communities will likely also yield feedback on the quality of food in the cafeteria, the availability of books in the bookstore, or the need for tutors in difficult first-year subjects like math and science.

CONCLUSION

This book highlights the research and practice that can make a difference in terms of the success of first-year college students. Much attention has been paid recently in higher education to pedagogy, curriculum, assessment, and structures that promote good teaching and deeper learning. Smith (2001), in an article discussing learning communities as a national movement, talked about the relationship between learning communities and other undergraduate reform initiatives:

> What's notable about the learning community effort is that it has often joined forces with these other efforts, providing a broader structural platform for implementing these other powerful pedagogies. This has both deepened learning community pedagogy and aims, and broadened the audience and base of potential allies (p. 6).

Learning communities allow us to not only change teaching practices, but also affect how students learn and experience their first year in college. Learning communities create a welcoming, supportive, collaborative, and engaging environment for our students.

REFERENCES

Avens, C., & Zelley, R. (1992). *QUANTA: An Interdisciplinary Learning Community.* Daytona Beach, FL: Daytona Beach Community College (ERIC Document Reproduction Service No. ED 349 073)

Astin, A. W. (1993). *What matters in college: Four critical years revisited.* San Francisco, CA: Jossey-Bass.

Barefoot, B. O. (2002). *Second national survey of first-year academic practices.* Brevard, NC: The Policy Center on the First Year of College. Retrieved from http://www.brevard.edu/fyc/Survey2002

Brower, A. (1997). *End of year evaluation on the Bradley Learning Community.* Unpublished report, University of Wisconsin–Madison.

Bystrom, V. A. (1997). Getting it together: Learning communities. In W. E. Campbell & K. A. Smith (Eds.), *New paradigms for college teaching* (pp. 243–268). Edina, MN: Interaction Book Company.

Chickering, A. W., & Gamson, Z. F. (1987). Seven principles for good practice in undergraduate education. *AAHE Bulletin, 39*(7), 3–7.

Eby, K. K. (2001) Teaching and learning from an interdisciplinary perspective. *Peer Review, 3/4*(4/1), 4–8.

Ewell, P. (1997). Organizing for learning. *AAHE Bulletin, 50*(4), 3–6.

Felder, R. M., Beichner, R. J., Bernold, L. E., Burniston, E. E., Dail, P. R., & Fuller, H. (1997). *Update on IMPEC: An integrated first-year engineering curriculum at N.C. State University.* Paper presented at the annual meeting of the American Society for Engineering Education, Washington, DC.

Felder, R. M., Bernold, L. E., Burniston, E. E., Dail, P. R., & Gastineau, J. E. (1996). *IMPEC: An Integrated First-Year Engineering Curriculum.* Paper presented at the 1996 ASEE annual meeting, Washington, DC, Session 2230. Available online at http://www2.ncsu.edu/ncsu/pams/physics/PCEP/impec/ASEE-P2.htm

Gabelnick, F., MacGregor, J., Matthews, R. S., & Smith, B. L. (1990). Learning communities: Creating connections among students, faculty, and disciplines. No. 41: *New Directions for Teaching and Learning.* San Francisco, CA: Jossey-Bass.

Huba, M. E., Ellerston, S., Cook, M. D., & Epperson, D. (2003). Assessment's role in transforming a grass-roots initiative into an institutionalized program: Evaluating and shaping learning communities at Iowa State University. In J. MacGregor (Ed.), *Doing learning community assessment: Five campus stories* (pp. 21–47). National Learning Communities Project Monograph Series. Olympia, WA: The Evergreen State College, Washington Center for Improving the Quality of Undergraduate Education, in cooperation with the American Association for Higher Education.

Levine, J., & Degnan, J. (2000). *Learning communities retention study: 1994–1998 cohorts.*

Philadelphia, PA: Temple University. Available online at http://www.temple.edu/university_studies/reports.html

Levine Laufgraben, J. (2004). Learning communities. In M. L. Upcraft, J. N. Gardner, & B. O. Barefoot (Eds.), *Challenging and supporting the first-year student: A handbook for improving the first year of college*. San Francisco, CA: Jossey-Bass.

Levine Laufgraben, J., & Shapiro, N. (2004). *Sustaining and improving learning communities*. San Francisco, CA: Jossey-Bass.

MacGregor, J. (1987). *Intellectual development of students in learning community programs 1986–1987*. Occasional Paper No. 1. Olympia, WA: The Evergreen State College, Washington Center for Improving the Quality of Undergraduate Education.

MacGregor, J. Smith, B. L., Mathews, R., & Gabelnick, F. (2001). Learning community models (http://www.evergreen.edu/user/washcntr/lcmodelsMay2001.pdf)

Oates, K. (2003). New century college: Connecting the classroom to the world. In J. O'Connor (Ed.), *Learning communities in research universities* (pp. 47–52). National Learning Communities Monograph Series, Olympia, WA: The Evergreen State College, Washington Center for Improving the Quality of Undergraduate Education in cooperation with the American Association for Higher Education.

Oates, K. (2001). Developing the faculty we need. *Peer Review, 3/4* (4/1), 4–8.

Pascarella, E. T., & Terenzini, P. T. (1991). *How college affects students*. San Francisco, CA: Jossey-Bass.

Reumann-Moore, R., El-Haj, A., & Gold, E. (1997). *Friends for school purposes: Learning communities and their role in building community at a large urban university*. Philadelphia, PA: Temple University.

Schoem, D. (2003). Learning communities at the University of Michigan: The best of both worlds. In J. O'Connor (Ed.) *Learning communities in research universities* (pp. 43–46). National Learning Communities Monograph Series, Olympia, WA: The Evergreen State College, Washington Center for Improving the Quality of Undergraduate Education in cooperation with the American Association for Higher Education.

Shapiro, N. S., & Levine, J. H. (1999). *Creating learning communities: A practical guide to winning support, organizing for change, and implementing programs*. San Francisco, CA: Jossey-Bass.

Smith, B. L, MacGregor, J., Matthews, R. S., & Gabelnick, F. (2004). *Learning communities: Reforming undergraduate education*. San Francisco: Jossey-Bass.

Smith, B. L. (2003). Learning community snapshots. In J. O'Connor (Ed.), *Learning communities in research universities* (pp. 53–62). National Learning Communities Monograph Series, Olympia, WA: The Evergreen State College, Washington Center for Improving the Quality of Undergraduate Education in cooperation with the American Association for Higher Education.

Smith, B. L. (2001). The challenges of learning communities as a growing national movement. *Peer Review, 3/4* (4/1), 4–8.

Strommer, D. W. (1999). Teaching and learning in a learning community. In J. H. Levine (Ed.), *Learning communities: New structures, new partnerships for learning* (pp. 39–50). Columbia, SC: National Center for the First-Year Experience and Students in Transition.

Student Life Studies Abstracts. (1996). *A student success story: Freshman Interest Groups at the University of Missouri-Columbia. No. 1*. Columbia, MO: University of Missouri.

Template for First-Year Seminars at IUPUI. (2002). Retrieved from http://uc.iupui.edu/.

Tinto, V. (1994). *Leaving college: Rethinking the causes and cures of student attrition.* Chicago: University of Chicago Press.

Tinto, V. (1998). *Learning communities and the reconstruction of remedial education in higher education.* Paper presented at the Conference on Replacing Remediation in Higher Education, Stanford University. Author's website: http://soeweb.syr.edu/Faculty/Vtinto/Files/DevEdLC.pdf

Tinto, V., Love, A. G., & Russo, P. (1993). *Building learning communities for new college students: A summary of research findings of the collaborative learning project.* University Park, PA: National Center on Postsecondary Teaching, Learning, and Assessment.

Author Index

Subject Index